The International Business Blueprint

Business Blueprints

This series presents the latest developments and concepts in the key business disciplines in an accessible way. Each title concentrates on the most crucial subjects within its area and presents the critical issues in a format and style that helps managers to develop real business skills. Using short case studies and practical examples the *Business Blueprints* series shows practising managers and students of management how to apply current management theory and best practice.

The *Business Blueprints* series is unique in its merging of the latest developments and concepts in management thinking with actual applications of those concepts.

The International Business Blueprint

Sylvester O. Monye

First published 1997

Reprinted 2000

Blackwell Publishers Ltd
108 Cowley Road
Oxford OX4 1JF
UK

Blackwell Publishers Inc.
350 Main Street
Malden, Massachusetts 02148
USA

British Library Cataloguing in Publication Data

A CIP catalogue record for this book is available from the British Library.

Library of Congress Cataloging-in-Publication Data
Monye, Sylvetser O. The International business blueprint / Sylvester O. Monye.
        p.   cm. – (Business blueprints)
Includes bibliographical references and index.

ISBN 0–631–19665–X (pbk.)
1. International trade 2. International business enterprises.
3. International economic relations.
I. Title   II. Series
HF1379.M65 1997
658'.049 – dc 21   96-46727
                                                                          CIP

Typeset in 11 on 13 pt Palatino by On Screen, West Hanney, Oxfordshire
Printed in Great Britain by TJ International, Padstow, Cornwall

This book is printed on acid-free paper

Contents

PART II Functional areas of international business

PART III Managing international business

List of figures

List of tables

List of exhibits

Preface

The last ten years or so have witnessed the most intense and sustained debate on the pattern and direction of international business in modern time. This debate centres on the changing nature of the global market in the wake of advances in transport and telecommunications technology, increasing commonality in consumer awareness and behaviour across the world. Deriving from this debate are two schools of thought: those who believe that the emerging similarities among nations far outweigh the differences (thus, the future of multinational enterprises depends on their ability to offer standardized products and services in this global village); and those who believe that unique differences among nations still exist, and that firms must recognize and respect these differences as the key to competitiveness and long-term success. Although there are merits in these contending views, a pragmatic approach is adopted in this book and I believe it is simply a question of finding a balance between what is required to maintain profitability and the need to meet customers' expectations and desires.

The aim of this book is to provide a concise introduction to the complex, changing, multi-faceted character of international business in a modern world, problems and issues, and the environment in which international business is conducted, in a succinct and accessible way that unravels the key factors in this on-going debate. With a book of this size, it is not intended to cover all the topics in great depth; rather the aim is to treat all aspects of international business with clarity and in a user-friendly style. Key concepts, issues and developments are discussed alongside functional areas such as marketing finance and human resource management.

As with the other books in the Blueprint series, it is an ideal introductory text for undergraduate, MBA and MSc students of international business, and should also prove an invaluable reference book for practising managers.

The book is organized in three parts and consists of a total of twelve chapters. Each chapter is supported by a variety of illustrations, bullet points, exhibits, and discussion questions to reinforce the reader's understanding of the main issues. The illustrations are taken from real life experiences of international firms. The book is arranged as follows.

Part I deals with the general aspects of international business operation and includes:

- chapter 1 – An overview of international business – covering definitions, concepts, the nature of international business and the role of multinational corporations in the world economy;
- chapter 2 – International trade and economic theories – covering international trade theories and regulatory framework for international business;
- chapter 3 – International business 'environments' – covering economic, political, socio-cultural, legal and technological environments in which international business is conducted;
- chapter 4 – International market entry and development strategy – covering topics ranging from exporting, licensing, strategic alliances to foreign direct investment.

Part II deals with the functional aspects of international business and includes:

- chapter 5 – International marketing – covering issues such as multinational versus global marketing, international marketing research, product management and other elements of the marketing mix;
- chapter 6 – International finance – covering issues such as the international monetary system, the international financial system, financing international trade, and management of international finance;
- chapter 7 – International production – covering topics such as plant location, greenfield versus acquisition, and the new production environment;
- chapter 8 – International human resource management – covering issues such as organizational structures, management staff, home versus host country staff, women as international managers, and international labour issues.

Part III deals with the issues relevant to the management of international business and includes:

- chapter 9 – Global strategic management – covering topics such as international planning process, strategy planning tools, and alternative strategy dimensions;

- chapter 10 – Corporate responsibility – issues such as corporate governance, the environment, sustainable development, health and safety, and ethics in international business are discussed;
- chapter 11 – Implementing and controlling international business strategy – deals with issues relating to the implementation of global strategy, organizational configuration, location of authority, cultural diversity, managing change, performance evaluation and systems of controlling multinational operation;
- chapter 12 – The future of multinational business – discusses the MNE/host country relationship, areas of conflict and the changing nature of international competition.

Acknowledgements

In writing this book, I have benefited immensely from the generous support and cooperation of a number of individuals – too many to mention. But I would like to say a big thank you to Chris Simango for reading the manuscript and offering constructive suggestions on how to improve the work. I am also grateful to Sati Bedaysee for assisting me with the graphic work. Special thanks are also due to my students at South Bank University who have stimulated my thinking on the subject of international business. Finally, the support and encouragement from my wife Ifeoma have been inspirational in completing this book. The responsibility for the book in its final form, naturally, lies solely with the author.

Every attempt has been made to trace copyright holders. The author and publishers would like to apologize in advance for any inadvertent use of copyright material, and thank the following individuals and organizations who have kindly given their permission to reproduce copyright figures, tables and text: Addison Wesley Longman Ltd; the *Daily Mail*; The Financial Times Ltd; *The Economist*; McGraw-Hill Companies; Pitman Publishing; Prentice-Hall Europe; Prentice-Hall, Inc.; the Regents of the University of California; Sunday Business Newspapers Ltd; John Wiley & Sons, Inc.

PART I

International business: an overview

1

Introduction to international business

INTRODUCTION

International business is, arguably, as old as mankind. Although modern trade theory is generally traced to the ideas put forward by Adam Smith's work *The Wealth of Nations* first published in 1776, normally referred to as the principles of absolute advantage, it is noteworthy that the Egyptians, the ancient Greeks and Romans had been actively involved in international trade for centuries. According to Taggart and McDermott (1993), there is evidence to suggest that, over 2000 years before the birth of Christ, merchants from Mesopotamia, Greece and Phoenicia were sending trading ships around the known world. These early developments in international trade provide the basis for our understanding of the concept of modern international business operations. They also reinforce the fact that even in classical times, the principle of national interdependence was understood and accepted as the basis for national development and prosperity. This view was reinforced by Root (1990), who argued that no nation inhabits an economic vacuum: its industries, commerce, technology, standard of living, and all the other facets of its economy are related to the economies of foreign nations by complex flows of goods, capital, technology and enterprise.

Modern international trade began with the rise of the modern nation state at the close of the European middle ages. At the end of the fifteenth century, the old European trading system, which was based on the Mediterranean, began to break down and the seaboard of western Europe became the main focus of economic activity (Minchinton, 1969). Countries such as Spain, the Netherlands, France and England in the seventeenth and eighteenth centuries were able to exploit their favourable geographic location by using the developments in shipping and navigational techniques which had become available. Minchinton suggests that the divergence in factor endowments of territories within the wider trading area created new opportunities for trade based on comparative advantage.

At this point, political philosophers began to examine the nature and function of the nation, and trade with other nations became an area of considerable interest to their investigation. It is therefore not surprising that mercantilism figured in the earliest attempts to describe the functions of international trade within this highly nationalistic framework. Mercantilist analyses focused directly upon the welfare of the nation. Consequently, trade policy was basically to 'encourage exports, discourage imports, and take the proceeds of the resulting export surplus in gold'. The virtue of gold was regarded almost as an article of faith. Adam Smith's work was a radical departure from the mercantilists' perspective of international trade. In particular he emphasized the importance of specialization as a source of increased output and treated international trade as a particular instance of specialization.

International business as it is known today can be attributed to two important developments. The first is the momentum generated by the reconstruction of Western Europe at the end of the Second World War. The success of programmes such as the Marshall Plan in revitalizing the economies of Western Europe increased production to such an extent that by 1948 world industrial output regained its pre-war high. Keegan (1989) noted that for almost thirty-seven years since 1945, international trade and investment have been growing faster than gross world product. This sustained growth over such a long period has transformed a collection of relatively autonomous national economies into a highly interdependent world of international competition. The second development is the rapid global spread of multinational enterprises, which may be explained not only by reduced marketing opportunities in the industrialized markets but also by the appreciable increase in the level of industrialization and general economic development in the developing world. This raises the question of the validity of the view that convergence of standards and tastes is occurring at a global level.

INTERNATIONAL BUSINESS DEFINED

In its simplest form, any business transaction that involves persons or firms of more than one country may be described as international business. This term covers business activities at both macro- and micro-economic levels – international trade in goods and services, export, licensing of know-how and trademarks, foreign direct investment and international transfer of personnel. Definitions of international business abound in the literature. However, for the purpose of this book, Robinson's all-embracing definition is adopted. Robinson (1978) defines international business as a field of study and practice that encompasses public and private business activity affecting the persons or institutions of more than one national state, territory or colony. He notes that the effect of international business may affect people's economic well-being, political status, convictions, skills or knowledge. Thus, the term 'international business' describes a broad spectrum of business activities that transcends national frontiers.

WHY STUDY INTERNATIONAL BUSINESS?

The principles of business management are universal. Business studies cover all functional areas of management such as finance, marketing, purchasing, operations management and human resource management. These functions are no different from market to market. None the less, international business entails additional risks and responsibilities which are unique to the management of business in multiple and often complex environments. These include:

- ownership, transfer and management of income-generating assets in multinational, multi-linguistic and multi-cultural environments. Thus, managing international business requires different kinds of information and analytical tools;
- political and financial risks in the form of expropriation, exchange rate fluctuations, and host government hostility;
- physical distance, which may complicate a firm's capability to communicate clearly and efficiently;
- the huge capital investment which is required for foreign investment and marketing.

The study of international business enables individuals and firms to recognize the opportunities and risks of extra-territorial operations, the process of internationalization of business and the management of these businesses in complex environments. The various facets of international business study are shown in figure 1.1.

Over the years, research in international business has evolved along two complementary paths – the study of the nature of the multinational

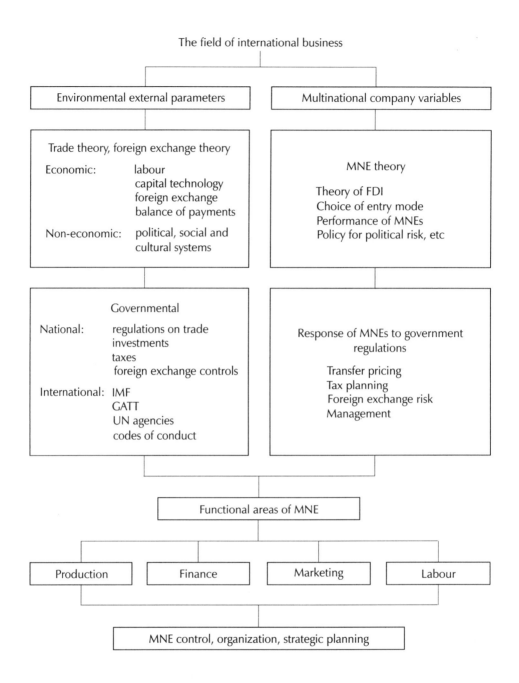

Figure 1.1 The nature of international business: MNEs and trade
Source: Rugman, A. M., Lecraw, D. J. and Booth (1985) *International Business: Firm and Environment*, p. 6. Copyright © 1985 McGraw-Hill. Reproduced by permission.

enterprise, and the theory and model of foreign direct investment. They are examined in this book.

THE INTERNATIONALIZATION PROCESS

The process of internationalization by firms is central to the concept of international business education, and has rightly received considerable attention in the literature. There seems to be a consensus that the primary explanation for internationalization is the growth of the firm. According to Akoorie (1993), it is believed that through expansion, growth and interaction in the world economy, firms ensure long-term survival and growth which ultimately brings benefits to the host nation as well as the home country.

There is, however, a difference between internationalization and growth in the home market. Welch and Luostarinen (1988) define internationalization as 'the process of increasing involvement in international operations'. Young *et al.* (1989) explain that this process includes the whole range of methods of undertaking business across national frontiers, some of which involve flows of goods and services between countries, some of which do not. Thus, the relationship between internationalization and forms of foreign market servicing is a close one (Buckley and Ghauri, 1993).

Although a number of scholars argue that the internationalization of the firm follows a logical and sequential process of acquisition, integration and use of knowledge about foreign markets (Johanson and Vahlne, 1977; Cavusgil, 1984), there is no conclusive evidence to suggest that all firms follow this approach in their decision to export, license or invest directly in a foreign market. For example, this sequential approach does not explain the follow-the-leader behaviour of multinational enterprises (MNEs) in their international activities. What is, however, clear is that firms are eager to satisfy the objectives of their operations in the host nation whether by exporting, licensing, franchising, joint venture or a wholly owned subsidiary. The choice of a particular market entry strategy is influenced by the availability of resources, and the level of interest and commitment in the market. The alternative methods of servicing foreign markets are examined in detail in chapter 4 of this book.

THE MULTINATIONAL ENTERPRISE

The terms 'transnational', 'multinational' and 'global' enterprises are used interchangeably in international business literature. Strictly speaking, there are differences in these terms which stem from the nature and character of companies which operate internationally:

- Transnational corporation (TNC): the origin of this term is rather recent and was popularized by the United Nations Centre on Transnational Corporations (UNCTC). According to Dunning (1993), it was adopted by the UNCTC in 1974 at the request of some Latin American countries, who wished to distinguish companies domiciled in one country of Latin America, which might invest in another, from those originating outside the region.
- Multinational enterprise (MNE): Hood and Young (1979) note that the essential elements of MNE operations are direct (as distinct from portfolio) investment abroad, giving a power of control over decision-making in a foreign enterprise, and the requirement that the income-generating assets be located in a number of countries. Furthermore, MNEs place a lot of emphasis on exploiting both real and perceived differences in global markets.
- Global enterprise: the term is used to refer to firms with geocentric orientation in their international operations. In other words, these firms seek global opportunities without regard to operating distances, host nation politics and culture. These firms tend to concentrate on the similarities in world markets rather than on the differences.

Although the three terminologies may be used in this book to describe different types of international operation, the term multinational enterprise (MNE) will be adopted because it provides a greater latitude for the discussion of international business.

The nature and characteristics of the MNE are a matter of academic debate. None the less, a number of fundamental characteristics are associated with MNEs:

- Ownership: to qualify for the label MNE, a firm must have ownership and control of subsidiary operations in at least five countries. This figure of five is rather arbitrary. Other figures such as two and ten have been mentioned by various scholars. In addition, it has been suggested that a firm must own at least 25 per cent of share capital in a foreign firm for it to be described as a subsidiary.

- Type of operation: MNEs engage in all sorts of value-adding activities both in production and services. Firms whose international activities are limited to exporting and portfolio investments abroad should not be described as MNEs.
- Size: MNEs are usually large corporations with substantial capital and technological resources. These resources often represent an important source of bargaining power and influence on host government policies towards foreign investors.
- Revenue: a substantial proportion of MNEs' revenue is accounted for by their international activities through a network of subsidiaries and affiliates. In some cases, this contribution to net sales can be as high as 70 per cent.

MNEs may be described as the most important business phenomenon to emerge after the Second World War, and they have generated a great deal of interest and scrutiny from academics, business communities and governments alike. This interest has manifested itself in a number of ways, including research and publications.

Academics have sought to explain the phenomenon with various theories. Pitelis and Sugden (1991) note that one explanation for the interest in MNE activities is the increased and increasing importance of such firms in the world economy. Studies of the MNE have focused first on the MNE as the primary institutional vehicle for international production and foreign direct investment (a particular characteristic of the MNE's foreign operations that is developed in chapter 7), and second the impact of MNEs on the global economy.

THE MULTINATIONAL ENTERPRISE IN THE WORLD ECONOMY

The world economy consists of a complex inter-relationships between multinational businesses, governments, economies and markets. The nature of this interaction is encapsulated in figure 1.2.

The impetus for the development and growth of the global economy is firmly anchored on the activities of the multinational enterprise. According to UNCTC (1992), multinational enterprises have become central organizers of economic activity in an increasingly integrated world

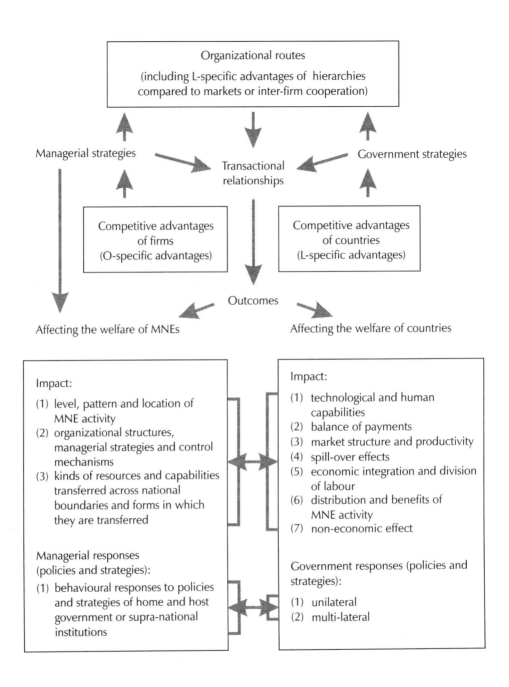

Figure 1.2 Schema for analysing the role of MNEs in the global economy
Source: Dunning (1993), p. xv. Reprinted by permission of Addison Wesley Longman Ltd.

Table 1.1 Stock of FDI, by country and region, 1987–92 (US$ billion)

Region/country		1987	1988	1989	1990	1991	1992
A.	Outward						
	France	41	56	75	110	134	151
	Germany, Federal Republic of	91	104	122	140	169	186
	Japan	78	112	156	204	235	251
	United Kingdom	135	172	208	226	244	259
	United States	339	353	379	408	438	474
	World	1,000	1,169	1,382	1,616	1,799	1,949
B.	Inward						
	Developed countries	787	920	1,088	1,260	1,369	–
	Western Europe	357	419	507	616	702	–
	North America	342	405	476	528	544	–
	Other developed countries	88	96	105	116	123	–
	Developing economies	212	241	270	300	338	–
	Africa	22	25	30	32	35	–
	Latin America and the Caribbean	84	95	104	114	129	–
	East, South and South-East Asia	106	121	136	154	174	–
	Central and Eastern Europe	–	–	–	–	–	–
	World	999	1,161	1,357	1,560	1,709	–

Source: UNCTC (1993), p. 14.

economy. It is suggested that about one-third of the world's private sector productive assets are under the common governance of MNEs.

The growing importance and influence of MNEs in the world economy can be assessed in terms of the stock of foreign direct investment (being a measure of the productive capacity of MNEs), the expansion in the range of their activities and the exponential growth in the total number of their subsidiaries as shown in tables 1.1–1.3.

The stock of foreign direct investment (FDI) by multinational enterprises headquartered in industrialized countries, reached nearly US$2,000 billion in 1992. This is illustrated in table 1.1. This represents the total capital employed and controlled by MNEs outside the domestic markets.

Table 1.2 Worldwide FDI and selected economic indicators (1991) and growth rates for 1981–5, 1986–90 and 1991 (US$ billion and percentages)

Indicator	Value at current prices, 1991	Annual growth (%)		
		1981–5	1986–90	1991
All countries				
FDI outflows	180	4	24	−22
FDI stock	1,800	7	16	11
Sales of transnational corporations	5,500	2	15	–
Gross domestic product at market prices	21,500	2	9	3
Gross domestic investment	4,900	0.5	10	3
Exports of goods and non-factor services	4,000	−0.2	12	2
Royalty and fee receipts	34	0.1	19	4
Developed countries				
FDI outflows	177	3	24	−21
Gross domestic product at market prices	17,200	3	10	5
Gross domestic investment	3,800	2	11	5
Exports of goods and non-factor services	3,000	2	12	1
Royalty and fee receipts	33	0.2	19	5
Developing economies				
FDI inflows	39	−4	17	24
Gross domestic product at market prices	3,400	0.2	8	−2
Gross domestic investment	800	−3	9	−2
Exports of goods and non-factor services	930	−3	13	4
Royalty and fee payments	2	−1	23	−26

Source: UNCTC (1993), p.15.

The combined domestic and foreign net assets of these MNEs was esti-mated at about US$5,000 billion for the same year. It is noteworthy that the annual flows of foreign direct investment remain substantial, and have contributed to a significant growth in the global stock of foreign direct investment. According to Dunning (1993), estimates of the sales and

Table 1.3 Number of parent transnational corporations and foreign affiliates, by area and country (1990–3)

Area/economy	Parent corporations based in country	Foreign affiliates located in country	Year
Developed countries	33,500	81,800	
Australia	1,036	695	1992
Austria	679	2,221	1990
Belgium and Luxembourg	96	1,121	1978
Canada	1,308	5,874	1991
Denmark	800	647	1992
Finland	1,300	1,000	1992
France	2,056	6,870	1990
Germany, Federal Republic of	6,984	11,821	1990
Greece	–	798	1981
Iceland	14	28	1991
Ireland	30	956	1992
Italy	263	1,438	1992
Japan	3,529	3,150	1992
Netherlands	1,426	2,014	1992
New Zealand	201	1,078	1991
Norway	1,321	2,854	1990
Portugal	684	6,680	1992
South Africa	–	1,884	1978
Spain	744	6,232	1992
Sweden	3,529	2,400	1991
Switzerland	3,000	4,000	1985
Turkey	–	267	1989
United Kingdom	1,500	2,900	1991
United States	3,000	14,900	1990
Developing economies	2,700	71,300	
Brazil	566	7,110	1992
China	379	15,966	1989
Colombia	–	1,041	1987
Hong Kong	500	2,828	1991
India	187	926	1991
Indonesia	–	1,064	1988
Mexico	–	8,953	1989
Oman	–	1,489	1989
Pakistan	57	560	1988
Philippines	–	1,952	1987

cont.

Table 1.3 *(cont)*

Area/economy	Parent corporations based in country	Foreign affiliates located in country	Year
Republic of Korea	1,049	3,671	1991
Saudi Arabia	–	1,461	1989
Singapore	–	10,709	1986
Taiwan Province of China	–	5,733	1990
Former Yugoslavia	112	3,900	1991
Central and Eastern Europe	400	21,800	
Bulgaria	26	114	1991
Commonwealth of Independent States	68	3,900	1992
Former Czechoslovakia	26	800	1992
Hungary	66	2,400	1992
Poland	58	3,800	1992
Romania	20	6,900	1992
World	36,600	174,900	

Source: UNCTC (1993), pp. 20–1.

value added generated by the stock of FDI suggests that MNEs accounted for up to 30 per cent of the GDP of the world's market economy in the mid-1980s. They were also responsible for around three-quarters of the world's commodity trade, and four-fifths of the trade in technology and managerial skills.

Table 1.2 shows the rate of growth of FDI between 1981 and 1991. This was a modest 4 per cent for all countries between 1981 and 1985. It grew more rapidly between 1986 and 1990, averaging 24 per cent per year during this period. Worldwide outflows of FDI declined in 1991 for the first time since 1982, with investment totalling US$180 billion – down from over US$230 billion in 1990. This was explained largely by the economic slowdown in the major developed regions, particularly Japan and Western Europe (UNCTC, 1993).

Estimates by the UNCTC (1993) suggest that 170,000 foreign affiliates of some 37,000 parent firms generated approximately US$5,500 billion in worldwide sales in 1990. This compares with world export of goods and non-factor services of US$4 billion, of which one-third took the form of intra-firm trade. As might be expected, over 90 per cent of these MNEs originate from or are headquartered in developed countries. Table 1.3 shows the extent of MNEs' global operating network.

Undoubtedly, the impact of MNEs on the global economy is substantial. They have been able to contribute to global economic growth and integration as a result of two but related factors: (1) their inherent attributes such as ownership, types of operation, size and resources; and (2) their structure and operating strategies which enable them to respond to the economic and policy environments in which they operate. With the advent of privatization sweeping through most developing and formerly communist East European countries, it is expected that the impact of MNEs on world economy will increase further.

EMERGING DEVELOPING COUNTRIES' MULTINATIONALS

Ownership of multinational enterprises is commonly associated with the industrialized countries of the West. This is understandable given that MNEs are usually very large firms with affiliates all over the world, and with minimum annual sales greater than the GDP (gross domestic product) of most developing countries. Before the oil price boom of the 1970s, no single developing country firm could boast of annual sales to the tune of US$1 billion. However, by 1985, multinationals from developing countries had achieved a position of eminence in terms of their contribution not only to the stock of foreign direct investment, but also their sales performance. For example, MNEs registered or headquartered in developing countries/newly industrialized countries (NICs) owned and controlled about 9 per cent of worldwide stock of foreign direct investment in 1992 (UNCTC, 1993).

The development and growth of NICs' multinationals have followed three predictable pathways based on location-specific advantages. These may be categorized as follows.

- Natural resources have provided developing countries with the ready-made route to multinationalism. In most of these countries, state-owned firms with effective control over natural resources such as oil, copper, tin and gold boast tremendous export earnings which provide them with the capital to invest and control assets abroad. For example, the Kuwaiti national oil company owns and controls a network of petrol stations across Europe under the trade name Q8.

EXHIBIT 1.1

Hyundai plans £2.4 billion plants in Scotland

Hyundai, the Korean electronics company, announced on Monday, 7 October 1996, that a £2.4 billion investment was to be made in Scotland, UK, over the next year. This represents Europe's largest inward investment, and it is expected to create over 2,000 jobs in the Fife region, which was hit by the government's decision to remove all nuclear submarine refitting work from the Rosyth dockyard and move it to Davenport. It is expected that more jobs will be created in allied industries.

Hyundai's investment marks the culmination of years of diplomatic efforts by the British Embassy in Seoul, the Korean capital. The embassy had been cultivating Hyundai for several years when the company approached diplomats with the proposal to build semiconductor production plants. Meetings were quickly arranged for visiting officials from the Department of Trade and Industry. Subsequently, a visit for company officials was arranged by the embassy to look at a number of potential sites in Britain.

The Foreign Office's largest single activity – costing £100 million a year – is to support British companies' overseas business and attract inward investment to Britain.

Discussion questions

1. How would you describe the basis for South Korea's attractiveness to international investors?
2. Explain why it is important for the Department of Trade and Industry to actively seek to attract inward investment.

- Skilled labour force: a number of developing countries with highly educated, disciplined and skilled, and relatively cheap labour forces have been very successful in converting these attributes into national competitive advantages, particularly in certain industries such as electronics and engineering. The assembly of electronics is labour intensive. The availability of a skilled and disciplined labour force is an important location-specific factor which has encouraged the influx of satellite plants owned by multinationals such as Hewlett-Packard, Philips and Hitachi into countries such as Hong Kong, Malaysia, Singapore, Taiwan and Korea. It is noteworthy that these countries have extended their capability beyond assembly of electronics into more technical engineering areas such as car manufacturing and construction. With small domestic markets, firms registered in these countries do not really have other meaningful survival and growth options other than internationalization of their activities. In this category are companies such Daewoo Industrial South and Samsung, LG (formerly Lucky Goldstar) and Hyundai from South Korea.

- Large domestic markets: a number of firms from NICs with large domestic markets have used these markets to perfect their production and marketing capability and have applied these skills as launch platform for internationalization. In a number of cases, MNEs from developing countries have transferred technology originally acquired from developed countries, after adaptation to the circumstances in other NICs. Example of companies in this category include General Motors do Brasil and Ford Brasil of Brazil; and BHarat Heavy Electricals and Steel Authority of India.

SUMMARY

In this chapter, we have examined the nature of international business and the role of the multinational enterprise. International business as a field of study and practice covers a broad spectrum of business activities that transcends national frontiers and affects all aspects of our lives. One unresolved issue in international business is finding a universally acceptable definition which describes the characteristics of the companies dominating the global economy. One thing that is clear, however, is the impact of MNEs on the global economy. Finally, the chapter also shows that the global economy consists of complex inter-relationships between multinational businesses, governments, economies and markets.

DISCUSSION QUESTIONS

1. Define and explain the nature of international business. Why should international business be regarded as a separate field of study?
2. The terms international, multinational and global firms are often used interchangeably. In strict terms, differences exist. What are these differences?

3. Examine the impact of MNEs on the global economy.
4. The dominance of MNEs from industrialized countries in the global economy is being challenged by emerging MNEs from developing countries. Discuss.

REFERENCES

Akoorie, M. 1993: 'Patterns of foreign direct investment by large New Zealand firms', *International Business Review*, Vol. 2, No. 2, pp. 169–89.

Buckley, P. J. and Ghauri, P. N. 1993: *The Internationalization of the Firm.* London: Academy Press.

Cavusgil, S. T. 1984: 'Differences among exporting firms based on their degree of internationalization', *Journal of Business Research*, Vol. 12, pp. 195–208.

Dunning, J. H. 1993: *Multinational Enterprises and the Global Economy.* Wokingham, UK: Addison-Wesley.

Hood, N. and Young, S. 1979: *The Economics of Multinational Enterprise.* New York: Longman.

Johanson, J. and Vahlne, J. E. 1977: 'The internationalisation process of the firm: a model of knowledge development and increasing foreign market commitments', *Journal of International Business Studies*, Vol. 8, No. 1, pp. 23–32.

Keegan W. J. 1989: *Global Marketing Management*, 4th edn. London: Prentice-Hall.

Minchinton, W. E. 1969: *The Growth of English Overseas Trade in the Seventeenth and Eighteenth Centuries.* London: Methuen.

Pitelis, C. N. and Sugden, R. 1991: *The Nature of the Transnational Firm.* London: Routledge.

Robinson, R. D. 1978: *International Business Management: A Guide to Decision Making*, 2nd edn. Hinsdale, IL: The Dryden Press.

Root, F. R. 1990: *International Trade and Investment.* Cincinnati, OH: South-Western Publishing.

Rugman, A. M., Lecraw, D. J. and Booth, 1985: *International Business: Firm and Environment.* New York: McGraw-Hill.

Taggart, J. and McDermott, M. 1993: *The Essence of International Business.* Hemel Hempstead: Prentice-Hall.

UNCTC 1992: *World Investment Report: Transnational Corporations as Engines of Growth.* New York: United Nations.

UNCTC 1993: *World Investment Report: Transnational Corporations and Integrated International Production*. New York: United Nations.

Welch, L. S. and Luostarinen, R. 1988: 'Internationalization: evolution of a concept', *Journal of General Management*, Vol. 14, No. 2.

Young, S., Hamill, J., Wheeler, C. and Davies, J. R. 1989: *International Market Entry and Development*. Hemel Hempstead: Harvester Wheatsheaf.

2

International trade and the nation state

INTRODUCTION

It is an accepted fact of life that no nation can achieve a completely independent existence because of the differences in factor endowment of nations. The global economy is an epitome of interdependence characterized by a complex flow of goods and products between countries, normally referred to as international trade. The term 'international trade' is broadly defined as transactions between sovereign nations which include the purchase and sale of consumer services, such as travel; industrial raw materials and services; producer and capital goods, such as plant and machinery; securities in the form of promissory notes and stock-ownership certificates; and natural resources such as crude oil, gold and other minerals. International trade provides the opportunity for less endowed countries to acquire goods and products that are either not available or in short supply within the local economy.

The impetus for international trade stems from the knowledge that, although most nations may have a sufficient variety of productive factors to produce almost every kind of good and product, they would not be able to produce each product and service with equal level of effectiveness (Root, 1990; Robock and Simmonds, 1989). The global economy thrives on the basis of national interdependence. The aims of this chapter are to examine (1) the theories of international trade; (2) international trade arrangements; and (3) the nature of state interference in international trade.

INTERNATIONAL TRADE THEORIES

Over the years, theories have evolved to explain the nature, importance and direction of international trade in the global economy. Although these theories are by no means conclusive in their explanation of international trade issues, they are none the less useful in articulating the likely composition and direction of trade. These theories have had a major effect on the formulation of trade policies by national governments. The main trade theories are examined in the following sections.

Mercantilism

The earliest attempt to explain the role of international trade in a nation's economy was dubbed mercantilism. The basic tenets of mercantilism were founded on the belief that there is a correlation between national wealth, power and security. The mercantilist influence upon European thought reached its peak in the sixteenth and seventeenth centuries. The focus of mercantilist analysis was the acquisition of wealth, particularly in gold, because it was felt that the power and influence of a nation could only be demonstrated by the size its accumulated wealth – preferably in the form of gold. Not surprisingly, mercantilist trade policy was fundamentally nationalistic in orientation with the primary aim of accumulating the wealth and power of the state by encouraging exports and discouraging imports. The proceeds from exports are then repatriated in gold. The principle of mercantilism is based on the belief that one nation can increase its trade only at some cost to other nations. It is the role of governments to control international trade by encouraging the exports of finished goods and imports of raw materials, and prohibiting the importation of finished goods.

Mercantilist philosophy was not without limitations. Its assumptions that international trade can only produce winners and losers, and that the accumulation of gold is synonymous with accumulation of wealth have been roundly criticized. These assumptions are fundamentally flawed and unsustainable and led to other studies and theories of international trade.

Absolute advantage

The limitations inherent in the philosophy of the mercantilist school of thought attracted considerable reaction from the English School of classical economics founded by Adam Smith (1723–90). Almost simultaneously, a group of French economists known as Physiocrats were demanding liberty of production and trade in France. The basic underlying principle of anti-mercantilist thought is that trade policies should be based primarily on cost considerations and not on nationalism. In 1776, Adam Smith published the *Wealth of Nations*, in which he articulated the advantages of importing goods where these could be obtained more cheaply than by domestic manufacture. This classical theory is now generally known as the theory of absolute advantage. As nations possess absolute advantages in the production of different goods, Smith suggested that each nation should specialize in the production of goods it was particularly well equipped to produce. Furthermore, he argued that part of the output should be exported, taking in exchange those goods that the country could not readily produce with equal levels of efficiency and effectiveness. If this principle were replicated in every country, discernible mutual benefits would arise.

The theory of absolute advantage has been found unsatisfactory by other economists. The main criticism focuses on the assumption that all nations have absolute advantage in the production of one product or the other. This has raised a number of questions. For example, Root (1990) posed the following questions. Suppose a country did not have absolute advantage in any product? Suppose a country had absolute advantage in producing all goods? Would there still be the need for international trade on both counts? These unanswered questions have undermined the relevance of the theory of absolute advantage as the basis for international trade policies.

Comparative advantage

Although the theory of absolute advantage was an important development in liberalism, Adam Smith did not expound on the theme at much length. This was later done by David Ricardo (1772–1823), the second great classical economist. In 1817 Ricardo published the classic *On the Principles of Political Economy and Taxation* in which he introduced the concept of comparative advantage. Ricardo's contention was that international trade could still be beneficial to all countries whether a country possessed absolute advantage in producing goods or not. He argued that if one country could produce all goods more efficiently than another, it should specialize in and export that product in which it was comparatively more efficient. For clarity and simplicity this principle is normally illustrated with two countries and two products. The two countries here are labelled A and B, and the two commodities wine and cloth. The labour unit required to produce either item in either country is as follows:

	Country A	Country B
Wine (1 unit)	0.5	1
Cloth (1 unit)	1	3

This shows that in the production of the two products, country A has absolute advantage over country B. It might therefore appear that if the two countries were to trade with each other in those products, country B would be worse off. But Ricardo insisted that this conclusion was not correct. He argued that the critical factor was that country B's disadvantage was less pronounced in wine production. This meant that country B would have a comparative advantage in wine production. Ricardo argued that the two countries would benefit from international trade if each country specialized in producing and exporting products in which it had comparative advantage, and imported those products in which it had a comparative disadvantage.

Although Ricardo's argument seemed plausible, his theory has a number of basic limitations. The concept of comparative advantage has been criticized for making a number of simplistic assumptions about the distribution of gains and losses accruing from international trade, the full employment objectives of nations, and for its concentration on production to the total exclusion of trade in services (Grimwade, 1989; Root, 1990; Khambata and Ajami, 1992).

Factor endowment theory

The factor endowment theory, normally referred to as Heckscher–Ohlin (H–O) theory, is based on the original work of the Swedish economists Eli Heckscher and Bertil Ohlin in which they tried to explain why differences in productivity exist between countries, and the impact of these differences on international trade. The basic tenet of the H–O theory rests on two fundamental assumptions. Countries differ in their relative factor endowments; and industries differ in their relative factor intensities. Therefore, trade encourages specialization in those activities requiring factor inputs in proportions similar to a country's natural and technological endowment. In other words, countries will have a comparative advantage in producing the goods using their abundant factor relatively intensively, and each country will export its abundant-factor good in return for imports of the good which uses its scarce factor relatively intensively (Pomfret, 1991; Heffernan and Sinclair, 1990; Sodersten and Reed, 1994)

Leontief paradox

No empirical study has cast more doubt on the H–O theory of international trade than the Leontief paradox (Root, 1990). Wassily Leontief, a

Russian-born economist, conducted a series of studies and published the results in the mid-1950s. Leontief tested the proposition that the USA, which is generally accepted as having a comparative advantage in the production of capital-intensive goods, was expected to export such goods and import labour-intensive goods, in which it has comparative disadvantage. Using 1947 international trade data, he examined the composition of factor-input of goods imported and those exported in that year. Leontief found that the capital to labour ratio for the export industries was US$14,010 per man-year and for the import-competing industries US$18,180 per man-year. Given that the USA is regarded as the most capital abundant country in the world, it is paradoxical that the USA was importing capital-intensive goods, thus contradicting the H–O theorem. The result of this study later became known as the *Leontief paradox*.

The Leontief paradox generated a great deal of interest and reactions from economists. Doubts and questions were raised concerning the accuracy of the data used in the study and the appropriateness of the year chosen for the study. It is noteworthy that subsequent studies by Leontief himself and other economists on the US economy in the 1950s and 1960s reaffirmed the paradox. The studies were replicated in Japan by Tatemoto and Ichimura in 1959, and in Canada by Wahl in 1961 with paradoxical results. However, other studies by Stolper and Roskamp in 1961 in East Germany and Bharadwaj in India did not show paradoxical results.

These mixed results have cast further doubts and confusion on the validity and usefulness of the H–O theorem. It is, however, true to say that the H–O theorem provides an analytical framework for predicting the likely pattern of trade between countries.

STATE INTERFERENCE IN INTERNATIONAL TRADE

The comparative advantage and factor endowment theories have been quite useful in exposing the virtues and benefits of unrestricted trade between sovereign nations. Despite these theoretical expositions, all nations, in one way or the other, interfere with international trade by controlling its nature, composition and direction. The extent of control, however, depends on the nature of the products in question and their perceived importance to the nation's economic well-being. As a result, types of control of international trade differ considerably from country to country. State interference in international trade may manifest itself either in the form of import/export tariffs, or quantitative restrictions in the form of quotas or even the outright ban on imports or exports of a product.

A tariff is a tax levied on goods when they are moved across national frontiers. The debate among economists over the merits and justification of state control of international trade through tariffs has a long history and still continues. The main element of this debate hinges on the concept of imperfect competition. Brander and Spencer (1981) suggest that one important aspect of imperfect competition is that the price charged for a product exceeds the marginal cost of production. As a result, a country importing such a product usually pays a monopoly rent to the exporting firm. Thus, tax policy becomes the standard instrument for extracting monopoly rents from imperfectly competitive firms in international trade.

From a policy standpoint, tariffs may be imposed either for protective reasons such as to shield domestic firms from unfair competition from abroad by ensuring that imported goods are exorbitantly priced, or for revenue considerations. Tariffs may be expressed as a specific tax payable on each unit imported or as a percentage of the total value of the goods imported – generally referred to as *ad valorem*.

There are other forms of trade control which are neither quantitative restrictions nor levies. These include government regulations and practices (procurement policy, health regulations, tests and standards, and valuation procedures) and quotas or quantitative restrictions (which impose a limit on the amount of goods being imported); they are normally collectively described as non-tariff barriers.

The impact of state control, regardless of its form, on international trade is undoubtedly significant; but it can be difficult to measure. None the less, two important effects are worth noting. First, it erodes the potential benefits of free trade as postulated in the various liberal theories of international trade. Second, it is generally argued that the amount of a tariff does not necessarily determine its restrictive effect. However, the potential worldwide benefits from free trade cannot be realized with state interference in the process.

TRADE AGREEMENTS

Trade agreements are contractual arrangements between sovereign nations on matters relating to their trade relationships. These agreements may be between two independent nations – bilateral – or between a group of nations – multilateral. Of all the trade agreements and economic cooperation between nations, the General Agreement on Tariffs and Trade (GATT) and subsequently, the World Trade Organization (WTO) has emerged as the most important reference point and charter governing world trade.

The economic depression of the 1930s led to an upsurge of trade restrictions, and of regional or imperial systems of preferential treatment of trade. Following the end of the Second World War, the United Kingdom and the United States, together with other countries, began to plan for a new and more viable basis for trade relations in the global economy with a view to avoiding the errors of the past. In 1944 a conference was convened at Bretton Woods, New Hampshire, where it was decided that the central coordinating bodies of the new economic order would be the International Monetary Fund (IMF) (to take care of short-term problems with international liquidity); the International Trade Organization (ITO) (to deal with trade relations among nations); and the International Bank for Reconstruction and Development (IBRD) (to assist with the post-war reconstruction).

In 1946, at a meeting of ITO in Geneva, there was a consensus between a group of twenty-three countries (which among them accounted for 80 per cent of world trade), on the need to reduce tariffs in order to facilitate world trade. This led to an agreement which was signed in Geneva on 30 October 1947, and dubbed the General Agreement on Tariffs and Trade (GATT).

GATT is a multilateral trade agreement which was signed on the basis of reciprocity and mutual advantage in world trade. Following a series of conferences organized with a view to lowering tariffs and trade barriers, the number of signatories to GATT has now grown to over ninety. The principles of GATT consist of four basic elememts:

- There shall be no trade discrimination of any kind between participating countries.
- As a rule, there is to be no protection other than that provided by the customs tariff (the 'national treatment' principle).
- Customs unions and free trade groupings are considered legitimate means of trade liberalization, provided that, taken as a whole, such arrangements do not discriminate against third countries.
- Members of GATT are entitled to levy the following charges on imports:
    (1)   an import tax equal in amount to internal taxes on the product concerned, subject only to the general national treatment principle above;

EXHIBIT 2.1

Japan to tackle unfair taxes on Scotch

The Japanese government announced Thursday, 3 October, 1996, that it intends to narrow the gap between tax levied on imported Scotch whisky and locally produced spirits. Unfair taxes on imported Scotch whisky have been a perennial problem for exporters to Japan, making these products very expensive and uncompetitive.

The move follows a ruling by the newly established World Trade Organization (WTO) in Geneva which found the current tax system in place in Japan to be unfair and unsatisfactory.

The cheapest imported Scotch in Japan sells for about US$30.00. Locally made *Shochu*, a spirit similar to vodka, costs no more than US$12.00.

Discussion questions

1. Explain why the Japanese government is now taking action to deal with this perennial problem.
2. Do you believe that the WTO will be more effective in dealing with international trade problems than GATT? Give reasons for your answer.

---

(2)   'anti-dumping' duties in the case of imported products that are being sold at a loss or are benefiting from an export subsidy;
(3)   fees and other proper charges for services rendered.

It is noteworthy, however, that these are only the basic rules under the GATT regime. There are a number of important exceptions to these rules which may be invoked in special circumstances, such as having to deal with problems of (1) balance of payment disequilibria, (2) serious and unexpected damage to domestic production, and (3) national security.

Following the success of the 1947 conference, GATT has organized a series of follow-up conferences for the purpose of encouraging trade liberalization by lowering trade barriers at Annecy (1949), Torquay (1950–1), Geneva (1956, 1960–1 and 1964–7), Tokyo (1973–9), Geneva (1982) and Punta de Este, Uruguay (1986–93). The outcome of these negotiations has not been unqualified success. It is expected that conferences and negotiations will continue until the potential benefits of global development and growth are achieved through trade liberalization.

WORLD TRADE ORGANIZATION

The Uruguay Round of negotiations commenced in 1986 with an inaugural meeting of trade ministers held at Punta de Este, Uruguay. (Although no negotiations actually took place in Uruguay, the 'Round' was none the less named after the country.) Following seven years of intensive negotiations, the Round was concluded in December 1993. The Final Act – a document containing the various agreements – was signed at Marrakesh, Morocco, in April 1994. Most of the agreements in the Final Act became effective 1 January 1995, albeit with different implementation periods for different groups of countries.

One of the main achivements of the Round was the agreement to establish the World Trade Organization (WTO) as an international body with permanent existence with effect from 1 January 1995, replacing GATT. WTO is now responsible for providing a framework for trading relationships between countries and will play a role similar to those of the International Monetary Fund (IMF) and World Bank. One significant difference between the new organization and GATT is that the latter is not an organization, but rather a treaty which countries signed to become contracting parties but not members. It is believed that the lack of permanence of GATT (as it offers only provisional application) reduced its effectiveness as the basis for a rule-based system of world trade. This apparent weakness in GATT provided the impetus for the agreement to establish WTO. It is expected that the new organization will strengthen the management of trading relationships between nations, particularly the enforcement of decisions.

Article 1 of the Agreement establishing WTO states that 'the new organisation is to provide the common institutional framework for the conduct of trade relations among its members' to encompass all the agreements and associated legal instruments contained in the Final Act. These agreements cover:

1.   the Agreements on Trade in Goods. This includes the so-called 'GATT 1994' (the Uruguay Round Protocol GATT 1994). This consists of the provisions contained in GATT 1947 'as rectified, amended or otherwise modified'.

EXHIBIT 2.2

Tariff-cutting deal lifts hopes for Uruguay Round

There was no shortage of superlatives in Tokyo when the ministers of the Quad group of countries unveiled their tariff-cutting deal to the world's press on 7 July 1993. Even the most jaundiced veteran of successive 'breakthroughs' in the seven-year history of the Uruguay Round of multilateral trade negotiations found it difficult not to be impressed by the package unveiled by negotiators from the USA, the European Community, Japan and Canada. The Quad package envisages substantial tariff cuts for manufactured products, including:

- complete elimination of tariffs and non-tariff measures in pharmaceuticals, construction equipment, medical equipment, steel, beer, and subject to certain exceptions, furniture, farm equipment and spirits;
- harmonization of tariffs at low rates for chemical products. The negotiators hope further negotiations will lead to more harmonization in other areas;
- tariff cuts of up to 50 per cent for 'high tariff' products, which carry tariffs of 15 per cent and above;
- tariff cuts averaging at least one-third for other products. These include wood, paper and pulp, and scientific equipment which some members of the Quad group had unsuccessfully earmarked for zero-for-zero tariff treatment.

In the area of services, progress has been more opaque. The report prepared by the Quad ministers for the G7 summit said there were many existing offers to improve market access for services. These covered sectors such as insurance, banking, securities, construction, distribution, tourism, software and computer services, professional and business services, including consulting, engineering, accounting and legal services.

In basic telecommunications the way ahead appeared somewhat clearer. The Quad ministers said they would 'pursue a multilateral liberalization' of the sector within the framework of a draft trade in services agreement and on the basis of a common detailed agenda that they had developed.

Discussion questions

1. What are the benefits of eliminating tariff and non-tariff barriers to the global economy?
2. Would the successful conclusion of the Uruguay Round lead to lower product prices?

Source: Adapted from Peter Norman and Michiyo Nakamoto, *Financial Times*, 8 July 1993. Reprinted by permission.

2. the Agreements on Trade in Services (GATS);
3. the Agreements on Trade-related Aspects of Intellectual Property Rights including trade in counterfeit goods (TRIPs);
4. the Understanding on Rules and Procedures Governing the Settlement of Disputes;
5. the Trade Policy Review Mechanism.

A member of WTO has to adhere to all and not just some of these agreements – a significant difference from GATT. GATT agreements allowed countries to comply only with those agreements they were contracted to. Countries not wishing to be bound by all the agreements in the Final Act have the option not to join. However, a country that is contracted to GATT 1947 but does not wish to become a member of WTO will continue to enjoy the protection of GATT 1947 with the obligations imposed by the membership of WTO. This is possible because GATT 1947 is legally distinct from GATT 1994.

It is clear that much depends on the new organization. The success or failure of WTO will depend on its effectiveness in managing world trade issues.

SUMMARY

In this chapter, we have discussed the nature of international trade and its effects on the global economy. In particular, the examination of the various theories of international trade has shown they are by no means definitive in explaining international trade. They are, however, useful reference points for policy makers in recognizing the benefits of global interdependence. In order to ensure that these benefits are achieved, nations are relying on GATT as the main body governing the conduct of international trade. Although the number of signatories to GATT has increased over the years, its aims and purposes remain the same: reciprocity and mutual advantage in global trade.

DISCUSSION QUESTIONS

1. Using the factor endowment theory (Heckscher–Ohlin) of international trade, explain how the less developed countries could benefit from international trade liberalization.

2. 'No empirical study has cast more doubt on the conventional theory of international trade than the Leontief paradox' (Root, 1990). What is the Leontief paradox? What are the arguments against it?
3. One of the stated objectives of GATT is to aid the development process in less developed countries. From the developing countries' standpoint, how successful has GATT been in the pursuit of this objective?
4. Distinguish between tariff and non-tariff barriers. Discuss the argument that non-tariff barriers are more effective in protecting markets than tariff barriers. Illustrate your answer with examples.

REFERENCES

Brander, J. A. and Spencer, B. J. 1981: 'Tariffs and the extraction of foreign monopoly rents under potential entry', *Canadian Journal of Economics*, Vol. 14, No. 3, pp. 371–89.

Grimwade, N. 1989: *International Trade: New Patterns of Trade, Production and Investment*. London: Routledge.

Heffernan, S. and Sinclair, P. 1990: *Modern International Economics*. Oxford: Blackwell.

Khambata, D. and Ajami, R. 1992: *International Business: Theory and Practice*. New York: Macmillan.

Norman, Peter and Nakamoto, Michiyo 1993: 'Tariff-cutting deal lifts hopes for Uruguay Round', *Financial Times*, 8 July, p. 2.

Pomfret, R. 1991: *International Trade: An Introduction to Theory and Policy*. Oxford: Blackwell.

Robock, S. and Simmonds, K. 1989: *International Business and Multinational Enterprises*, 4th edn. Homewood, IL: Richard D. Irwin.

Ricardo, D. 1971: *Principles of Political Economy and Taxation*. Harmondsworth: Penguin.

Root, F. R. 1990: *International Trade and Investments*, 6th edn. Cincinnati, OH: South-Western Publishing.

Sodersten, B. and Reed, G. 1994: *International Economics*, 3rd edn. Basingstoke: Macmillan.

3

The international business environment

INTRODUCTION

In chapter 1 we examined the nature of international business and why it should be studied as a separate field of study. It was also noted that international business activities take place in multiple and complex environments. These include forces that affect a firm's immediate operating environment such as customers, suppliers, competitors, labour market; and the remote environment which consists of economic, political, sociocultural, technological and legal considerations. Although these indirect external factors are referred to as the remote environment, their impact on international business activities is by no means remote. Indeed, they have a direct impact on the performance of the MNE. For example, the economic environment of a host market has direct implications for a company's strategic planning and profitability. It is the aim of this chapter to examine the nature of the external environment and its impact on international business.

THE ECONOMIC ENVIRONMENT

The economic environment in which international business must be conducted is perhaps the most important aspect of the remote environment which impacts on the activities of the firm as it considers a market's potential. It consists of both the domestic or national and international or global elements, as these are intertwined. The domestic economic environment affects business activities within a country, while the international economic environment affects business activities between and among nations.

Domestic economic environment

There are a number of general and useful indicators that are needed for assessing an economic environment in which MNE operational activities are contemplated. These must, however, include an assessment of population; per capita income; income distribution; and the type of economy.

- Population: market size is primarily a function of the population and purchasing power propensity. As a general rule, the larger the population, the better the market. Although it is rational to suggest that there is no correlation between population size and sales potential, it is noteworthy that population is the primary indicator of the size of any market. It is particularly pertinent for certain product categories. For consumer products such as food, drugs and other basic but essential products, the higher the population the greater the demand. Thus, India is usually considered as an important market because of the size of its population.

  In addition, the geographic distribution of population within a country is important, as it has significant marketing and logistics implications for international marketing planning. In most countries urban centres tend to be more densely populated than the rural areas because of the attractions of urbanization, such as better developed infrastructure, transport and housing. Similarly, age distribution is an important consideration when the structure and composition of the population is being examined. This is particularly essential in the marketing of products that are susceptible to age differential. Examples of products in this category include fashion and horticultural products.

- Per capita income: is probably the commonest statistical indicator of a country's economic potential that international firms consider when investment decisions are being made. Per capita income measures the performance of an economy in relation to the size of the population. Where low population is supported by high gross domestic product, the per capita income will be high. The per capita income of Libya is comparable with that of the USA, Germany and Japan. Similarly, although India is a rapidly developing country, the size of its population (over 850 million) means that per capita income is low. However, it is misleading to rely entirely on per capita income in evaluating a country's marketing potential. This can be illustrated on the one hand, by Libya's developing nation status despite its high per capita income. On the other hand, despite its low per capita income,

India is considered as an important market for every conceivable type of product. In particular, it offers a considerable number of very affluent customers.

- Income distribution: although per capita income indicates the basic economic potential of a country, it is generally misleading and perhaps dangerous for international firms to rely solely on this indicator in assessing any market. The Pareto rule often applies in both the income distribution and the demand pattern in any market. This rule suggests that, for certain products such as non-basic and luxury items, 80 per cent are bought by only 20 per cent of the population. In some desperately poor countries where wealth is concentrated in the hands of a tiny minority of the population, the demand for and consumption of luxury products can be unbelievably high and comparable to the pattern of demand in fairly affluent countries. For example, the very high demand for luxury products such as Louis Vuitton travel accessories, Mercedes-Benz cars and other designer products in Nigeria has no correlation with that country's low per capita income.
- Type of economy: economies may be categorized according to a number of characteristics such as the level of development, the predominant economic activities, availability of economic and technological infrastructures, and the degree of urbanization. These characteristics are useful indicators of the type of market which a country offers and its marketing implications. These indicators are also important in evaluating the level of development, type of production techniques and the nature of consumption in a country, as these have direct relevance for the marketing of certain products.

THE POLITICAL ENVIRONMENT

The political environment in which international business is conducted consists of three important elements that are generally complex and intertwined – the home country political environment, the host country political environment, and the global political environment. Each of these political elements may have either a direct or an indirect influence, and may also be favourable or hostile to the activities of the international firm. Phillips *et al.* (1994) noted that in an ideal world, the business community would prefer a political environment that was fully supportive of the interests of business and which followed policies that were consistent and predictable. But this is not an ideal world and political environments are not always supportive of business or even consistent in their policies.

Home country political environment

These are the domestic politics of the firm's country of incorporation. In an ideal world, one would not normally expect domestic politics to affect a firm's international activities. However, they may have far reaching consequences for a firm's activities. This is particularly pertinent for certain product categories, such as frontier military and nuclear technology, and scientific innovations with possible military applications. The export of these products may either be banned completely or subject to export control by the home country government. This type of control was a commonplace at the height of the cold war between the West and the former Soviet Union. Even with the collapse of Soviet Union, the West has not relaxed its control over trade in certain technologies. It is feared that, without proper control, there are risks of proliferation and the development of nuclear technology by some ambitious and unstable developing countries, which may spell disaster for global security. Even the export of less potent technologies is equally controlled. In 1991 the directors of a British company, Matrix Churchill Engineering in Coventry, England, were prosecuted by the British government for exporting heavy steel pipes because they were suspected to have possible military applications in Iraq.

Domestic firms that continue to invest and manufacture abroad while ignoring their home country are often accused of exacerbating domestic unemployment problems and may be subject to political pressure from the government of the day. Finally, the international activities of a firm may be criticized by its home country government if these activities generate international outcry.

Host country political environment

Host country politics are those of the foreign market in which a firm may be conducting its activities away from home. Host country policies governing the activities of foreign firms can range from the welcoming and supportive to the outright hostile. The political atmosphere tends to be hospitable where both the perceived and actual benefits of hosting foreign firms outweigh their costs. The construction of manufacturing facilities which create employment opportunities and create other social benefits in the host market will attract support from labour organizations and the government. Where foreign firms are perceived to contribute little or nothing to the well-being of the nation, this may produce hostile behaviour from the business community and labour organizations, which may put pressure on the government to take necessary steps to extract more economic rent from these firms. In extreme cases, this may lead to either nationalization or the expropriation of the assets of foreign firms. Similarly, a breach of a stipulated code of conduct by international firms in a host market can lead to more than proportionate reprisals from the government. In 1978, the Nigerian government nationalized the assets of British Petroleum when it was revealed that the company was clandestinely selling Nigerian crude oil to the apartheid regime in South Africa, despite an embargo against such activities.

Global political environment

This may be described as the combined politics of the home, host and third countries. The political atmosphere in a third country can have a major impact on the activities of international firms in ways that may not

---

EXHIBIT 3.1

China orders Microsoft to stop selling 'Windows 95'

On Monday, 30 September 1996, Beijing announced it had ordered the US computer giant, Microsoft, to stop sales of the Mainland version of 'Windows 95'. Chinese officials say it contains politically offensive material including the phrases 'communist bandits' and 'Taiwan independence'. It also has a map depicting China without Taiwan.

Microsoft blames programmers in Taiwan who were subcontracted to produce the operating system for the problem. The company has offered to update the software eliminating the references in order to assuage officials in Beijing. It further promised to provide the revised version free to those who had bought the original Mainland version.

Discussion questions

1.   What is the political significance of a map of China without Taiwan?
2.   Examine the business implications of Beijing's irritation with Microsoft.

be immediately apparent. Multilateral agreements between international organizations such as GATT, the United Nations and the Commonwealth may constitute an impediment to free trade as well as to the nature and scope of the operation of international firms. The economic embargo on Iraq by the Security Council of the United Nations in 1991 meant that conducting trade with that country became illegal for all international firms.

SOCIO-CULTURAL ENVIRONMENT

With the increasing wave of interest in globalization, it must be emphasized that lack of understanding of the vital role of culture in shaping consumer attitudes, lifestyle and behaviour may be catastrophic for the multinational firm. Instances where MNEs have failed to recognize the significance of cultural differences between home and foreign markets in planning and executing their international marketing activities, with disastrous consequences, abound in international business literature. When companies move beyond their national frontiers they are confronted with a new set of values and lifestyles that are, in some cases, quite different from those they are familiar with. The performance of a company in the international arena partly depends on how well the marketing mix elements fit into the culture of the host market. So what is culture? Although there is no definitive definition, it may be described as the totality of the complex and learned behaviour of members of a given society. The elements of culture include belief, art, morals, law and custom. Jain (1990) suggests that culture develops through recurrent social relationships that form patterns that are eventually internalized by members of the entire group and must have the following three characteristics:

- It is learned: acquired by people over time through their membership in a group that transmits culture from generation to generation.
- It is interrelated: one part of the culture is deeply connected with another part such as religion and marriage, business and social status.
- It is shared: tenets of a culture extend to other members of the group.

Culture is, perhaps, one of the most important determinants of consumer behaviour. It influences the process of decision making in the day-to-day buying habits of consumers. Culture is central to how products and the process of marketing are viewed. Thus, there is a need for cross-cultural

EXHIBIT 3.2

McDonald's battles for survival in Israel

Benjamin Netanyahu was elected Prime Minister of Israel in a most dramatic fashion in May 1996. He defeated the incumbent Prime Minister, Shimon Peres, with 50.5 per cent of the votes. As Israelis voted for the two candidates for the top job, they were also, for the first time, electing new members of Parliament independent of the two candidates for the top job.

As soon as the Election Committee announced the results of the election, political horsetrading for the formation of a new right-wing Israeli coalition Cabinet began in earnest. The triumphant religious parties demanded the closure of the popular 'non-kosher' McDonald's in the heart of Jerusalem and thousands of other establishments in breach of Jewish law as their price for joining the coalition government.

McDonald's, recently opened in Jerusalem's Shamai Street, has become the symbol of the transformation of Israeli society under the four years of Labour rule which religious deputies want reversed by the Prime Minister-Elect, Benjamin Netanyahu. To outsiders, the depth of passion that can be engendered by the eating of a cheeseburger and the breaching of the Jewish dietary law of not mixing meat with dairy products is hard to fathom. Other non-kosher delicatessens are also threatened with closure, but not without a fight from owners. As one owner puts it: 'This could lead to civil war. The new government has to remember that almost half of the country voted to continue the [Shimon] Peres way. There are also Christians and foreigners in the city.'

One of the hardline deputies elected on the platform of National Religious Party (NRP), Mr Yigal Bibi, said his group would be demanding that McDonald's should either be shut or forced to become kosher under rabbinical supervision. He added that the NRP and the two other religious parties would also be demanding that the new administration close down shopping malls, restaurants and other places breaching the sabbath. Such establishments have been doing a roaring trade in all parts of the country under Labour. 'It is unacceptable that in the state of Israel, people are being forced to work seven days,' Mr Bibi said.

Many young Israelis are appalled at the prospect of an imminent end to the Western-style life that they enjoyed under the Labour-led administration, with Jerusalem on Friday nights now throbbing to techno rhythms from dozens of sabbath-breaking nightclubs and bars.

Discussion questions

1. How would you describe the threat facing McDonald's from an international business standpoint? *cont.*

> 2. Would you advise McDonald's to withdraw from Israel in the light of this threat from the ultra-orthodox religious parties?
> 3. If not, what are the options available to McDonald's?

understanding because of the significant differences in attitude, belief, motivation, perception and lifestyle between nations.

The social dimension of culture is receiving serious attention as a critical determinant of international management behaviour. The socio-cultural environment for international business refers to the set of factors which shape the material and psychological development of a nation, and represents the primary influence on individual lifestyle, attitudes, predisposition and behaviour as consumers in the market. The socio-cultural environment consists of those physical, demographic and behavioural variables which influence business activities in a given country as depicted in figure 3.1. The central argument for the need to examine the significance of the socio-cultural dimension of the internationalization of the firm is that management views tend to be influenced or, in some cases, determined by culture and ethnocentric by implication. Bradley (1991) suggests that the growing use of anthropology, sociology and psychology in international marketing analysis is an explicit recognition of the non-economic bases of market behaviour.

The most important task of the international marketer is to identify relevant similarities and differences among target markets. This task is not easy and is made even more complicated because experts and business people disagree over whether buyer behaviour is converging or diverging globally (Toyne and Walters, 1993). The convergence school of thought believe that there are some universal cultural traits and that, essentially, the same product can be sold with similar promotional appeals in all overseas markets. This line of thought is particularly attractive to those firms seeking to pursue global strategies. The primary task, therefore, is to identify and build on the cultural similarities across markets. On the other hand, the divergence school of thought believes there are distinctive national cultural traits, and that these unique national characteristics cannot be ignored. Advocates of this belief suggest that companies must seek to identify and recognize these national characteristics with a view to satisfying unique market needs and wants.

These two schools of thought are inherently idealistic as they represent extremes of international marketing strategies' continuum. International marketers must develop marketing programmes that recognize the similarities and differences between markets as the basis for competitive success.

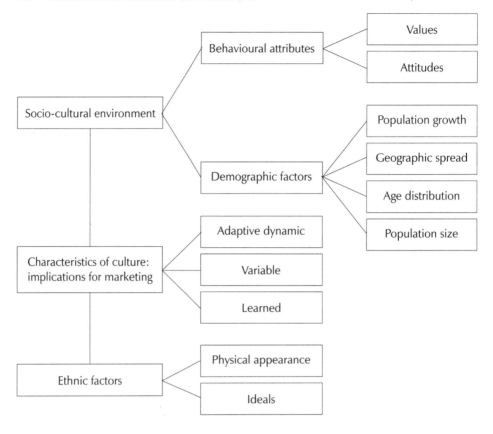

Figure 3.1 The socio-cultural environment and marketing implications
Source: Bradley (1991), p. 111. Copyright © Prentice-Hall 1991. Reproduced by permission.

THE IMPACT OF THE SOCIO-CULTURAL ENVIRONMENT ON INTERNATIONAL BUSINESS

The socio-cultural environment in which international business is conducted affects all aspects of marketing: it affects the consumer perception of products, distribution, pricing, and communications policies and strategies. The cultural impact is better illustrated with practical examples.

- Product: the utility value of a single product may differ considerably from country to country because of differences in beliefs, values and lifestyles. Fast foods such as Kentucky fried chicken, McDonald's

EXHIBIT 3.3

Elements of consumer behaviour analysis in a cross-cultural setting

1. Determine underlying values and their rate of change within the relevant market. What values are generally held strongly within the general market and the intended market segment? What is the rate and direction of value changes taking place within the relevant culture?
2. Evaluate the product concept as it relates to this culture. Is this product concept one that harmonizes with current and evolving values? If there are value conflicts with ownership of this product, can the product be changed to fit these values? How can the product be effectively identified with positive values? What needs does the product satisfy for members of the culture? Are these needs important? How are competitive products and brands currently satisfying these needs?
3. Determine characteristic purchase decision-making patterns. How do consumers make decisions for this product? Which family members are involved in purchase decision-making and use of this product? What role does each member typically play in the process? What purchase criteria and sources of information do consumers use in making buying decisions for this product? What is the cultural attitude toward acceptance of innovations? What cultural values might be congruent with or conflict with purchase and use of this product?
4. Determine appropriate promotion methods. What means of communications exist for advertising to consumers? How is advertising perceived among those in the culture? Must different languages be used to reach various cultural groups? What are the most relevant appeals for this product among the culture? What taboos (such as words, themes, colours or pictures) may impinge on our sales or advertising strategy? What is the role of the salesperson in this culture?
5. Determine appropriate distribution channels. What are the characteristic distribution channels for this product? Are capable institutions available for handling this product? Might new channel opportunities exist which would be readily accepted by consumers? What is the nature of the shopping process for this product?
6. Determine appropriate pricing approaches. Are consumers aware of prices in the product category? Are they sensitive to differences in prices between brands? How important is price in consumers' purchasing decisions?

beefburgers and pizza have a higher utility value in modern societies than in traditional societies. Similarly, branding and packaging are very susceptible to cultural bias.

- Pricing: products are bought in markets on the basis of either perceived or real utility value. Products from certain parts of the world such as Western Europe and the United States command premium prices in developing countries because they possess higher perceived quality, and thus value, than locally manufactured products. In Nigeria, certain locally manufactured goods are known to be marketed with labels 'Made in England' – or USA, or Japan – to facilitate acceptability in the market.
- Promotion: culture is perhaps the most powerful influence in determining effectiveness and acceptability or otherwise of advertising copy, design and other elements of marketing promotion in international markets. The fact that advertising copy and design are successful in the domestic market is not a guarantee they will be successful in all international markets. In 1994, Laboratoire Garnier, a French cosmetic company, developed a successful pan-European advertising campaign for its shower gel – Neutralia. However, when it was shown in the UK, there was a considerable protest from viewers, who felt uncomfortable about viewing an advertisement showing exposed nipples. The advertisement was later modified for the UK market to mask the offending nipples.
- Distribution: certain distribution strategies may be affected by local norms and practices that derive from culture. In Spain, mail-order shopping which enables individuals to shop from catalogues in the privacy of their homes does not work because packages cannot be delivered to private addresses by the post office.

Thus, at a time when globalization of businesses is fast becoming the rule rather than the exception, cross-cultural understanding is absolutely vital in helping international marketing executives to recognize and appreciate the significance of business norms and practices, and the motivation for consumer behaviour in host markets.

TECHNOLOGICAL ENVIRONMENT

Technology and its application have become the key factors in determining the international competitiveness of the firm in the conduct of international business. Indeed, differentiation strategies based on the

EXHIBIT 3.4

Shower of complaints

The first commercial on British television to feature a woman's exposed nipple has created a storm of protest. Viewers – mostly women – have complained to television watchdogs about the advert, which shows a blonde massaging shower gel on to her bare breasts. The French-made commercial has been shown in ten other European countries, reportedly without a single complaint. But more than forty British viewers have complained to the Independent Television Commission (ITC) since it was first shown last week. Scores of others have protested directly to their local stations, according to the ITV Network Centre. Viewers have objected to bare breasts being shown in a TV commercial and claim the advert is offensive, sexist and degrading to women.

The French comestic firm Laboratoire Garnier, which makes Neutralia shower gel, was given permission to screen the advert only if it went out after the 9 pm family viewing watershed. A nipple-free version is shown earlier in the day. Virginia Lee, a spokesman for the ITC, said: 'This complaint is quite significant. We are monitoring the advert to see if it breaks our guidelines on taste and decency. If it does, we have the power to pull it.' TV watchdogs have so far decided not to ban the advert because bare breasts on a programme shown after 9 pm would not normally offend viewers. Virginia Lee said: 'Most people watching a programme after 9 pm are no longer shocked at some degree of nudity, but in adverts the reaction seems to be different.'

A spokeman for Laboratoire Garnier said, however: 'We have complied with all the regulations. It will be part of an on-going advertising campaign.' In 1993, the ITC ruled that a Gossard bra advert could be aired at any time of the day provided no nipple shape could be seen through the fabric.

The complaints come as advertisers have been asked to take account of reactions to an ultrabra commercial. It features a woman who has padded with tissue, trying to get the attention of the man – only to have the padding removed by a rival female wearing an ultrabra. Twenty-seven viewers complained to the ITC that the advert 'perpetuated the image of women as sex objects' but although it asked advertisers to take note, it decided not to ban the advert.

Discussion questions

1. Discuss the factors influencing the attitude of British viewers towards nudity on television and its impact on pan-European advertising.
2. Do you agree with the assertion that the advert perpetuates the image of women as sex objects? Give reasons for your answer.

Source: Adapted from V. Orvice, 'Bare breasts in French advert outrage viewers', *Daily Mail*, 13 May, p.12. Reprinted by permission.

exclusive mastery of a technology or a set of technologies are those which generally give the firm the greatest competitive advantage (Dussuage *et al.*, 1992). Technological leadership is only achieved through a consistent programme of intensive research and development, which can be very costly. Thus, costs of successful innovations are recovered more swiftly by internationalization of the know-how.

The technological revolution of the 1980s and 1990s simply means that no firm, and certainly no industry, can be insulated from its impact on both domestic and international business. Dussuage *et al.* (1992) suggest that as the impact of technology increases, the significance of local and regional differences is diminished. Thus, technological evolution and the growing importance of technology in many industries encourage global-ization of markets. Levitt (1983) writes: 'a powerful force drives the world toward a converging commonality, and that force is technology. It has proletarianized communication, transport and travel. It has made iso-lated places and impoverished peoples eager for modernity's allure-ment.' The evolutionary nature of technology implies that companies that are able to maintain their technological activities will remain competitive.

There are managerial implications in the emergence of new technologies. Management must deal with the problems of technical and structural changes associated with their diffusion, and their wider impact on society.

THE LEGAL ENVIRONMENT

The legal environment in any market relates to the laws and regulations governing the conduct of business activities in that market. It may be expressed as a function of the socio-cultural, political and ideological ori-entation of a country, and the perceived role of multinational enterprises in a nation's economy and development. Thus, every sovereign nation has a legal system that reflects its socio-cultural and political values and beliefs. Multinational enterprises have to deal with varied and sometimes complex legal systems across the world.

The international legal environment has three aspects: home country laws, host country laws, and international laws.

Home country laws

Home country laws and regulations deal with two important issues – the conduct of the firm in the domestic market and trade with third countries.

These laws and regulations do not discriminate between domestic and international operators as they are designed to protect the domestic consumers, national interest and security. However, for the international operators, there are additional controls on exporting to third countries. These relate to the types of country and the nature of products for which export authorization might be denied. The export of high technology products with military applications is normally controlled to ensure they do not get into the wrong hands. Nuclear technology falls into this category.

Host country laws

Multinational enterprises have to deal with myriad regulations on their activities in host countries. The most obvious areas with stringent control includes investment regulations, tariffs and duties, anti-dumping regulations and the protection of local industries (the infant industry argument). One of the reasons for the control of foreign firms derives from the need to protect less developed local industries from unfair competition from the more industrialized countries. In most developing countries, foreign firms are either excluded from competing with domestic firms in certain sectors of the local economy or their involvement is severely restricted. Similarly, tariffs and duties are used to fulfil two important objectives: to discourage importation of non-essential products in order to conserve foreign exchange and maintain a favourable balance of trade; and to generate revenue for the government.

International laws

Terpstra (1983) defines international law as the collection of treaties, conventions and agreements between nations, which have, more or less, the force of law. They are usually multilateral among many nations. National parliaments normally ratify these treaties and conventions to provide them with the force of law and they have considerable international implications. International laws are particularly relevant in areas relating to patents and trademark protection and piracy laws, UN resolutions, multilateral trade agreements such as GATT and Codes of conduct for multinational enterprises.

Firms are motivated to continue with research and development activity at considerable costs by the knowledge that inventions and discoveries can be registered and exploited exclusively by the inventors and know-how owners. Registered intellectual properties and inventions are protected in international law under the auspices of the World Intellectual Property Organization (WIPO). Infringements are vigorously contested by patent owners. Similarly, multilateral agreements such as GATT have become the force governing international trade.

SUMMARY

The environment for international business is multifaceted, stratified and highly intertwined. An international firm has to deal with multiplicity of complex aspects of the environment such as political, socio-cultural, legal and technological issues. This chapter shows that:

- Both the domestic and international economic environment affect international business.
- Understanding cultural differences between nations is vitally important for international competitiveness.
- The legal environment is a function of a country's socio-cultural, political and ideological orientation.

DISCUSSION QUESTIONS

1. Examine the role of culture in international marketing planning.
2. To what extent can per capita income be relied upon as an indicator of a market's potential?
3. International firms have to deal with multiple set of laws in the course of their operation. Discuss the implication of these laws in international business.
4. Describe the impact of technology on international competitiveness.

REFERENCES

Bradley, F. 1991: *International Marketing Strategy*. London: Prentice-Hall.
Dussuage, P., Hart, S. and Ramanantsoa, B. 1992: *Strategic Technology Management*. Chichester: John Wiley.

Jain, S. C. 1990: *International Marketing Management*, 3rd edn. Boston: PWS-Kent Publishing.

Levitt, T. 1983: 'Globalization of markets', *Harvard Business Review*, May/June, pp. 92–102.

Loudon, D. L. and Della Bitta, A. J. 1993: *Consumer Behaviour*, 4th edn. New York: McGraw-Hill.

Orvice, V. 1994: 'Bare breasts in French advert outrage viewers', *Daily Mail - UK*, 13 May, p. 12.

Phillips, C., Doole, I. and Lowe, R. 1994: *International Marketing Strategy: Analysis, Development and Implementation*. London: Routledge.

Terpstra, V. 1983: *International Marketing*, 3rd edn. Chicago, IL: The Dryden Press.

Toyne, B. and Walters, P. G. P. 1993: *Global Marketing Management: A Strategic Perspective*, 2nd edn. Needham: Allyn and Bacon.

4

International market entry strategies

INTRODUCTION

Although the internationalization of firms may manifest itself in a variety of ways, firms choose entry strategies that represent diverse levels of commitment to the host market and organizational capacity in terms of structure, finance and personnel (international experience, skills and training). Contrary to popular views in international business literature that the internationalization of the firm is a sequential process, starting with exporting, licensing and eventually foreign direct investment (Tookey, 1969; Wind *et al.*, 1973; Johanson and Weidersheim-Paul, 1975), empirical studies suggest that bigger multinational firms may adopt a variety of entry methods in servicing international markets at any point in time (Turnbull, 1987). This chapter examines the range of market entry methods in international business, as well as benefits and costs of each market entry strategy.

EXPORTING

Exporting is the oldest and most basic form of international business activity and may be defined as the process of servicing foreign markets from a home country facility. Exporting is arguably the least risky method of involvement in international business because of the limited resources that may be committed in the process. A firm simply uses its domestic capacity to produce for export markets. There are two major forms of exporting, direct and indirect. Each of these is summarized below.

Indirect exporting

Indirect exporting may be treated as domestic sales since it involves selling of products on an ex-works basis to international trading companies whose responsibility it is to sell the products abroad. Although the firm is aware of its products being sold abroad, it has neither interest nor control over these products in the foreign market. McKinnon (1989) explains that indirect exporting relieves the manufacturer of the effort, expense and worry of international distribution; but he must accept lower prices and smaller sales than may be obtained by direct exporting. Shogo Shosha, the Japanese trading company, offers considerable export opportunities for smaller Japanese companies lacking in size, resources, and international distribution experience. Similarly, the British trading company United African Company (UAC) offers the greatest coverage of the African markets for any prospective exporter. Indirect exporting offers a number of important benefits, particularly to smaller exporters. Indirect channels may be equated to the export sales departments of the manufacturer, but without without the cost of maintaining an in-house export department. Indirect exporting enables a manufacturer with limited resources and expertise to benefit from export activities without any capital outlay. Export sales are treated as if they were domestic sales. Consequently, manufacturers that are involved in indirect exporting are not exposed to foreign exchange risks. Finally, the use of indirect channels enables a manufacturer to have a presence on a wider network of markets than he could possibly afford with a direct channel.

The use of indirect channels for exporting is not without its limitations. Some of these limitations include the inability of an indirect exporter to gain access to markets other than those being serviced by the intermediaries. Intermediaries may not be willing to incur the market development costs which may be necessary for market penetration. Furthermore, intermediaries are only interested in product lines that guarantee the highest possible return. Consequently, the full range of a manufacturer's products may not be given international exposure. Finally, given that export sales are treated as if they were domestic sales, manufacturers do not share from the success of their products in international markets.

Variants of indirect exporting are discussed in the following sections.

The piggyback scheme

Piggybacking enables a manufacturer (the rider) to take advantage of the foreign distribution systems of other manufacturers (the carriers) offering complementary products. This is usually a mutually beneficial arrangement for the partners. As the rider gets access to foreign markets through established channels, the carrier is able to spread the overhead costs of its marketing operations. A good example of a successful piggyback arrangement is that of the Singer Sewing Machine Company, which supports fabric manufacturers and pattern designers through its network of distribution outlets.

Export management companies

Export management companies may be described as the 'external export department' of a firm. These companies may take full responsibility for the entire export activity of a manufacturer who is unable or unwilling to undertake such a task. As export management companies do not take title to goods they simply sell on behalf of manufacturers on commission basis.

Direct export

The use of foreign distributors indicates an increasing level of involvement and commitment to a foreign market. The firm undertakes the export activity itself, and builds up contacts, undertakes market research, handles documentation and transportation, establishes price, etc. (Young *et al.* 1989). Direct exporting is normally attractive to medium to large manufacturers with better resources and experience, who wish to control their international activities. The main benefit of direct export is that it reverses the limitations of indirect exporting. It further enables a manufacturer to establish the depth and breadth of its international marketing activities, and develop strategies accordingly. The main disadvantage of direct exporting is the huge costs associated with such activities.

Direct exporting may be conducted either by appointing foreign distributors or setting up own sales offices in the host markets.

Foreign distributors

By appointing foreign distributors, the manufacturer deals directly with local merchants who buy on account and take title to goods. It provides the manufacturers with shorter channels to the foreign market and better information flow. Cateora (1993) explains that using foreign distributors moves the manufacturer closer to the market and involves the company more closely with problems of language, physical distribution, communications, and financing. Foreign distributorship is particularly useful where (1) the market is huge and good coverage is needed; (2) capital requirements and patterns of cash flow exclude smaller middlemen such as agents or brokers; and (3) initial installation and after-sales service are required.

Identifying foreign distributors is usually a very difficult task and can be time consuming. It involves the identification of credible and willing distributors. It is advisable for manufacturers to follow a systematic procedure in order to ensure that the best distributors are appointed. Cateora suggests a four-stage process of identifying and screening prospective distributors in the following sequence:

1. A letter including product information and distributor requirements in the official business language is sent to each prospective middleman.
2. A follow up is made to the best respondents for more specific information concerning lines handled, territory covered, size of firm, number of salespeople, and other background information.
3. A check of credit and references from other clients and customers of the prospective middleman is carried out.
4. If possible, a personal check is made of the most promising firms.

Other methods of identifying foreign distributors include personal visits to trade fairs/exhibitions in the foreign market, talking to visitors, and asking relevant questions relating to buyers and users of the products in the country in question.

Foreign sales office

A firm may establish a sales office in the host market to coordinate the activities of distributors and retailers, and maintain direct contact with buyers and users in the market. This method of servicing a market should be considered where the potential is substantial and the firm seeks a long-term relationship with the market because of the resource implications. It signifies commitment to the host market, and a desire to control marketing activity. Having a foreign sales office provides the flexibility and freedom needed by overseas representatives to decide on marketing policies as they see fit.

Licensing

Licensing arrangements allow for the use of a firm's technology, patents, trademarks, or other firm-specific advantages by another in exchange for

EXHIBIT 4.1

The twelve most common mistakes of potential exporters

1. **Failure to obtain qualified export counselling and to develop a master international marketing plan before starting an export business**
    To be successful, a firm must first clearly define goals, objectives, and the problems encountered. Secondly, it must develop a definitive plan to accomplish an objective despite the problems involved. Unless the firm is fortunate enough to possess a staff with considerable export expertise, it may not be able to take this crucial first step without qualified outside guidance.

2. **Insufficient commitment by top management to overcome the initial difficulties and financial requirements of exporting**
    It may take more time and effort to establish a firm in a foreign market than in domestic ones. Although the early delays and costs involved in exporting may seem difficult to justify when compared to established domestic trade, the exporter should take a long-range view of this process and carefully monitor international marketing efforts through these early difficulties. If a good foundation is laid for export business, the benefits derived should eventually outweigh the investment.

3. **Insufficient care in selecting overseas distributors**
    The selection of each foreign distributor is crucial. The complications involved in overseas communications and transport require international distributors to act with greater independence than their domestic counterparts. Also, since a new exporter's history, trademark and reputation are usually unknown in the foreign market, foreign customers may buy on the strength of a distributor's reputation. A firm should therefore conduct a personal evaluation of the personnel handling its account, the distributor's facilities, and the management methods employed.

4. **Chasing orders from around the world instead of establishing a basis for profitable operations and orderly growth**
    If exporters expect distributors to actively promote their accounts, the distributors must be trained, assisted, and their performance must be continually monitored. This requires a company marketing executive to be permanently located in the distributor's geographic region. New exporters should concentrate their efforts in one or two geographical areas until there is sufficient business to support a company representative. Then, while this initial core area is expanded, the exporter can move into the next selected geographical area   *cont.*

5. **Neglecting export business when the home market booms**
   Too many companies turn to exporting when business fall off in the home market. When domestic business starts to boom again, they neglect their export trade or relegate it to a secondary place. Such neglect can seriously harm the business and motivation of their overseas representatives, strangle the home company's own export trade and leave the firm without recourse when domestic business falls off once more.

6. **Failure to treat international distributors on an equal basis with domestic counterparts**
   Often, companies carry out institutional advertising campaigns, special discount offers, sales incentive programmes, warranty offers, etc., in the home market but fail to make similar assistance available to their international distributors. This is a mistake that can destroy the vitality of overseas marketing efforts.

7. **Assuming that a given market technique and product will automatically be successful in all countries**
   What works in one market may not work in others. Each market has to be treated separately to ensure maximum success.

8. **Unwillingness to modify products to meet regulations or cultural preferences of other countries**
   Local safety and security codes, as well as import restrictions, cannot be ignored by foreign distributors. If necessary modifications are not made at the factory, the distributor must do them – usually at a greater cost and, perhaps, not as well. It should also be noted that the resulting smaller profit margin makes the account less attractive.

9. **Failure to print service, sale and warranty messages in locally understood languages**
   Although a distributor's top management may speak English, it is unlikely that all sales personnel have this capability. Without a clear understanding of sales messages or service instructions, these people may be less effective in performing their functions.

10. **Failure to consider use of an export management company**
    A firm decides it cannot afford its own export department (or has tried unsuccessfully), it should consider the possibility of appointing an appropriate export management company (EMC).

11. **Failure to consider licensing or joint venture agreements**
    Import restrictions in some countries, insufficient personnel/financial resources, or a too limited product line cause many companies to dismiss international marketing as unfeasible. Yet, many products that can compete

cont.

on a national basis in the home market can be successfully marketed in most markets of the world. A licensing or joint-venture arrangement may be the simple, profitable answer to any reservations. In general, all that is needed for success is flexibility in using the proper combination of marketing techniques.

12. **Failure to provide readily available servicing for the product**
A product without the necessary service support can acquire a bad reputation in a short period, potentially preventing further sales.

Source: Adapted from INTERNATIONAL BUSINESS: THEORY AND PRACTICE by Khambata/Ajami, Copyright © 1995. Adapted by permission of Prentice-Hall, Inc., Upper Saddle River, NJ.

valuable consideration (Monye, 1989). In broad terms, international licensing includes a variety of contractual arrangements whereby the transfer of intangible assets is accompanied by technical services to ensure proper utilization of these assets. The core of a licensing agreement is the transfer of intangible property rights and this is what distinguishes licensing from other contractual arrangements such as management contracts and technical service agreements (Root 1987). Because of the distinct nature of know-how licensing, payment may be made in any form that is mutually acceptable to the parties concerned. According to Oman (1984), compensation for a licensing arrangement may be any of the following:

- initial lump-sum fee;
- a percentage of sales;
- royalties;
- share of equity (and hence profits);
- goods bought at a discount in a counter-purchase or buy back arrangements; or
- access to any technological improvements or adaptations the licensee may make;
- any combination thereof.

Licensing offers a number of benefits to both the licensor and the licensee. In some industries where substantial investment is required for research and development – for example, high technology industry – it may be appropriate for firms with limited resources to consider acquiring technology through licensing rather than embarking on the tortuous route of research and development which is largely a hit or miss affair. This is particularly important where there are appropriate and willing licensors.

Bradley (1991) identifies a number of benefits of licensing in international markets. These include:

- access to difficult markets;
- low capital risk and low commitment of resources;
- information on product performance and competitor activities in different markets at little cost;
- improved delivery and service levels in local markets;
- important in diversification strategies.

In international business literature, opinion is divided as to when it is most feasible to use licensing in the internationalization process. However, two main schools of thought are easily identifiable: one school includes Dunning, and Rugman, Lecraw and Booth; and the second school includes Johanson and Weidersheim-Paul, and Thunman.

According to Dunning (1979), FDI is a superior strategy compared with the external sale of proprietary assets through licensing arrangements, *ceteris paribus*. The strength of his argument lies in the internalization strand of Dunning's so-called 'eclectic paradigm' of international production which holds that: 'the basic incentive of a firm to internalise its ownership endowments is to avoid disadvantages, or to capitalise on the imperfections of one or the other of the two main external mechanisms of resource allocation – the market or price system and public authority fiat (order or decree)'. Dunning suggests that market imperfections arise wherever negotiation or transaction costs are high, wherever the economies of interdependent activities cannot be fully captured, and wherever information about the product or service being marketed is not readily available or is costly to acquire. The concept of internalization then becomes relevant to the choice between licensing and FDI. Licensing is thus thought to be attractive at the last stage of the technology cycle, consequent on the standardization of the product or process.

Rugman *et al.*'s model of the internationalization process (1985) underlines Dunning's eclectic paradigm. The main thrust of this model is that the net profit from any one mode of entry changes at a rate different from others, and that the multinational enterprise will choose the mode that will maximize the net present value of all future cash inflows. It is also suggested that the choice will depend on the length of time it is anticipated that the market will be serviced.

Rugman *et al.* explain that in a perfect world, exporting will be the first option. Yet when foreign nations impose tariffs or erect other barriers with the risk of dissipation to the MNE, the host nation may be best serviced by direct investment rather than host country production by a licensee. It is only when the host nation imposes regulations on the MNE which are greater than the benefits of FDI that the MNE turns to licensing as a mode of entry into the host nation. If the costs of regulation are less than the benefits of FDI, the MNE sticks to FDI. The conditions assumed in the Rugman *et al.* model would suggest the following pattern in the internationalization process: exporting → FDI → licensing.

The second school of thought suggests that licensing is likely to be the second stage in the internationalization process. Johanson and Weidersheim-Paul (1975) observed that most firms without extensive knowledge of foreign markets adopt stages of development approach to international expansion. Each stage in the process represents a successively larger resource commitment and also leads to a quite different market experience and information for the firm. The contention here is that licensing follows exporting before FDI as a sequential progression: exporting → licensing → FDI.

Thunman (1982) also suggests that licensing can represent a firm's first step into a new market, where for example, the licensor may at a later stage buy the licensee. He argues that licensing is particularly important to small firms from countries with small domestic markets such as Sweden, since they may lack the broad spectrum of capabilities and resources required for successful international marketing. Other factors that encourage licensing at the early stage of the internationalization process include restricted access to a market through direct investment or where the size of a market does not justify the substantial capital commitment required for FDI.

It is clear from the above discussion that whichever approach one finds convincing, there is evidence to suggest that licensing activity is a dynamic and growing part of international business (see Buckley and Davies, 1979; Young, 1987; Young *et al.*, 1989).

Limitations of licensing

Licensing is by no means without its shortcomings. Licensing of intellectual property is characterized by a number of problems, primarily arising from the intangible nature of intellectual property and limited information in the transaction process. This makes each licensing arrangement unique. Caves *et al.* (1983) suggest that the lack of adequate information in licensing transactions is a result of market imperfection. It is therefore difficult to pick and choose licensing deals with a reasonable level of awareness of prevailing terms and conditions. Market imperfection is perhaps the main source of problems in licensing transactions. These problems may be summarized as follows:

1. One of the major problem areas in international licensing relates to its pricing. Pricing of technology is determined by, among other things, cost of research and development, the relative bargaining power of the parties involved, and the perceived need for the technology by the licensee (Monye, 1989). Developing countries maintain that MNEs systematically overcharge them for the technologies that are supplied. Hood and Young (1979) note that host countries are inevitably at a disadvantage because they cannot know all there is to know about what is being bought until the technology has been purchased.

2. The costs of a licensing transaction may constitute a barrier to the willingness of prospective licensors to engage in international licensing. McGee (1966), Teece (1976) and Lovell (1979) suggest that the transaction costs involved in transferring technology are quite significant. They believe that the resource cost of transferring technology constitutes between 2 and 59 per cent of the recipients' project total costs, and averages about 19 per cent, thus affecting profitability.

3. A licensor with multiple licensees may find it attractive to pursue a strategy of uniform royalties and conditions of sale to all licensees. However, uniform royalty may not yield the desired results; but at the same time, discriminatory royalties alone may not work unless different licensees are spatially separated with imperfect knowledge, on the part of the buyers, of the market and pricing structures. The monopolistic licensor with perfect information and perhaps no transaction costs could write licensing agreements to extract maximum rents from competing licensees.

4. Know-how licensing is susceptible to the possible risk of loss of control by the licensor. The licensor may lose proprietary control of the technology, with the attendant risks of unauthorized disclosure. There is then the opportunity cost of profits forgone from foreign investment when the licensing works out badly, and the emergence of a new competitor when it works out well.

5. There is also the debate on the appropriateness of transferred technology. The technology-receiving developing countries often feel that the technology transferred may be ill suited to the factor endowment of their environments (see Contractor and Sagafi-Nejad, 1981).

6. Finally, a technology's economic performance is uncertain. A licensee may make a substantial investment in physical facilities and market-

ing outlays on the 'uncertain' prospect that a licensed technology will perform as promised. However, the technology may not work properly in the new location, the demand for the product that embodies it may change, or newer technologies may displace it. These factors reinforce the fact that potential returns to the technology licensed abroad are simply uncertain.

FRANCHISING

Despite the rather recent escalation of publicity surrounding it, franchising is not a new phenomenon. Indeed, it is frequently seen as a recent 'import' into Europe, particularly from the United States (Bradley, 1991). None the less, evidence abounds to suggest that it has been in use since the eighteenth century (Young *et al.*, 1989; Stern and Stanworth, 1988). Franchising is an all-inclusive contractual arrangement which enables the franchisee (receiver of the privileges) to use a proven and successful business formula in operation and marketing, a package of goods and services, and permission to trade with franchisor's (parent company or owner) trademark or brand name for a fee. In return, the franchisor receives payment for the use of trademark or brand name, training, and for merchandise supplied. One important distinction between licensing and franchising is that the latter is very prescriptive.

Franchising is a very important marketing and growth strategy in the service and hospitality industry, particularly the fast food chains. The most popular examples of companies that have been very successful, using franchising as the mainstay of their growth strategy include Kentucky Fried Chicken, McDonald's, Burger King, Hilton, Body Shop, Kwik Fit, Avis, Hertz and Benetton, to mention but a few.

Nature of franchising

There are two types of franchising – basic franchise and business format franchise. The basic franchise enables the franchisee to produce or sell products identified by a brand or trademark. Examples will include distribution franchise, and soft drinks bottling agreements. The basic franchise is similar but not identical in concept to licensing.

A business format franchise may be described as a 'total business concept'. It includes both the marketing of goods identified by a brand name and trademark and the preparation of a 'blueprint' of all aspects of conducting a successful business, including site selection, equipment supply, training, techniques for preparing products/service, marketing, publicity and customer care.

Ayling (1988) lists the following as some of the common characteristics of franchising:

- There is a legal contract outlining the terms and obligations agreed between franchisor and franchisee.
- The franchisor initiates and trains the franchisee in all aspects of the business, prior to its opening.
- After the franchisee's business is opened, the franchisor maintains a continuing interest in providing the franchisee with support in all aspects of the operation.
- The franchisee is permitted, albeit under the control of the franchisor, to operate under a given brand name, business format and procedure, and with the benefit of the goodwill generated by the franchisor.
- The franchisee makes a substantial capital investment from his own resources
- The franchisee owns his own business.
- The franchisee pays the franchisor for the acquired rights through a front-end 'licence fee' and on-going management services fees for continuing support.
- The franchisee will generally be granted (by the franchisor) a geographical territory and/or a vertical market sector in which to operate.

The growing interest in franchising

A number of factors are responsible for the growth in franchising agreements worldwide over the last twenty years. One of the key reasons for this phenomenon is its apparent success rate compared with other types of small business start-ups. Ayling suggests that the Pareto's 80/20 rule applies to small businesses and franchising, citing the Power Research Associates' report. The survey showed that after a five-year period, 80 per cent of all small businesses have ceased trading, for various reasons. On the other hand, well in excess of 80 per cent of franchised businesses are still trading after ten years, demonstrating how franchising appears to substantially reduce the failure rate of small businesses. Ayling attributes this success rate of franchising to number of factors:

- The greater involvement of the major clearing banks has lent greater stability to the franchise industry.
- The image of franchising has improved significantly through the activities of the major clearing banks and the International Franchise Associations, and by the emerging acceptance and accreditation procedures of the Newspaper Publishers Association.
- Recent government policies in the UK have improved the general climate for small businesses as a means of stimulating employment.
- There has been steady growth of new shopping centres where lease requirements are so heavy that they can eliminate small independent businesses.
- There has been a gradual decline of the population of small towns and therefore a decline in the number of independent stores serving those communities.

Limitations of franchising

Franchising, like any other method of doing business, has a number of limitations, some of which are similar to those of licensing. Additionally, there are limitations which are intrinsic in the very nature of franchised operations and can be summarized as follows:

- Although the franchisee is the owner of a franchised operation, s/he is merely operating with and developing the goodwill and reputation of the franchisor. If the contractual arrangements are terminated, the franchisee will have nothing to show for his/her contribution towards the development of franchisor's goodwill and reputation. Arguably, the cost of terminating a franchising agreement is higher to the franchisee.
- Franchisors take risks when they enter into contractual arrangements with franchisees. There is no guarantee that brand name and image of the franchisors will be protected by the franchisees.
- International franchising may be problematic particularly in developing countries where there are regulatory controls that may impinge on the implementation of the franchise agreement.

MANAGEMENT CONTRACT

A management contract is a form of contractual arrangement which enables a firm with capital and personnel but limited management know-how to seek managerial expertise and developmental support from another firm in specific areas of its operation, for a fee. By choosing a management contract, the receiving firm expects to accomplish two objectives: to secure the managerial know-how necessary to run an efficient business; and to train local managers who will continue with the management of the business at the end of the contract period.

Management contracts are particularly popular in developing countries where there is the capital and manpower to set up either manufacturing or leisure facilities such as a refinery and hotels, but necessary managerial expertise is lacking for efficient operation. Management contracts are often made in conjunction with other contractual arrangements such as licensing and franchising to ensure their effective utilization. The French leisure group Club Med has been so successful partly as a result of its management contracts in holiday resorts around the world.

The main limitation is that by transferring know-how and training local personnel in different markets, global competitors are being created, thus limiting the opportunity for possible future investment in these markets.

CONTRACT MANUFACTURING/INTERNATIONAL SUBCONTRACTING

The terms 'contract manufacturing' and 'international subcontracting' denote an arrangement where the production of branded goods is contracted out to independent manufacturers, to be produced in accordance with the specifications provided by trademark owners, in the host market or in locations with a cheaper labour supply. The two terms are therefore used interchangeably in this book. Contract manufacturing has become an increasingly important strategy for assembly and manufacturing operations in certain industries such as electronics and textiles. In the electronics industry, where certain stages of production are labour-intensive, high technology components and other semi-finished products are manufactured by trademark owners and shipped to developing countries with a cheap and skilful labour supply for the final assembly. Countries such as Hong Kong, Malaysia, Singapore and Taiwan are very popular locations for contract manufacturing for Japanese, American and West European companies.

Dicken (1992) suggests that international subcontracting may be subdivided into three types according to the motivation of the principal firm (the one placing the order). He describes these as:

- Speciality subcontracting which involves the carrying out, often on a long-term or even a permanent basis, of specialized functions which the principal chooses not to perform itself but for which the sub-contractor has special skills and equipment.
- Cost-saving subcontracting, which is based upon differentials in pro-duction costs between principal and subcontractor for certain processes or products.
- Complementary or intermittent subcontracting, which is a means adopted by the principal firm to cope with occasional surges in demand without expanding its own production capacity.

Contract manufacturing may be attractive for firms operating in inter-national markets in preference to direct investment where the host market is not considered either large enough to justify substantial capital invest-ment or too risky for direct investment.

Benefits of contract manufacturing

In contractual agreements between a principal and a foreign market-based manufacturer who produces branded products, both the principal and subcontractor expect to benefit. For the principal, contract manufacturing offers access to raw materials and cheap labour supply, flexible prod-uction planning, and the opportunity to circumvent restrictive employ-ment legislation in the host country. For the subcontractor, there are a number of benefits; the opportunity to create and sustain additional employment, and manufacture to international standards. In cases where manufactured products are re-exported to third markets, contract manu-facturing is encouraged by the host government as it contributes to improved balance of trade.

Limitations of contract manufacturing

Contract manufacturing has a number of drawbacks. It may be very diff-icult to find suitable subcontractors in the host market whose facilities, equipment and know-how are compatible with the requirements of the principal. Even where they can be found, the principal may not have direct supervisory control over the manufacturing process. This can lead to serious problems of quality control. Second, contract execution and supply of merchandise may be disrupted either by local political upheavals or industrial relations difficulties in the host market. For a sub-contractor largely dependent on one principal, termination of contract by the principal could cause short-term difficulties and might lead to bankruptcy in the long run.

STRATEGIC ALLIANCE

A strategic alliance may be described as a long-term non-equity relationship between two firms from different countries seeking to achieve specific strategic objectives by combining know-how, resources and commitment. Strategic alliances may arise when firms realize that they lack the technological know-how or resources to compete successfully alone in the global markets. Indeed, it is generally recognized that in some industries, it is simply impossible for a single company to undertake all the necessary research and development work on a given technology without losing time and proprietary secrets to competitors. Consequently, the need for some form of collaboration becomes vital.

Strategic alliance is significantly different from equity investment joint ventures in a number of ways. Unlike conventional collaborative arrangements where there is little or no competition between collaborating firms, Young *et al.* (1989) point out that the partners in a strategic alliance will often be competing in the same product/geographical markets, as well as cooperating in various ways. Examples of successful and better known strategic alliances which are shown in exhibit 4.2 reinforce this assertion.

Strategic alliances are not a new phenomenon but have been given additional impetus by rapid globalization of markets and competitive pressures have created many new challenges for managers of industrial R&D. Annual R&D trends surveys conducted by the Industrial Research Institute have noted an increasing emphasis on external interactions, especially strategic alliances and technology licensing. Such technology sourcing activities are expected to grow and become more systematic (Chatterji and Thomas, 1993). It is therefore clear that in future, surviving the intense global competition will require some form of leveraging as a key strategic consideration for international firms. Rosenbaum (1993) suggests that the very survival of a business and the industry will depend among other things, on the ability (1) to leverage skills that were developed elsewhere; (2) to exploit synergies and economies of scale with other parts of business operations; and (3) to develop strategic and complementary alliances with others – especially customers.

EXHIBIT 4.2

Examples of international strategic alliances

Partners	*Products*
General Motors/Toyota	Automobiles
British Leyland/Honda	Automobiles
American Motors/Renault	Automobiles
Chrysler/Mitsubishi	Automobiles
Ford/Toyo Kogyo	Automobiles
Alfa Romeo/Nissan/Fiat	Automobiles
ATT/Olivetti	Office equipment; computers
Amdahl/Fujitsu	Computers
ATT/Philips	Telecommunications equipment
Honeywell/L.M. Ericsson	PBX systems
General Motors/Fanuc	Robotics
AEG Telefunken/JVC	VCRs
General Electric/Matsushita	Electrical appliances
Corning Glass/Siemens	Optical cables
Hercules/Montedison	Polypropylene resin
United Technologies/ Rolls-Royce	Aircraft engines

Source: Adapted from Young, S., Hamill, J., Wheeler, C. and Davies, J. R. (1989) International Market Entry and Development: Strategies and Management, Copyright © Prentice-Hall 1989. Reproduced by permission.

Strategic alliances offer a number of significant benefits to the partners such as:

- improved prospects for success of partners in exploiting technological advantages;
- achieving economies of scale in research and development by combining resources and commitment;
- a pragmatic and accessible means to achieve set business objectives;
- opportunity for further growth by providing access to global markets and distribution network;
- opportunity for cost effective procurement on a global basis.

Enabling conditions for successful strategic alliances

Managing strategic alliances can be a complex operation, particularly if the partners are not carefully chosen. Thus, prerequisites for long-term success of strategic alliances must include extensive knowledge of industry, product, and market trends. Sakai (1994) identifies a number of important elements which are essential to ensure success. These include:

- a strong and visible commitment by the top management of both partners;
- mutual trust and respect between the partners;
- a clear understanding of each partner's true motivation for the partnership;
- similarity and compatibility in business philosophies;
- valued contributions to the alliance from each partner;
- clarity and agreement on the goals and objectives of the partnership;
- competent and experienced management to operate the strategic alliance;
- a clear understanding of each partner's expectations and definitions of success;
- recognition of and respect for cultural differences; and
- on-going communication between the partners at all levels of the organization.

The essence of strategic alliance is to bring together complementary partners to achieve economies of scale. Therefore, it is vitally important for firms to undertake certain intelligence activities to ensure that wrong or incompatible partners are not selected. According to Thayer (1994), strategic alliances can strengthen the partners, but all too often ill-conceived unions collapse under the weight of unfulfilled expectations.

Limitations of strategic alliances

Despite the major benefits identified above, strategic alliances can and do go wrong, leading to all sorts of problems. One of the main problem areas in strategic alliances is the expectations of the partners. Although, by definition, strategic alliances are utilized with a view to yielding long-term benefits, the insistence of some partners on short-term results can be a source of tension in the relationship. In general, most of the problems of strategic alliances are similar to those found in licensing and franchising arrangements. Strategic alliances also have to deal with the following problems:

- Often, partners are reluctant to commit enough resources necessary to make the arrangement work.
- Cooperative arrangements are usually difficult to manage.
- Partners to strategic alliances are exposed to the risks of leakage of proprietary technology, which in turn can facilitate the creation of more powerful competitors than the company had to deal with, prior to the alliance arrangements.
- There can be difficulty in producing a quantifiable and balanced reward for all partners.
- In a mentor–protégé relationship, the balance of bargaining power may shift to the weaker partner once the venture commences. This may cause the larger partner to withhold vital resources and commitment to the joint venture.

JOINT VENTURES

The term 'joint venture' covers a wide variety of collaborative agreements between firms (Young *et al.*, 1989). As a result, definitions abound in the literature. For example, Onkvisit and Shaw (1989) define a joint venture as simply a partnership at corporate level; it can be domestic or international. Similarly, Harrigan (1985) contends that a joint venture is formed when two or more firms form a third to carry out a productive economic activity. However, for the purpose of this book, a fairly broad view of the term is adopted. A joint venture is therefore defined as any business arrangement in which subscribers commit capital, technology and managerial resources for a stake in the ownership and control of a new enterprise. Ownership of the joint venture is proportionate to the perceived or real value of the contribution of each subscriber. These contributions may be in the form of capital, technology or even managerial expertise that help to further the objectives of the joint venture. Exhibit 4.3 illustrates a joint venture arrangement between two partners with different motivations.

Firms enter into joint venture arrangements for a variety of reasons which may be grouped into four categories:

EXHIBIT 4.3

AMIC, Daewoo establish white goods joint venture

Anglo-American Industrial Corporation (AMIC) of South Africa and the South Korean Daewoo group have established a 50–50 joint venture to manufacture high-value consumer goods and exploit international technology market. Leslie Boyd, Chairman of AMIC, the industrial arm of the Anglo-American group, said the deal with Daewoo was part of AMIC's strategy to reduce its dependence on cyclical commodity markets.

The alliance with an Asian partner is an important one for AMIC, which has traditionally found its partners in Europe. Daewoo–AMIC, the new company, will make an initial investment of about R20million ($6 million) to take a 29.99 per cent stake in Gentech, a company that manufactures and distributes household electrical appliances. The basis of the venture includes growth potential in the Southern African white goods market and Daewoo's extensive technology base and exposure to consumer durables.

The establishment by the new company of a local colour picture tube (CPT) manufacturing facility for televisions is being considered. Given the reasons for the Daewoo tie-up, Mr Boyd said AMIC needed Daewoo's specific technology and international marketing skills to establish itself 'boldly in downstream consumer industries'.

Daewoo saw South Africa as a developing consumer market, and needed AMIC's financial partnership and operating skills. South African companies suffered during the sanction era from the lack of transfer of technology. Part of AMIC's reason for seeking a Korean partner was the idea that Korean investors were more willing to accept the risks of the South African environment than US, Japanese or European investors.

Korea is also felt to be better attuned to the needs of developing countries, particularly regarding how to use labour-intensive manufacturing methods without sacrificing international competitiveness.

Altech, AMIC's electronic associate, has a tie-up with the French group, Alcatel, while Samcor, the motor manufacturer in which AMIC has a 19 per cent stake, has close ties with Ford.

Discussion questions

1. Define and explain the term joint venture.
2. Outline the benefits of AMIC's link up with Daewoo.
3. What are the limitations of having a 50–50 joint venture?

Source: Adapted from *Financial Times*, 6 July 1993. Reprinted by permission.

- The most widely quoted reason for joint ventures is that they offer firms the opportunity to combine resources and know-how with a view to reducing each firm's costs and obtaining economies of scale by consolidating production and marketing activities. A joint venture also helps firms to reduce their risks in proportion to their involvement, particularly in projects involving a large capital investment.
- In certain markets, host governments may legislate or pressure multinational firms into accepting local partner in their subsidiary operations because this offers greater opportunity for effective transfer and diffusion of technology to the host economy. For example, in India, the Foreign Exchange Regulations Act of 1973 outlawed wholly owned subsidiary. It is believed that by sharing in ownership and management of an enterprise, relevant technical and managerial skills are transferred to host country nationals. In other developing country markets where controls on ownership of subsidiaries exist, joint venture represents one of the few feasible methods of entering these markets. According to Young *et al.* (1989), while the motivations underlying early international joint ventures were associated with risk sharing and the combination of financial resources, the growth in joint venture activity during the 1960s and 1970s was less voluntary.
- Multinational firms may require a partner in order to obtain knowledge of new and unfamiliar host country environment. For example, Sony Corporation and Prudential Insurance Company formed a joint venture to sell insurance policies in Japan.
- A local partner may provide the multinational firm with access to local resources, raw material materials and channels of distribution otherwise denied it. In Nigeria, natural resources such as oil and gas may only be exploited by multinational firms in partnership with indigenous firms.

Disadvantages of joint ventures

Joint ventures have a number of limitations. The first disadvantage stems from possible risks of loss of control of management. By definition, joint venture partners must reach decisions concerning strategic issues by consultations, compromises and agreements. This may considerably slow down the decision-making process. Secondly, joint ventures may lead to loss of control over proprietary technology. This is one of the factors responsible for IBM's general policy of across-the-board internalization. In the 1970s IBM had to withdraw from the huge and lucrative Indian market rather than take on a local partner. Thirdly, a joint venture may fail because of cultural differences between partners, divergent short- and long-term objectives, and real or perceived unsatisfactory contribution to the venture by one partner.

WHOLLY OWNED SUBSIDIARY OPERATION

Ownership, management and control of a subsidiary operation is largely determined by the level of capital investment and commitment of the parent company in the subsidiary venture, the bargaining power of the MNE and the host country, and whether the MNE is a technological leader or follower. Thus, a wholly owned subsidiary operation is defined as 100 per cent ownership and control by a parent company headquartered, usually but not exclusively, in a foreign country. It offers the greatest opportunity for profit maximization when things work out well and poses a higher level of risks than other methods of market entry, if it fails. In most cases, choosing the wholly owned subsidiary operation as an entry method into a foreign country by a multinational firm amounts to a vote of confidence in the host country given the level of commitment and capital investment that is required for such an alternative. In other cases, a company with a broad policy of complete internalization may insist on wholly owned subsidiary. IBM has successfully and consistently pursued this policy over the years. Therefore, the decision concerning ownership and control of subsidiaries in host nations has to be viewed within the context of two primary determinants – economic considerations and internalization policy.

According to Young *et al.* (1989), while wholly owned subsidiaries are characterized by complete ownership by the parent company, different types of subsidiaries exist and that these may vary along several dimensions, including the following:

1. the nature of activity – whether sales/marketing, extraction, assembly and manufacturing;
2. the orientation of investment – market oriented, cost oriented or raw material oriented;
3. the age of the subsidiary – which may affect plant status;
4. the method of establishment – whether 'greenfield' or acquisition;
5. subsidiary performance – and the measures used to assess subsidiary performance (cost centres versus profit centres);

6. organization and control – and centralization/decentralization of decision-making *vis-à-vis* production, marketing, research and development, etc.

Benefits and costs of a wholly owned subsidiary

There are significant benefits and costs associated with the strategy of establishing wholly owned subsidiaries in foreign markets. The advantages include the following:

- Total control by the international headquarters is necessary to accomplish corporate objectives, whether they can be defined in terms of maximization of corporate profit, return on investment, growth, geographical spread, or market share (Robinson, 1978).
- By establishing wholly owned subsidiaries, secrecy surrounding proprietary technology can be maintained.
- Establishing a wholly owned subsidiary eliminates problems such as those associated with joint ventures.
- Wholly owned subsidiary operation ensures consistency of policy, strategy, product quality and marketing programme between the subsidiary and headquarters.

Despite the benefits outlined above, the strategy of a wholly owned subsidiary is not without its drawbacks. Some of the limitations include:

- The parent company bears all the costs and associated risks of establishing a wholly owned subsidiary
- Developing host nations view the benefits arising from wholly owned subsidiary operation with scepticism. This can lead to the imposition of all kinds of control on the activities of these subsidiaries.
- The operation of wholly owned subsidiaries is usually subject to close scrutiny by governments. Consequently, even legitimate activities such as repatriation of profits and other assets can be a sensitive issue and may lead to accusations of exploitation.

Host country response to wholly owned subsidiary operation

One aspect of multinational operations that has attracted the most attention is the ownership and control of tangible and intangible assets in the host nation. The worry stems from the perceived impact of multinational operation in a host nation, particularly if it is a developing economy. Jenkins (1989) identifies two schools of thought on impact of multinational investment on a host country – the advocates and the critics. On the one hand, advocates of direct investment argue that the foreign resources which it provides are a supplement to locally available resources. On the other hand, critics argue that because of its 'package' nature and the monopoly power of multinational companies, such investment often leads to displacement of local resources. The views of the critics are born out of genuine concerns over the exploitative power of multinational companies. Robinson (1978) notes that there is a strong undercurrent of feeling that foreign investors have an obligation to respect national susceptibilities and to conform to policies of countries in which they are located, particularly in respect to the abuse of a dominant or monopolistic position. This has led to continuous calls for legally enforceable international codes of conduct for multinationals under the auspices of some United Nations' agencies. Essentially, developing countries want international control of multinationals because this would force a more equitable distribution of income, wealth, and power between North and South.

Developing countries also believe that additional measures are needed to curtail the power and influence of multinationals in their countries. Such measures include the placing of an upper limit on the equity ownership by multinationals in their subsidiaries. Consequently, most developing countries have placed mandatory equity limitations on foreign-owned firms. In special circumstances, however, such limitations may be waived by the host government. For example, as a result of political and economic pressure on the Mexican government, IBM was allowed 100 per cent ownership of its subsidiary in that country.

TURNKEY CONTRACT

The exact status of turnkey contracts as a market entry strategy is unclear in international marketing literature. While some academics regard them as export sales, others see them as a direct investment strategy. However, in this book, a turnkey contract is regarded as a one-off export sale requiring an extended period for its execution. The duration of a turnkey contract can last up to five years. Turnkey contracts do contain elements of a one-off export sale and of long-term contractual arrangements. In terms of formal definition, a turnkey contract may be described as 'an agreement by a seller to supply a buyer with a facility fully equipped and ready to be operated by the buyer's personnel, who will be trained by the seller' (Onkvisit and Shaw, 1989). Other definitions include 'a package deal in which the MNE constructs a production facility and provides training for the personnel necessary to operate it, such that the facility is ready to begin operations on the completion of the project' (Rugman *et al.*, 1985).

Turnkey contracts are normally used in large-scale construction and engineering projects such as fertilizer and cement manufacturing plants, and waste incinerators. Turnkey contracts are often accompanied by other contractual arrangements such as licensing, training and management contracts. This form of international business has been growing steadily over the years. Young *et al.* (1989) noted that the major boost to this form of activity came with the oil price rises of the 1970s, when some of the OPEC countries used turnkey operations to establish entire industrial complexes. Turnkey projects are normally used by rich industrializing countries.

The benefits arising from turnkey contracts include (1) the opportunity to sell both components and other intangible assets; (2) host government patronage which ensures that payments are made promptly and may also lead to mutually beneficial relationship in other areas; and (3) for the host nation, the opportunity to build industrial complexes and train local personnel. These advantages must, however, be balanced against the disadvantages which include the fact that by building an industrial complex in a host country, the possibility of exporting to or making other forms of investment in the market is effectively lost; and that turnkey contracts may result in the purchase of inappropriate technology. Designing and building complex and advanced industrial facilities in a host country may require the permanent attention of the suppliers, thus perpetuating management and other contractual arrangements to the detriment of the owner/purchaser.

FADE-OUT AGREEMENTS

In previous sections the difficulties in establishing wholly owned subsidiaries were highlighted. Occasionally, these developing countries may allow multinational companies to establish wholly owned subsidiaries in special circumstances. One of these circumstances would be when the multinational company agrees in advance to a planned and systematic programme of divestment by the host government. Effectively, the company will commence operation in the host country as a 100 per cent owned subsidiary of a foreign based international company, with an understanding and agreement to dilute its equity interest to an acceptable level by taking on local partners over a period of time.

Decisions about whether to enter into such an agreement with a host government have to be based on careful assessment of its pros and cons. In addition, the benefits must be easily realizable in the short rather than long term. Robinson (1978) suggests that for any investment to be advisable, the company must feel relatively certain that it can recapture its investment, plus an appropriate return, within a period of time during which it can demonstrate that its ownership is in the interest of the society, both as presently perceived and in reality.

The main drawback to fade-out agreements stems from the volatile nature of most developing countries. Given that some countries change governments frequently, agreement with one government may not be honoured by its successor. Similarly, local pressures on the government by influential individuals and labour organizations may force the government to review the agreement once investments have been made.

CROSS-BORDER ACQUISITIONS

Foreign production through greenfield investment is a difficult and time consuming process. It is estimated that it takes a minimum of three years to complete arrangements in a greenfield start up, from the time when a site selection decision is made to the commencement of production. For companies wishing to make an immediate impact in a market, greenfield investment may not be an attractive method of market entry. Normally such companies would prefer to acquire existing facilities in the host market as a way of establishing instant presence in the market.

It is therefore, not surprising that in the 1980s and the first half of 1990s, the rate of international acquisitions was breathtaking, surpassed only by the rate of domestic acquisition. Examples of some of the more popular acquisitions are presented in exhibit 4.5. The critical strategic question is: what is the driving force behind the upsurge of interest in cross-border acquisition? Perhaps the most obvious and outstanding reason for this is the excitement and prestige associated with globalization, and the attendant speed of market entry. Bengtsson (1992) identifies the following factors as additional motivation for the acquisition mania:

EXHIBIT 4.4

Asia's brand barons go shopping

Stroll along Orchard Road, Singapore's main shopping street, and you will be besieged by brands. All the big names shout (elegantly, of course) from shop windows: Gucci, Louis Vuitton and Gianni Versace from some, Calvin Klein and Dolce and Gabbana from others. Rolex, Cartier and Christian Dior glitter expensively alongside the conservative tailoring of Burberrys and Aquascutum. Exhausted shoppers compare trophies over a cup of DKNY coffee.

The cacophony of brands has long been familiar in Japan. But the determination of the region's burgeoning middle class to wear the right thing and eat in the proper places means that it is increasingly found in other Asian countries, besides the traditional shopping paradises of Singapore and Hong Kong. And invariably, the label shoppers crave is a Western one.

This has made Asia the fastest-growing market for most of the West's top brands. Those in the luxury-goods and fashion business reckon that roughly a third of their sales are now to Asia (including Japan). For instance, sales in the region by members of the Committee Colbert, an association of France's top seventy-five luxury-goods producers, rose from 20 per cent of their total sales in 1984 to 35 per cent last year. Some retailers predict that, within a decade, Asia will make up half of the world's luxury-goods market.

By then, Asians may own many of the brands they covet. As the region's retailers and wholesalers turn into powerful international groups in their own right, they are no longer content merely with the franchise to sell Western branded goods in their home market. Most expect to sell throughout the region, and many want to design and make their own products for the brands they are pushing. This has led some Asian groups to take stakes in foreign brands, or even to buy them outright.

Consider Ong Beng Seng, a publicity shy Singaporean who runs Hotel Properties, a large property group. Together with his wife Christina, Mr Ong is assembling a formidable portfolio of clothing and food brands. The Ongs represent more than forty top America and European brands – not just in Asian, but also in Australia and Britain. They increasingly own large chunks of the businesses. For example, last year the Ongs formed a joint venture (in which they are thought to have a controlling interest) with DKNY, a fashion brand founded by Donna Karan, a New York designer. The venture will build a string of boutiques in Japan and other parts of Asia.

Mr Ong may also make more money from the fashionable Planet Hollywood restaurant chain than its famous founders, who include such show-biz glitterati

cont.

as Sylvester Stallone, Arnold Schwarzenegger and Bruce Willis. Mr Ong's companies own some 10 per cent of Planet Hollywood, which was listed in New York in April; and 50 per cent of the chain's master franchise-holder for the Asia-Pacific region, the Middle East and South Africa. Mr Ong is also the partner in Singapore and Hong Kong for the Hard Rock Café and Häagen-Dazs ice cream. Other Singaporeans are out brand-hunting. The Hour Glass, a watch retailer listed on the Singapore stockmarket, recently bought controlling stakes in two of Switzerland's most exclusive watch makers: Daniel Roth and Gerald Genta. The two companies produce watches that range in price from US$3,000 to US$2 million.

Hong Kong, too, has its share of brand barons. Joyce Ma the founder of Joyce Boutiques, is one of the world's largest buyers of designer clothing. Her company is opening stores and restaurants throughout South-East Asia. In January YGM Trading, a Hong Kong retailer which represents such foreign brands as Valentino, Daniel Hechter and Pierre Cardin, bought Hang Ten, an American brand of leisure clothing (which takes its Chinese-sounding name from the number of toes a good surfer places on the edge of a surfboard).

Dickson Poon, another dedicated follower of fashion, snapped up his first European brand in 1987 when he bought S. T. Dupont, a classy French producer of lighters and other accessories. Mr Poon is the founder of Dickson Concepts, a Hong Kong-based wholesaler and retailer that has graduated to buying department stores: in June, he acquired the Seibu department stores in Hong Kong and Shenzhen, China, from their Japanese owners. Five years ago he bought Harvey Nichols, a posh British department store, which was listed on the London Stock Exchange in April. He is now casting his eye over its New York equivalent, Barney's, which filed for protection from creditors in January.

Discussion questions

1. Why is brand image very important in Asia?
2. Why are the Asian brand barons not contented with franchising arrangements?

Source: Adapted from *The Economist*. Copyright © *The Economist*, London, 10 August 1996.

- Prestige of international profile: few companies ever admit, even in private, to perhaps the least laudable reason for acquiring abroad – prestige. Yet this is the thinly disguised motive for a lot of foreign ventures. For some chief executive officers (CEOs) having organizational presence in certain international markets can be a matter of personal crusade. With print and broadcast interests in Australia, North America, Europe and Asia, the global ambition of Rupert Murdoch's News International typifies this type of corporate egoism.

- Geographical risk spreading: spreading risks geographically is a popular solution to fears about the parent company's domestic market. With a saturated domestic market, firms are forced to internationalize their operation by cross-border acquisition.
- International synergies: synergy is the most widely quoted reason for cross-border acquisition. This is the reason given for BMW's acquisition of the Rover Group in 1994. Undoubtedly, synergies may be achieved through international acquisitions, it is important to recognize that in most cases, superficial compatibilities mask fundamental dissimilarities. BMW is now beginning to discover for itself that the acquisition of Rover may have been a major mistake. Only time will tell!
- Product acquisition: the process of research and development, and the launch of a new product, is a hit or miss affair and can take years to reach fruition. Some international acquisitions are made in order to circumvent the difficult stages of new product development with the acquisition of a certain winner. A good example of this is Nestle's acquisition of Smarties from Rowntree, and the subsequent acquisition of the company itself, with successful brands such as Kit-Kat.
- Strengthening core business: it is generally accepted that core businesses can be strengthened by successful strategic cross-border acquisitions. This is particularly attractive for firms wishing to protect their sources of material input or even the supply outlet.
- Production costs and economies of scale: lower production costs are an attractive and valid motive for investing abroad. Similarly, acquisition of prospective competitors in host markets will hasten the entry process and offer opportunities for costs savings through consolidation and economies of scale in production, distribution and marketing.

Despite these seemingly overwhelming benefits of acquisition, cross-border acquisitions are more complex than domestic deals because of the differences in culture, business practices, and management styles and philosophy. As Bengtsson observes: 'Asia, Japan and Africa are less dangerous than Europe and North America because we expect them to be different.' Seductive similarities in economies, political, socio-cultural norms, and even language can often conceal nasty surprises. Therefore, in order to enjoy the benefits of acquisition and achieve the stated objectives, each situation must be assessed on its own merits and according to the circumstances of such takeovers at the time. Bengtsson cautioned that generalized justification is not enough for growth through acquisition. Each company has to be certain that it is the right way for them, and that the potential target will meet their requirements.

EXHIBIT 4.5

Examples of cross-border acquisitions

Predators	**Victims**
BMW (Germany)	Rover Group (UK)
Nestle (Switzerland)	Rowntree (UK)
Ford (USA)	Firestone (USA)
Kodak (USA)	Sterling Drug (UK)
Matsushita (Japan)	MCA (USA)
Sony (Japan)	Columbia Pictures (USA)
HSBC Group (Hong Kong)	Midland Bank (UK)

SUMMARY

In this chapter, we have examined a wide range of market-servicing alternatives in international business, moving from export activities through a variety of contractual arrangements to direct investment alternatives. The nature and characteristics of each method have been evaluated, outlining benefits and limitations. While it is not possible to prescribe 'the best' alternative for foreign market entry and development, it is noteworthy that these alternatives are not mutually exclusive. The choice of entry method or combination of methods is largely dependent on a number of factors such as the nature and size of the foreign market, availability of capital and other resources, risks and long-term objectives of the company.

DISCUSSION QUESTIONS

1. Define the term 'exporting'. Distinguish between direct and indirect exporting. Examine the reason why a company may combine different market entry methods in the internationalization process.
2. Outline and discuss the six most common mistakes of potential exporters.

3. Define the term 'know-how licensing'. How important would licensing be in international business strategy in the twenty-first century? Identify and examine the limitations of licensing.
4 Explain the term 'strategic alliance'. Why would a firm choose to enter into an alliance with a competitor? What are the enabling conditions for successful strategic alliances?
5. 'There is no one best method of servicing a foreign market.' Discuss.

REFERENCES

Ayling, D. 1988: 'Franchising in the UK', *The Quarterly Review of Marketing*, Summer, pp. 19–24.

Bengtsson, A. M. 1992: *Managing Mergers and Acquisitions: A European Perspective*. Aldershot: Gower.

Bradley, F. 1991: *International Marketing Strategy*. New York: Prentice-Hall.

Buckley, P. J. and Davies, H. 1979: *The Place of Licensing in Theory and Practice of Foreign Operations*. Discussion Paper. University of Reading, No. 47.

Cateora, P. R. 1993: *International Marketing*, 8th edn. Homewood, IL: Irwin.

Caves, R. E., Crockell, H. and Killing, J. P. 1983: 'Imperfect market for technology licensing', *Oxford Bulletin of Economics and Statistics*, Vol. 45, No. 3, pp. 249–67.

Chatterji, D. and Thomas, M. A. 1993: 'Benefiting from external sources of technology', *Research-Technology Management*, Vol. 36, No. 6, pp. 21–6.

Contractor, F. J. and Sagafi-Nejad, T. 1981: 'International technology transfer' *Journal of International Business Studies*. Fall, pp. 113–35.

Dicken, P. 1992: *Global Shift: The Internationalisation of Economic Activity*. London: Paul Chapman.

Dunning, J. H. 1979: *International Production and The Multinational Enterprises*. London: Allen and Unwin.

Harrigan, K. R. 1985: *Strategies for Joint Venture Success*. Lexington, MA: Lexington Books.

Hood, N. and Young, S. 1979: *Economics of Multinational Enterprise*. London: Longman.

Jenkins, R. 1989: 'The impact of foreign investment on less developed countries: a cross-section analysis vs. industry studies'. Paper presented to the Academy of International Business, UK Regional Annual Conference, at the University of Bath, 7–8 April.

Johanson, J. and Weidersheim-Paul, F. 1975: 'The internationalization of the firm: four swedish case studies', *Journal of Management Studies*, October, pp. 305–22.

Khambata, D. and Ajami, R. 1992: *International Business: Theory and Practice*. New York: Macmillan.

Lau, R. 1994: 'Why everyone wants to know more about strategic alliances', *Broker World*, Vol. 14, No. 2, Febuary, pp. 48–54.

Lovell, E. B. 1979: *Appraising Foreign Licensing Performance*. Studies in Business Policy, New York Conference Board, No. 128.

McGee, J. S. 1966: 'Patent exploitation: some economic and legal problems', *Journal of Law and Economics*, Vol. 9, No. 1.

McKinnon, A. C. 1989: *Physical Distribution Systems*. London: Routledge.

Monye, S. O. 1989: *International Technology Transfer: The Case of Licensing in Nigeria*. PhD thesis. Glasgow: University of Strathclyde.

Oman, C. 1984: *New Forms of International Investment in Developing Countries*. Development Studies, Paris: OECD.

Onkvisit, S. and Shaw, J. J. 1989: *International Marketing: Analysis and Strategy*. London: Merrill Publishing.

Robinson, R. D. 1978: *International Business Management*, 2nd edn. Hinsdale, IL: Dryden Press.

Root, F. R. 1987: *Entry Strategies for International Markets*. Lexington, MA: Lexington Books.

Rosenbaum, J. 1993: 'Strategic alliances in the global marketplace', *Managing Intellectual Property*, No. 35, pp. 17–25.

Rugman, A. M., Lecraw, D. J. and Booth, L. D. 1985: *International Business: Firm and Environment*. New York: McGraw-Hill.

Sakai, J. T. 1994: 'Japan as an attractive alliance partner', *Directors and Boards*, Vol. 18, No. 2, pp. 42–4.

Stern, P. and Stanworth, J. 1988: 'The development of franchising in Britain', *National Westminster Quarterly Review*, May, pp. 38–48.

Teece, D. J. 1976: *The Multinational Corporation and The Resource Cost of International Technology Transfer*. Cambridge, MA: MIT Press.

Thayer, J. D. 1994: 'The tender trap', *Journal of European Business*, Vol. 5, No. 3, pp. 34–8.

Thunman C. G. 1982: *Swedish Licensing in World Markets*. Research Reports, Marketing Techniques Centre, Stockholm, No. 11.

Tookey, D. 1969: 'International business and political geography', *British Journal of Marketing*, Vol. 3, No. 3, pp. 18–29.

Turnbull, P. 1987: 'A challenge to the stages theory of the internationalization process', in P. J. Rosson, and S. D. Reed (eds.), *Managing Export Entry and Expansion*. Westport, CT: Greenwood.

Wind, Y., Douglas, S. and Perlmutter, H. 1973: 'Guidelines for developing international marketing strategies', *Journal of Marketing,* Vol. 37, pp. 14–23.

Young, S. 1987: 'Business strategy and the internationalisation of business: recent approaches', *Managerial and Decision Economics*, Vol. 8, No. 1.

Young, S., Hamill, J., Wheeler, C. and Davies, J. R. 1989: *International Market Entry and Development: Strategies and Management.* London: Harvester Wheatsheaf.

PART II
Functional areas of international business

5

International marketing

INTRODUCTION

Although international marketing is not a new area of business activity – companies such as IBM, Ford, Singer and Unilever have been involved in international marketing operations almost since their establishment – its popularity and acceptance as the focus of international activity increased after the Second World War (Monye, 1995). International marketing has hitherto been considered as merely a routine functional activity, and not meriting special effort or additional resources in the development and management of this activity by firms operating in foreign markets. Bradley (1991) notes that companies in most industries are now concerned with developments in international markets: banks, communications and transport, manufacturing and retailing.

An overview of marketing management is necessary in order to capture the nature and essence of international marketing. Definitions of marketing abound but for the purpose of this book, marketing as defined by the British Chartered Institute of Marketing (CIM) will suffice. CIM define marketing as 'the management process responsible for identifying, anticipating and satisfying customer requirements, profitably'. Thus, the purpose of marketing is simply to identify the basis for customer satisfaction and deliver it with a view to making profit. Accordingly, international marketing may be described as the extension of this domestic marketing objective into a multi-country, multi-linguistic and multi-cultural global market. Cateora (1990) defines international marketing as 'the performance of business activities that direct the flow of a company's goods and services to consumers or users in more than one nation for a profit'. However, there is no definitive definition of international marketing.

In extending business activities beyond national frontiers, firms have to cope with myriads of uncertainties in these foreign markets. The task of the international marketer is to manage the firm's international activities within the constraints of these uncontrollable elements in a way that enhances international competitiveness. The nature of these external factors is encapsulated in the framework for international marketing, as shown in figure 5.1. For the international marketer, these external factors are further complicated by the fact that different countries present different environmental conditions for the same product, a fact which is illustrated with exhibit 5.1 and covered in chapter 3. It is the uniqueness of each country's environmental characteristics that fundamentally distinguishes international marketing from domestic marketing. Robinson (1978) writes that

> different national sovereignties generate different legal, monetary, and political systems. Each legal system implies a unique set of relevant rights and obligations in relation to property, taxation, control of monopoly, business organisation, and contract. These in turn require the firm to consider new organisational relationships, acquire new skills, and adopt new accounting and control procedures; new, that is, in the sense of being different from that required in a purely domestic setting.

The increasing globalization of business activities and the establishment of regional economic integration among nations would suggest that firms operating in the complex global environments will require a broad understanding and knowledge of these environments to facilitate effective international marketing planning; and have to develop managerial expertise in intra- and inter-cultural marketing and foreign language skills. These are necessary to ensure that an international marketing manager is able to execute an effective international strategy that enhances a firm's international competitiveness. Taggart and McDermott (1993) suggest that the international marketing management function has to fulfil a number of requirements such as:

- using international marketing research to identify the various possible end-users for the service or product;
- classifying the identified potential customers using segmentation methods;
- modifying products (or creating new ones) to produce customer satisfaction in the markets thus established (product strategy);
- setting an international pricing strategy to determine the range of selling prices that will help the firm establish a sustainable competitive edge in its chosen foreign markets;
- developing a promotional strategy to inform potential customers of the attributes and benefits of the product;
- arranging an international distribution system that ensures a satisfactory level of service to foreign customers.

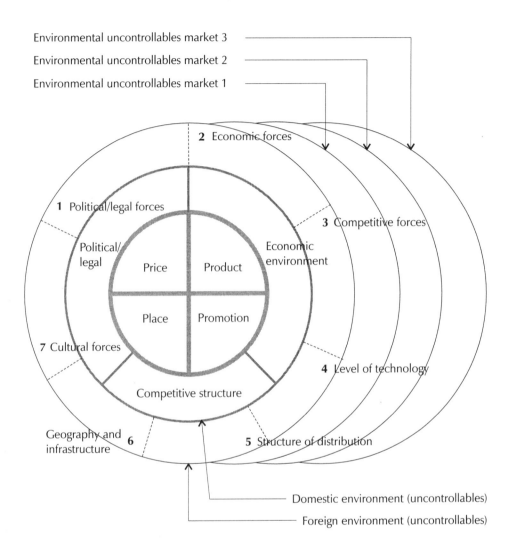

Environmental uncontrollables market 3
Environmental uncontrollables market 2
Environmental uncontrollables market 1

2 Economic forces

1 Political/legal forces

3 Competitive forces

Political/
legal

Price | Product

Economic
environment

Place | Promotion

7 Cultural forces

4 Level of technology

Competitive structure

Geography and
infrastructure 6

5 Structure of distribution

Domestic environment (uncontrollables)
Foreign environment (uncontrollables)

Figure 5.1 The international marketing task
Source: Adapted from Cateora (1990), p. 10.

EXHIBIT 5.1

Japan : the ultimate market

Changes are afoot in the economic powerhouse of the Far East. An appreciating yen has forced Japanese producers to incorporate relatively cheaper foreign suppliers into their production process. This, together with international pressure to lower their trade surplus, has encouraged the Japanese to open their markets to the rest of the world. According to the Japanese Ministry of International Trade and Industry (MITI), Japan's major importing firms are planning to increase overseas purchases by 15 per cent this year.

An increasing number of British firms are benefiting from this new openness: exports to Japan in the first seven months of 1989 were up 31 per cent over the same period in 1988, and passed the £2 billion mark for the first time last June.

The Opportunity Japan Campaign, a cooperative effort of the British Overseas Trade Board and the Department of Trade and Industry, looks set to achieve its goal of doubling British exports to Japan by the end of 1990. Launching the campaign in January 1988, the then Secretary of State for Trade and Industry, Lord Young, called on British business to shift its perception of Japan from problem to opportunity. 'Learn to profit from the new Japan', he said. 'Given long-term commitment and the right approach, opportunity and profit are there as never before.' Lars Janneryd, deputy managing director of Crossfield Electronics, agrees: 'It is not that the problem of exporting to Japan are not real – they do exist – but they are not insurmountable. If approached well, Japan can be a very lucrative market.'

Crossfield has made a successful foray into the Japanese market with its computerized systems for the graphics, design and communications industries. 'You might think trying to sell such high tech products to the Japanese would be like sending coal to Newcastle', says Janneryd. But Crossfield now has 30 per cent of the Japanese market in sophisticated digital scanners and almost one-third of the market in computerized design systems – despite the fact that one of the four major international manufacturers of this equipment is Japanese.

Janneryd credits Crossfield's success to commitment and patience. 'The first requisite for success in this area is one of attitude. It is necessary to have wholehearted commitment to the Japanese market or one's initiative will rapidly run out of steam', he says.

Marketing in Japan invariably begins with formal introductions followed by a long process of building relations with customers and trading partners. 'It is almost impossible to cold call in Japan', says Ruta Noreika, a director at the Scottish Centre for Japanese Studies. *cont.*

The approach

'Whether negotiating with potential suppliers or prospective customers it is vital to address things in a way that appeals to a Japanese sensibility,' says Noreika. 'What goes down as a good presentation in Britain may not impress the Japanese.' 'In English speaking countries, for example, being articulate is seen as a virtue, but in Japan if you talk too much you only sound glib. Westerners are also quick to say they can do something, while the Japanese tend to minimize their ability and avoid attracting attention to themselves', she says. Modest, low key but persistent presentations are generally the best received. 'If you have limited time to prepare, it would be better spent learning about the culture and basic business etiquette than trying to learn the language,' she adds. 'Business can be done in English, with an interpreter if necessary, but an understanding of how things are done is essential.'

Consumer tastes

Exporters must be prepared to alter their products to suit Japanese tastes. 'The Japanese are very quality conscious and very brand conscious,' says Noreika. Presentation is paramount. As one cynic noted – 'If you want to sell it in Japan – put it in a nice box.' Not surprisingly many of the more successful British imports have been luxury branded goods, such as Scotch whisky, crystalware and fine woollens.

Says Noreika: 'The Japanese often like things to be tailor-made: successful exporters are those that have been willing to work with Japanese partners and customers and alter their products accordingly.' The French-based food multinational BSN Gervais Danone learned a salutary lesson about the difficulties of imposing global tastes when it suffered losses totalling more than the initial capital investments of ¥2.5 billion (£11.1 million) trying to enter the Japanese yogurt market. The irony is that the company seemed to be doing everything right: lots of marketing research, entering the market very slowly, careful selection of a partner for a joint venture. Research showed that yogurt beverages were very popular but there appeared to be huge potential for solid yogurt sales, as they made up only 25 per cent of the total. After a market survey running for six months, BSN had visions of sales growth as high as 100 per cent annually. When sales fell far short of even the most conservative estimates, the company was forced to reassess its approach. There seemed to be two main problems. Marketing professionals had not been prepared for the extreme politeness of the Japanese, who may say a product is good even if they don't like it.

The market

Breaking into the market is less than half the battle. Says Noreika: 'The Japanese internal market is extremely competitive.' Scotch whisky importers discovered

cont.

this last year. The formal import barriers came down when the Japanese government was obliged to comply with GATT ruling to tax imported whisky at the
same rate as the domestic product. Scotch whisky imports jumped by 39 per
cent in the space of a few months – only to trigger competition from a glut of
cheaper Japanese imitations.

British goods must also find their way through Japan's complicated distribution system. Wholesaling tends to be multi-layered and retailing is fragmented –
DTI statistics show that the average Japanese shop serves about 70 people, as
opposed to 240 in the UK.

Those who have cracked the market barriers are optimistic. Says Janneryd:
'What has probably deterred many UK manufacturers is the perception that
Japan is so alien a market as to be inaccessible to British goods. In reality, the
only fundamental obstacle is the quality of those goods.'

Source: Adapted from *Marketing Business*, February 1990, pp. 12–14.

MULTINATIONAL VERSUS GLOBAL MARKETING

The concept of global marketing is a fairly recent phenomenon, used
glibly and grossly misunderstood. To some firms, it is the buzzword or
fashionable term for multinational marketing. Consequently, the terms
multinational and global marketing are sometimes used interchangeably,
thereby removing any distinction between them. To others, global marketing represents a new perception of the world market. At the heart of the
matter is the orientation and strategy of firms in servicing international
markets. Levitt (1983) argues that:

> a powerful force drives the world toward a converging commonality, and
> that force is technology. It has proletarianized communication, transport,
> and travel. It has made isolated places and impoverished peoples eager for
> modernity's allurements ... the result is a new commercial reality – the
> emergence of global markets for standardised consumer products on a pre-
> viously unimagined scale of magnitude ... thus globalization of markets is at
> hand. With that, the multinational commercial world nears its end, and so
> do the multinational corporations.

This raises the question of the distinction between multinational
marketing and global marketing. There is consensus in the literature
that global marketing is different from multinational marketing

(Cateora and Hess, 1988; Albaum *et al.*, 1989; Toyne and Walters, 1993). What is, however, unclear are the distinguishing features. According to Levitt the multinational corporation operates in a number of countries, and adjusts its products and practices in each – at high relative costs. The global corporation operates with resolute constancy – at low relative cost – as if the entire world (or major regions of it) were a single entity; it sells the same things in the same way everywhere. Keegan (1989) goes further to argue that the concept of multinational corporation is obsolete, suggesting that the death of the multinational is not just a change in terminology. The global corporation is distinctively different: it has a different focus, vision, orientation, strategy, structure, R&D policy, human resource policy, operating style, communications pattern, financial policy, sourcing policy, and a new product development policy and investment policy.

Thus, it would seem that cost considerations are paramount in the concept of global marketing. This argument was amplified by Jatusripitak *et al.* (1985) in their seminal article. They suggest that in order to become a global marketer, the company must establish plants around the world and decide which plants should be used to manufacture which products for which markets to obtain the lowest costs of production and distribution.

Levitt and Keegan believe the era of multinational marketing is over simply because globalization offers significant economies of scale. The debate has to be broadened to incorporate all the pros and cons of globalization. For example, does it necessarily mean that any firm that does not have plants around the world is not global? Have international consumers become culturally and economically homogeneous? Does the concept of globalization apply equally to all industries and every type of product or service? The debate needs to be put in perspective. Given that the characteristics of buyers and users differ, it is evident that no single type of marketing programme is likely to succeed in all situations even for the same product. Thus, it will be myopic or perhaps suicidal for every type of firm to jump on the globalization bandwagon without due consideration for the nature of its product or service and the characteristics of the consumers in a target market.

The recent wave of interest in globalization has been attributed to a range of factors, but the key ones are:

* Mobility of consumers: developments in transport, telecommunications and information technology are facilitating easy travel and information flow in a 'shrinking world', thereby providing the necessity for global brands.

- Convergence of consumer tastes: Levitt (1983) suggests that consumers everywhere want all the things they have heard about, seen, or experienced via new technologies.
- Savings in production and marketing costs: intense competitive pressures mean that firms are forced to respond by undertaking cost control measures designed to permit the spreading of R&D costs over longer production runs.
- The lowering of trade barriers under the auspices of the General Agreement on Tariffs and Trade (GATT) over the last thirty years.

Undoubtedly, there are substantial gains to be made by pursuing the strategy of globalization. The benefits may be summarized as:

- lower costs: the most widely mentioned benefit of globalization is the cost savings to be derived from economies of scale in R&D, production and marketing;
- the creation of a consistent global brand and image;
- consistency in product policy and other aspects of the marketing strategy.

On the other hand, critics of globalization argue that few industries or indeed firms can truly be described as being global. Most firms talk about globalization glibly. The main limitations of this strategy are:

- It ignores the differences in national characteristics, tastes and preferences.
- It undermines the basic tenets of marketing: segmentation based on differences in consumer preferences; and profitability based on consumers' wants, choice and satisfaction.
- It is cost driven and not customer centred.
- The so-called cost savings are not usually passed on to the consumers in the form of lower prices.
- It undermines the need for subsidiary executives to make inputs in the strategy planning process based on their local market knowledge. Globalization reinforces the centralization of authority at the headquarters, which in turn, breeds an autocratic style of management.

From the preceding discussion, it is clear that a wide range of benefits are to be derived from pursuing a strategy of globalization. But these benefits should not be overstated and must be put in perspective. The strategy must not be pursued without due consideration for specific host market conditions and needs. For companies to be successful, they must think global but act local.

INTERNATIONAL MARKETING RESEARCH

International marketing decisions are preceded by two primary questions: which markets to enter and how to succeed in those markets. The answers to these questions lie in international marketing research. Seemingly, the unfamiliarity of foreign markets does increase the risks for international marketing activity. Thus, only marketing research information can improve a company's knowledge of a foreign market and accordingly, minimize the problem of uncertainty.

Kinnear and Taylor (1991) define marketing research as 'the systematic and objective approach to the development and provision of information for the marketing management decision-making process'. Thus, information is the key to making meaningful decisions *vis-à-vis* organizational performance. This point is relevant whether in a domestic or an international setting. Douglas and Craig (1983) explain that in the international environment, however, not only are the decisions facing management more complex, but the actual task of conducting research is also more difficult. Jain (1990) goes further to identify three major ways in which international marketing research differ from purely domestic marketing research. He contends that:

- The effects of the international environment on the whole company as a profit-oriented unit are considered. For example, the marketing research project concerned with the ramifications of a substantial price hike in a particular country must consider questions that do not apply to the domestic market; for example, will the company's subsidiary be nationalized if prices are increased beyond a certain level?
- Many concepts and frameworks (i.e. market segmentation), which constitute the core of marketing decision-making in the domestic arena, may be unusable in international marketing, not because the concept cannot be transferred, but because the information necessary to make such a transfer is not available. For example, if there is a lack of current income distribution data on a country, any analysis of the demand for a product will assume incorrect income categories and, therefore, cannot mean much for practical purposes.

- The ethnocentric nature of marketing makes cultural differences among nations a significant factor. Thus, culture in a domestic market can be considered to be naturally understood, but in international marketing the culture must be fully investigated.

Jain contends that these factors raise a variety of conceptual, methodological and organizational issues in international marketing research relating to:

- the complexity of research design, caused by operation in a multi-country, multi-cultural and multi-linguistic environment;
- the lack of secondary data available for many countries and product markets;
- the high cost of collecting primary data, particularly in developing countries;
- the problem associated with coordinating research and data collection in different countries;
- the difficulties of establishing the comparability and equivalence of data and research conducted in different contexts;
- the intra-functional character of many international marketing decisions;
- the economies of many international investment and marketing decisions.

These complexities notwithstanding, Douglas and Craig (1983) maintain that since decisions such as selection of target markets, segmentation strategy, or standardizing marketing mix tactics cover several countries, it is important that the information on which such decisions are based must be comparable and consistent from one country to another.

Thus, given the complex nature of international marketing decisions, it is essential that every aspect of a host country is examined. A number of academics and business consultants have developed systematic schemes for screening international markets. As long as the key information requirements are covered, any of these schemes will suffice. For example, table 5.1 lists the types of information that a company may require for assessing an international market. It shows the three categories of information that must be examined before a decision could be made to enter a foreign market: (1) the eliminating factors (useful in determining whether the market should be entered or not); (2) the general influencing factors (relevant to assessing market potential and investment conditions); and (3) specific influencing factors (for the individual company) – to determine sales potential.

Furthermore, there is need for company-specific primary information which provides the basis for formulating marketing plans and operational tactics in the host market. This category of information relates to the marketing mix elements and should include the following items.

Product research
- extend existing products to new market;
- adapt existing products for the new market;
- develop new products for the new market;
- government regulations;
- design requirements;
- packaging requirements;
- after-sales service required;
- brand name (international versus local brand names).

Pricing research
- elasticity and cross-elasticity of demand;
- profitability analysis;
- rate of inflation and its impact on pricing;
- exchange rate volatility;
- competitors' pricing policy and strategy.

Promotion research
- extend existing promotion campaign;
- modify existing message for the new market;
- create a new campaign for the new market;
- cultural and language barriers;
- host country regulations and controls;
- availability of marketing infrastructure;
- availability of advertising agencies;
- quality, reliability and cost of advertising agencies.

Distribution research
- direct versus indirect distribution system;
- location of distribution facility;
- difficulties or otherwise of appointing channel members;
- cost of distribution;
- availability and quality of distributors;
- transport cost;
- tariffs and customs charges;
- quality and cost of port facilities.

Table 5.1 Screening potential export territories

Screen 1 Eliminating factors

Unacceptable product	Standards, safety, socio-cultural factors
Political barriers	Boycotts, sanctions, local participation, state monopolies
Economic	Non-transferability of funds, barter trading, price levels
Legal	Anti-trust legislation, labour laws, patents, environmental control
Supply	Shortage of labour/material, distributors/servicing

Screen 2 General influencing factors by group

Factor	Weighting	Individual countries			
		A	B	C	D
		Rating total	Rating total	Rating total	Rating total

Economic

1. Size of GNP and rate of growth
2. Nature of development plan
3. Resistance to recession
4. Relative dependence on imports and exports
5. Foreign exchange position
6. Balance of payments outlook
7. Stability of currency, convertibility
8. Remittance and repatriation regulations
9. Balance of economy (industry–agriculture trade)
10. Size of market for products; rate of growth
11. Size of population; rate of growth
12. Per capita income; rate of growth
13. Income distribution
14. Current or prospective membership in customs union
15. Price levels; rate of inflation

Political

16. Stability of government; its form
17. Presence or absence of class antagonism
18. Special political, ethnic, and social problems
19. Attitude towards private and foreign investment
20. Acceptability of foreign investment by government
21. Acceptability of foreign investment by customers and competitors
22. Presence or absence of nationalization threat

cont.

Table 5.1 cont.

Factor	Weighting	Individual countries			
		A	B	C	D
		Rating total	Rating total	Rating total	Rating total
23. Presence or absence of state industries					
24. Do state industries receive favoured treatment?					
25. Concentration of influence in small groups					
26. 'Most favoured nation' treatment availability					

Government
27. Fiscal and monetary policies
28. Extent of bureaucratic interference and administration
29. Fairness and honesty of administrative procedures
30. Degree of anti-foreign discrimination
31. Fairness of courts
32. Clear and modern corporate investment laws
33. Patentability of products
34. Presence or absence of price controls
35. Restriction on complete or majority ownership

Geographic
36. Efficiency of transport system and methods
37. Port facilities and level of costs
38. Free ports, free zones and bondage warehouses
39. Proximity to export markets
40. Proximity to suppliers, customers
41. Proximity to raw material sources
42. Existing supporting industry
43. Availability of local raw materials
44. Availability of power, water, gas
45. Reliability of utilities
46. Waste disposal facilities
47. Ease of exporting
48. Ease of importing
49. Cost of suitable land

Labour
50. Availability of managerial, technical personnel
51. Availability of skilled labour
52. Availability of semi-skilled and unskilled labour
53. Level of worker productivity

cont.

Table 5.1 cont.

Factor	Individual countries				
	Weighting	A	B	C	D
		Rating total	Rating total	Rating total	Rating total

54. Training facilities
55. Outlook for increase in labour supply
56. Degree of skill and discipline at all level
57. Climate of labour relations
58. Degree of labour involvement in management
59. Compulsory and voluntary fringe benefits
60. Social security taxes
61. Total cost of labour including fringe benefits
62. Compulsory or customary profit-sharing

Tax
63. Tax rates
64. General tax morality
65. Fairness and incorruptibility of tax authorities
66. Long term trend for taxes
67. Taxation of export income earned abroad
68. Tax incentives for new business
69. Depreciation rates
70. Tax loss carry forward and back
71. Joint tax treaties
72. Duty and tax drawbacks
73. Availability of tariff protection

Capital
74. Availability of local capital
75. Cost of local borrowing
76. Normal terms of local borrowing
77. Availability of convertible currencies locally
78. Efficiency of the banking system

cont.

Table 5.1 cont.

Factor	Weighting	Individual countries			
		A	B	C	D
		Rating total	Rating total	Rating total	Rating total

79. Government credit aids to new business
80. Availability and cost of export financing including insurance
81. Do normal loan sources favour investment

Business methods
82. General business morality
83. State of development of marketing and distribution system
84. Normal profit margins, for industry concerned
85. Climate of competition
86. Anti-trust and restrictive practices laws
87. Quality of life for expatriate staff

Screen 3 Specific influencing factors (for the individual company)

88. Company and trademark must be well known.
89. A good geographical network of distributor/service companies must exist.
90. No conflict must occur with corporate development elsewhere in company's market.
91. Reasonable level of local management sophistication.
92. Must not compete with company's customers also exporting/producing in the area.
93. Internal transport capable of handling products.

Score:

Source: Adapted from A. Wilson (1982), *Aubrey Wilson's Marketing Audit Check List: A Guide to Effective Marketing Resource Realisation*. Copyright © 1982 McGraw-Hill. Reprinted by permission.

SOURCES OF INFORMATION FOR INTERNATIONAL MARKETING

Sources of information available to a researcher are dependent on the nature of information being sought. Information necessary to examine the eliminating and general influencing factors can be obtained from a number of secondary sources. Secondary information is defined as data that have already been collected for other purposes and readily available, which can be utilized for the task at hand. The main advantages of secondary data are ready availability and relatively low cost. On the other hand, the main disadvantages are related to issues such as accuracy and reliability, fit, comparability, and currency. None the less, it is worth stressing that secondary information is a very useful starting point for any research. Sources of secondary information include:

* public sources: government publications; government-funded agencies; chambers of commerce; foreign trade missions; foreign embassies; OECD publications; United Nations publications; and European Union publications.
* private sources: private research organizations; banks; and trade associations.

Where the quality of secondary data is unacceptable, primary data may be needed for tactical decisions relating to product, pricing, promotion, and distribution in order to ensure that the right decisions are made. Douglas and Craig (1983) define primary data as information tailored to meet the specific information requirements of international management decisions. This type of information is available only to the researcher and may provide the additional information necessary for success in tactical planning. Primary data offer a number of fundamental advantages to the firm such as more specific information for the decision at hand; up-to-date information; and research results available only to the researcher. The disadvantages are numerous and include the high cost of data collection and the problems associated with conducting research in multi-country, multi-cultural and multi-linguistic environment, as discussed in the preceding part of this chapter.

INTERNATIONAL MARKET SEGMENTATION

The concept of international segmentation is based on the fact that no company can serve the global market satisfactorily in resource terms.

Similarly, with the degree of diversity in national characteristics (socio-cultural, political, economic and technological), the concept of global product and standardized international marketing strategy is realistically, limited in applications to certain product categories such as industrial products. Segmentation enables firms to concentrate their marketing resources on group of countries that exhibit considerable similarities in their responsiveness to marketing efforts. Thus, international market segmentation may be defined as a technique for separating the global market into largely homogeneous groups, with a separate marketing programme for each market group. Consequently, it is imperative that a firm screens these market segments to identify those that are most likely to respond to its marketing efforts in a particular manner. Segmenting the global market offers a number of benefits. Toyne and Walters (1993) contend that segmentation allows:

- foreign firms to be selected on the basis of their individual potential;
- foreign markets to be treated independently, as elements of an overall foreign market portfolio to be increased or decreased depending on individual profitability;
- products and product lines to be tailored to the particular needs and requirements of local markets;
- products and product lines to be priced according to local demand and competitive conditions;
- channels to be developed according to local competitive conditions and market circumstances;
- promotional themes and campaigns to be developed according to local competitive conditions and market circumstances.

CRITERIA FOR SEGMENTING INTERNATIONAL MARKETS

While there are no standard and universally accepted criteria for segmenting international markets, certain variables are, none the less, essential for meaningful segmentation. Some of the key segmenting variables are:

- Economic basis for segmentation: with this technique, countries are grouped together on the basis of the levels of their economic development and per capita income. These economic indicators are published regularly by United Nations. While this may be a useful criterion, it has to be used in conjunction with other variables.

- Geographic segmentation: this is the most widely used technique for segmenting markets by multinational firms because of its simplicity. It allows for the classification of world market along regional lines such as Europe, North America, Africa and the Far East. Given that trading blocs are organized along regional lines, it seems a viable way of segmenting international markets. It is, however, noteworthy that cultural and linguistic diversities within regions are ignored by using this technique.
- Political segmentation: countries are sometimes grouped on the basis of their political inclinations. Jain (1990) suggests that the concept of political segmentation may form the basis for a standardized marketing approach. Thus, in countries where certain business practices such as centralized buying and countertrade are particularly popular, it may be possible to apply a common marketing strategy.
- Cultural segmentation: culture is everything that is socially learned and shared by the members of the society and consists of material and non-material components such as knowledge, belief, art, morals and religion. Since culture is completely intertwined with lifestyle and hence consumer behaviour, it represents an important international market segmentation criterion. A standardized marketing strategy may be applied to a group of countries with a common culture.
- Multi-variable segmentation: given that the previous variables may not be individually viable as a basis for segmenting international markets, it may be necessary to combine some of them in order to establish a more viable segmenting framework. This will ensure that countries with similar socio-cultural, economic and political characteristics are grouped into segments.

While international market segmentation offers a number of important advantages, it is imperative that each potential market segment is evaluated with carefully developed criteria to ensure that (1) effective programmes can be formulated, and (2) the cost of special marketing programme will be less than the benefits of operating in the segment.

INTERNATIONAL PRODUCT POLICY AND PLANNING

Product decision is potentially the most important factor that determines the success or failure of any company whether in domestic or international markets. The other elements of the marketing mix are built around sound product policy and decisions. A product offering is the totality of all that a buyer or consumer perceives as being part of the product. This includes the core product, the product package (brand name, quality, design features and packaging) and augmented services (user manual, after-sales service and warranties). Intense global competition suggests that a company must seek to achieve competitive advantages by providing a product that meets market requirements better than ever. In particular, the need to keep prices down has resulted in more emphasis being placed on product strategy.

Once the decision to internationalize is made, managers must appraise the feasibility of standardizing the firm's product offering or consider alternative product strategies that are more host country-specific in terms of local conditions and tastes. For the international marketer, there are three options to introducing a product to a foreign market: (1) straight-forward extension (introduction of the same product sold in the domestic market without any adaptation); (2) product adaptation (modifying the domestic product to meet host market needs/wants, tastes and culture); and (3) new product development (developing a completely new product for the new market). No single approach may be completely satisfactory as each option offers a host of benefits as well as limitations and therefore needs careful evaluation. Although, since the mid-1980s and 1990s, the trend in international product policy has been towards standardization, it is noteworthy that certain factors are fundamental in making these decisions. Robinson (1978) and Jain (1990) suggest that a set of specific criteria must be applied to determine whether adaptation is desirable or not, and if so, the extent of the modification required. These would include:

- The nature of the product which will determine whether adaptation is necessary. Generally, industrial products are more likely to lend themselves to standardization than consumer products. Some international companies have discovered at considerable cost that consumer products such as food products have to conform to local tastes and eating habits.
- Cost–benefit analysis: depending on the nature of modification to be carried out, the cost of modifying existing products can be a major factor in decisions concerning standardization versus adaptation. Analysis will include costs associated with physical modification of the core product, design and styling, packaging and branding. These costs must be evaluated in relation to the expected benefits to be derived, particularly in terms of long-run profitability of the product in the host market.

- Legal requirements: host governments may impose mandatory standards which must be met by firms marketing in such countries. For example, the United States imposes stringent technical requirements on the importation of automobiles into the country. Similarly, following years of research into the impact of environmental pollution and the sources of such pollution on Lake Geneva, Swiss scientists confirmed that phosphate in detergents was harmful to marine life. Consequently, in 1986, Switzerland passed legislation banning the use of phosphate in detergents.

Albaum *et al.* (1989) suggest conditions under which adaptation or standardization would be appropriate. These conditions are listed in table 5.2.

PORTFOLIO APPROACH IN INTERNATIONAL PRODUCT PLANNING

Decisions relating to international product planning tend to hinge on its marketing potential in the host market and require careful analysis, as indicated above. A number of schemes can be used in the analytical process. One such scheme is the product portfolio analysis, for which the Boston Consulting Group (BCG) is pre-eminent. This approach classifies a firm's international performance on the basis of relative market share and growth rate. Larreche (1980) notes that product portfolio approach is particularly useful in formulating international marketing strategies. He argues that significant differences between countries in terms of market growth and structure will generally lead to the consideration of multiple market entries for given a product. Furthermore, a detailed product/market portfolio analysis will give a correct picture of the competitive situation and offers the following advantages:

- It offers a global view of the international competitive structure. The international product/market portfolio analysis provides a clear picture of the current competitive situation and its evolution in the future.
- It acts as a guide for the formulation of a global international marketing strategy. By considering international markets as basic investment units, generators or users of cash, the international product/market portfolio approach places the emphasis on the strategic issue of allocating scarce resources between these investment units in order to attain the stable long-term growth in sales and profits.

Table 5.2 Factors to consider for global product strategy

	Globalize when	Adapt when
Competitive factors		
Strength of competition	Weak	Strong
Market position	Dominant	Non-dominant
Market factors		
Homogeneity of consumer preferences	Homogeneous	Heterogeneous
Potential growth of currently small segments	Low	High
Consumer purchasing power	Uniform	Varied
Willingness of consumers to pay for differentiated products	Low	High
Need satisfied by product in market served	Shared	Individual
Conditions of use	Uniform	Varied
Product factor		
Importance of scale economies in manufacturing	High	Low
Opportunities to learn from small-scale production of innovative products	Low	High
Type of product	Industrial consumer	
Codes of restriction	Uniform	Varied
Company factors		
Scope of international involvement	Many or large markets	Few or small markets
Company resources (financial, personnel, production)	Limited	Abundant

Source: Adapted from Albaum *et al.* (1989).

- It acts as a guide for the formulation of marketing objectives for specific international markets. Imposed or self-assigned marketing objectives for specific international markets may be dysfunctional if the role of each market within the global marketing strategy is not well understood.

Despite these seemingly overwhelming advantages, the product/market portfolio model of analysing international markets has been criticized for its simplistic approach in dealing with the complex issue of international market evaluation. Albaum *et al* (1989) identified two main limitations of the product/market portfolio approach:

- The basic assumptions concerning the experience curve mechanism, that is, the links between market share and profitability, and the product life cycle as the driving force of market evaluation, are violated.
- The measurements are questionable. How much market segmentation? Which level of geography? Should the definition of product market be broad or narrow?

Albaum *et al.* argue that these questions are important for measuring the relative market share and growth rate, and so are the interpretations of the strategic bases for resource allocation.

PRODUCT POSITIONING

A firm's product is differentiated from those of its competitors partly by its quality and features, and partly by its positioning in the minds of consumers; these form the basis for achieving competitive advantage in the market. According to Kotler (1988), 'positioning is the act of designing the company's image and value offer so that the segment's customers understand and appreciate what the company stands for in relation to its competitors'. Thus, a positioning strategy has to be based on the aggregate benefits that consumers seek from a product class. Keegan *et al.* (1992) suggest that marketers have only two choices in developing their positioning strategy: go head to head in direct competition with other firms or try to differentiate your own product – make it so unique that it has no direct competition. Furthermore, these two approaches could be developed and exploited using the following criteria:

- Product positioning could be achieved by emphasizing the attributes of the products or the benefits that consumers seek. This is the most frequently adopted positioning strategy. For example, Toyota launched its Lexus range as very luxurious cars.
- Positioning by product category. This involves pitching a product against similar products with a view to highlighting the differences in

quality or price. For example, Unilever launched Radion in the UK as a detergent that removes stale odour in washed clothes and pitched it against other brands of washing powder.

* Positioning by use/user. Sometimes, products are positioned according to user characteristics and lifestyle. Rolex wrist watches are positioned as exclusive products for the wealthy or for special occasions.

The differences in international marketing environments discussed in the preceding sections of this chapter mean that each market is unique in character and presents different sets of marketing opportunities and problems. Therefore it is not unusual to find a single product positioned differently in each market. Perrier has successfully pursued a policy of differentiated positioning strategy globally. In France, its sparkling water is positioned as ordinary bottled water, while in the UK it is positioned as a substitute for soft drinks with snob appeal. This is reflected in its promotion and pricing strategies. In one of its recent advertising campaigns, the company even claimed that drinking Perrier water can improve your sex life – certainly an interesting claim for carbonated water.

Thus, it is necessary for marketers to strike a balance between a product's features, user characteristics and culture, and the benefits sought from a product in order to determine an ideal positioning strategy for each market. Ultimately it is the perception of consumers *vis-à-vis* a product that determines its desirability and marketability.

INTERNATIONAL BRANDING

A brand may be described as anything which identifies a firm's goods or services and distinguishes them from competing products or services. A brand acts as a symbol of quality, reliability, performance and assurance. Thus, a brand name is an essential part of a product mix which reinforces a firm's marketing efforts in areas such as advertising and pricing.

Finding a brand name that is both suitably attractive, and registerable, is a very difficult task. Picking an appropriate global brand is substantially more difficult than selecting a brand name for a single market because of linguistic and cultural diversities in international markets. Some marketing agencies specialize in assisting international firms with the selection of global brand names. These agencies are growing in number and popularity.

Given the need to evaluate the pros and cons of extending domestic brands into foreign markets, international firms expend considerable amounts of time and resources on the brand selection process. As part of the process, international marketers have to choose between extending domestic brands into foreign markets, and adopting completely different brand names. However, it has to be said that globalizing a local brand name has its limitations. For example, some well established local brands may not be acceptable when used in certain foreign markets: they may not be easily pronounceable; may be meaningless or even mean something unpleasant when translated into local languages. On the other hand, certain brand names such as Kodak and Coca-Cola have been successfully marketed internationally. Therefore extending a local brand name internationally calls for a close examination of its merits and demerits. Toyne and Walters (1993) list the following advantages of global branding:

- It promotes global product recognition and a consistent international product and corporate image.
- Although developing a new global brand name is not cheap, time and money may be saved because it is not necessary to develop new brands in individual overseas markets.
- Promotional benefits accrue when media overlap national boundaries.
- This policy complements a drive for standardization of other elements of the international marketing mix, particularly in the areas of product characteristics and advertising.

The following may be limitations on global brands:

- There may be considerable difficulty in identifying a global brand name that is pronounceable, meaningful and available in all foreign markets.
- The cost of promoting global brands is high.

BRAND COUNTERFEITING

Jeannet and Hennessey (1988) explain that because brand names or trademarks are usually backed with substantial advertising funds, it makes sense to register such brands for the exclusive use of the sponsoring firm. Sadly, many firms have found themselves subject of violation by imitators who use either the protected name or very similar one. This violation can come in a number of forms (as shown in exhibit 5.2) and are generally known as brand counterfeiting. Young *et al.* (1989) contend that counterfeiting involves the imitation of a product or service, without the permission of the legal owner, and the packaging of it to look like the original, with the result

---

EXHIBIT 5.2

Types of counterfeiting

1. Piracy: the design and trademark of the original good are copied and the fake is marketed as the genuine product. Rolex watches, Levi's jeans, and many brands of auto parts are good examples of frequently pirated products.
2. Design counterfeiting: the physical attributes of the original good are copied, and the product is then marketed under a different brand name. Apart from looking like the original, the counterfeit product often performs as well as the original. Products such as perfume and electronic equipment are susceptible to this form of counterfeiting.
3. Trademark or brand name counterfeiting: the fake is marketed using a well-known brand name but is physically different from the original. Clothing is commonly counterfeited in this way.
4. Clone strategy: modification of the design and brand name in such a way that the modified product is very similar to the original good. In the case of product design and performance, many personal computers are, for example, highly derivative of IBM machines.

Source: Adapted from Toyne and Walters (1993), p. 460.

---

that the consumer is misled. Brand counterfeiting has become more widespread than ever before and constitutes a serious menace for multinational companies, with well-known and desirable brand names such as Levi 501 and Rolex as the major victims. Unfortunately, combating counterfeiters is fraught with difficulties because of lack of international agreement on counterfeiting legislation. Even where there is legislation, the scope and effectiveness of the enforcement process varies from country to country. None the less, international firms are not relenting their effort to defeat the counterfeiters. In addition to legislation, international firms pursue a host of anti-counterfeiting measures in order to minimize its menace. Kaikati (1981) identified the following anti-counterfeiting strategies:

- Compete and attempt to overcome the opposition: the objective here is domination and forcing the counterfeiters out of the market. This may be a feasible strategy when the firm's stakes and power are relatively high.

- Avoid conflict and withdraw from the fray: this option may be feasible if what is at stake for the firm is of limited consequence.
- Accommodate the opposition, where the objective is appeasement: customers may switch to the opposition's brand if they knew the products they buy are faked. The victim of counterfeiting will hope that the problem may disappear.
- Collaborate: if other policies fail or are not effective, firms may consider the option of working with rather than against some counterfeiters. For example, when the counterfeiter is able to manufacture a clone at lower cost that performs as well as the original, a joint venture may make sense.

PACKAGING

Packaging is an important element of the product mix and has both a protective and a promotional role. Packaging offers protection for the content against changes in climatic conditions in the course of transport between and within markets. Effective packaging minimizes the risks of damage, which is known to cost international firms a fortune. In some countries, packaging is expected to meet government requirements both in terms of packaging materials and labelling. Some of these requirements may be imposed for safety reasons and to provide essential information about the product.

Similarly, the promotional role of packaging manifests in the attraction that it offers to customers. In certain product categories where differentiation is difficult to establish (such as toiletries and perfume), brand name and packaging can provide the competitive edge.

INTERNATIONAL PRICING

Of all the elements of the marketing mix, only price relates to the revenue of a firm, yet its competitive value was largely underdeveloped until fairly recently, when firms began to use price to achieve a number of objectives. One of the reasons for the passive role of pricing in the past was partly to do with the misplaced belief that once other elements of the marketing mix were properly developed, pricing would simply 'fit' in place. However the complex marketing conditions have shown that pricing has to be applied as a more active element of the mix. Becker (1980) writes that the change of status of pricing arises from both internal and external factors. He argues that internally, probably the strongest force that has propelled pricing to greater relative importance in the marketing mix is the adoption of the systems concept – the combination and synergistic effect of all the variables together. Externally, in a world of increasing competition, government regulation, accelerating inflation, and widely fluctuating exchange rates, management is simply forced to take heed of its pricing policy – especially in the international sphere.

Perhaps the most instrumental factor in amplifying the importance of effective pricing policy is the intensification of global competition, which has resulted in international firms re-examining the role of pricing as a competitive tool with more rigour. This point is illustrated with the change of pricing policy by one of the world's best known companies – Mercedes-Benz, as shown in exhibit 5.3. Mercedes-Benz has traditionally regarded pricing as a reflection of its product differentiation strategy. The firm hitherto believed its competitive advantages rested on non-price factors. It is noteworthy that firms have come to realize they can no longer compete effectively without due consideration of their pricing policy. This is consistent with the policies of other international firms. As a matter of economics, cost is the key propelling force behind the concept of globalization.

Pricing strategies

A number of possibilities exist for the international firm in terms of pricing strategies. Robinson (1978) suggests six possibilities based on three alternatives as shown in table 5.3: (1) a standard worldwide base price, which may be cost or market oriented; (2) a domestic price and a standard export price, which may also be cost or market oriented; and (3) a market differentiated price that is either cost or market oriented. The attractiveness of each alternative is dependent on the pricing objectives. For example, cost-oriented pricing is normally associated with either intra-firm transfers or with dumping.

Factors influencing pricing decisions

International pricing decisions are very complex and are often fraught with difficulties such as initial price setting, price changes as a reaction to competitors' behaviour and multiple product pricing. This is partly due to the multitude of factors that influence international pricing decisions. The obvious determinants are as follows.

EXHIBIT 5.3

Mercedes-Benz slaughters a sacred cow

Mercedes-Benz, one of the world's most prestigious and tradition-laden car makers, has taken its time to wake up to the daunting dimensions of the challenges it faces in the rapidly changing world car market of the 1990s.

But the Mercedes juggernaut is finally rolling. It arrived publicly at the starting line yesterday with an agenda for change which will astonish the rest of the world car industry. With a breathtaking abandonment of its traditional air of arrogance, the company set out a strategy for change aimed at transforming its fortunes and position in the world car market by the end of the decade.

The bearer of the dramatic tidings was Mr Helmut Werner, the 56-year-old former tyre industry executive who takes over officially as Mercedes-Benz chief executive on 27 May from the long-serving Mr Werner Niefer. He joined Daimler-Benz in 1987 from Continental, the tyre maker.

Mr Werner, a potential candidate for the chairmanship of Daimler-Benz when Mr Edzard Reuter retires in the mid-1990s, revealed that the new Mercedes-Benz management team was now ready to challenge virtually all of the most dearly-held tenets of one of the world's most exclusive car markers. There are to be no more sacred cows in Stuttgart. The company has accepted that radical changes in the world car market mean that Mercedes-Benz will no longer be able to demand premium prices for its products based on an image of effortless superiority and a content of the ultimate in automotive engineering.

With a disarming frankness and a devastating attack on Mercedes-Benz's most recent past Mr Werner admitted that if the company were to continue to 'over-engineer' its products it would be 'priced out' of its markets. In order to avoid this 'trap' the company has decided to turn on its head its whole product development strategy.

Instead of developing the ultimate car and then charging a correspondingly sky-high price as in the past, Mercedes-Benz is taking the dramatic and radical step of moving to 'target pricing'. It will decide what the customer is willing to pay in a particular product category – priced against its competitors – it will add its profit margin and then the real work will begin to cost every part and component to bring in the vehicle at the target price.

Such an approach is not entirely new. Chrysler has begun to use it to great effect to fuel its renaissance in the US, but at Mercedes-Benz this is the stuff of revolution. At the same time Mercedes-Benz is aiming to transform its range of product offerings by the end of the decade, changing from being 'a car manufacturer offering high quality vehicles in all segments of the market'.

Mr Warner disclosed that Mercedes would add to its present three car ranges during the 1990s with a small 'city car', possibly with electric propulsion as one variant, a 'people carrier' in the mode of the Renault Espace, and a modern four-wheel drive leisure/utility vehicle.

The people carrier, or multi-purpose vehicle, is closest to the market and would see Mercedes thus joining the fight in what promises to become one of the most fiercely contested segments of the European car market in the second half of the 1990s. Fiat and Peugeot are developing a plant for a rival vehicle in northern France, while Ford and Volkswagen are cooperating on a similar vehicle to be built at a jointly owned plant in Portugal.

Mr Werner said that Mercedes-Benz's new direction was being forced by a conviction that 'radical changes in the structure of the car market had necessitated the strategic reorientation of the company'. According to Mr Werner, 'the traditional vertical market structure defined by engine size is increasingly giving way to a horizontal market structure'. Under the influence of factors such as stricter traffic and environmental requirements and a growing subjective component in vehicle use, the division of the market into luxury class, medium class and small cars is becoming less and less meaningful.

With a proliferation of niche vehicles such as MPVs, off-road vehicles and roadsters, it was body shapes and forms of propulsion that were becoming the more important distinguishing features, rather than engine size and performance. 'Mercedes-Benz has to gear itself to a future market structured primarily around a diversity in vehicle concepts rather than around engine prestige value,' he said.

As car buyers forsake the conspicuous consumption of the 1980s and place more stress on a vehicle's functional use than on its role as a status symbol, Mercedes is also beginning to investigate radical new ideas of 'car ownership' and of selling cars.

By the late 1990s, Mr Werner suggested that personal car leasing programmes could be available, where the customer might have available several different vehicles during the year. The brave new world is not going to be won without pain and dislocation, however.

Source: Adapted from *Financial Times*, 27 January 1993. Reprinted by permission.

Cost

In determining an appropriate price for a product, one of the main factors influencing the final decision is cost. Cost is of particular importance in international marketing and has to be carefully evaluated to determine the type of costs to be included. The two possible options are full-cost

Table 5.3 Matrix of international pricing strategies

	Cost oriented	Market oriented
Standard worldwide price:		
with net price control		
with final price control		
Dual pricing (domestic/export):		
with net price control		
with final price control		
Market-differentiated prices:		
with net price control		
with final price control		

Source: Robinson (1978), p. 95.

pricing and marginal-cost pricing. Full-cost pricing will include R&D, distribution and marketing costs. The implication of full-cost pricing in international marketing is price escalation. Price escalation occurs as a result of successive additions of costs incurred in the course of exporting a product to a foreign market. These additional costs include transport, customs and excise duties, and distributors' margin. Price escalation could render a product uncompetitive. On the other hand, where marginal costing is used as the basis of the pricing strategy, the firm risks being accused of dumping by host nations. Dumping simply means fixing export prices lower than the domestic prices by excluding certain costs from the final price.

Demand and supply

The relationship between the demand for a product and its supply is crucial in determining the prices which can be set by the international firm. Where the demand for a product is greater than its supply, the price is likely to increase, and vice versa. For example, when video camcorders were first introduced in the markets in the early 1980s, there were only a limited number of suppliers. Consequently, camcorders were very expensive. By the late 1980s, Japanese manufacturers had flooded the markets with video camcorders, thereby depressing the prices. Similarly, the threat of disruption of supply of crude oil at the onset of the Gulf war caused the price of oil to rise.

Exchange rates

Although exchange rates are an irrelevant factor in pricing for domestic markets, they are one of the additional factors that the international marketer has to cope with in determining prices in foreign markets. Exchange rate unpredictability and volatility can have a damaging effect on both the competitiveness and profitability of a firm, particularly in the short run. Given that some currencies are more stable than others, the effect can vary considerably from country to country. Increasingly, international marketers are writing quotations either in their domestic currencies or the more stable currencies. Similarly, currency hedging has become very popular with international marketers. Phatak (1980) describes hedging as meeting future commitments or protecting future income by buying or selling a forward contract to offset or minimize the exchange risks of loss on assets or liabilities which are denominated in a foreign currency. A forward contract refers to the sale or purchase of a specified amount of foreign currency at a fixed exchange rate for delivery or settlement on an agreed date in the future.

Competition

As firms do not operate in a vacuum; competition remains a formidable factor in international pricing decisions. According to Jeannet and Hennessey (1988), the nature and size of competition can significantly affect price levels in any given market. A firm acting as monopolist in any market will have greater pricing flexibility.

INTERNATIONAL DISTRIBUTION

The importance of international physical distribution to the success of any international marketing operation cannot be overemphasized as it has a direct impact on how a market is served and the cost of doing so. Consequently, international distribution decisions are inherently more complex than those for purely domestic distribution operations. In international physical distribution, goods are subject to multiple modes of transport and possibly delays at borders, cover longer distances, involve higher costs, and require more extensive documentation. One of the most important strategic decisions facing the international marketer is who is to be entrusted with the distribution responsibility in each market – whether this function should be performed in house or contracted to an outside organization. Each market has to be treated differently in terms of distribution strategy. The choice of strategy will depend on a number of important factors such as size of the market and profit potential; the firm's resources and commitment to the market; and the level of control required on the marketing mix elements in the market.

Developing a distribution strategy

The logical starting point in determining an efficient and effective distribution strategy is to establish the company's objectives and the marketing efforts required in each market; and to evaluate the environmental factors (size of the market, location of consumer conurbations, geography of the market); infrastructures (warehousing facilities, availability of efficient transport system and other facilitating organizations); and competition (the distribution strategy of competitors and its effectiveness). These factors will determine the distribution strategy. A firm may choose an indirect system of international physical distribution where a lot of uncertainties exist. In this case, export activities are undertaken by specialist facilitating organizations such as export houses, export co-operatives, international trading companies and export management companies. Although the risks with this method of exporting are reduced to bare minimum, the rewards are equally limited. On the other hand, exporters controlling their own distribution network in foreign markets must establish a system that takes into account the stockholding and bulk-breaking functions. McKinnon (1989) suggests that the following systems may be considered:

- Direct system: this is a distribution system that permits the centralization of stocks in the home country and where deliveries are made directly to foreign buyers. Its main advantage is that it eliminates the need for foreign warehousing and allows for greater centralization of inventory. On the other hand, its disadvantages include longer order lead times; in some cases, the urgency of deliveries may limit the scope for achieving economies of scale in larger loads.
- Transit system: with this system, exports are channelled through a

non-stockholding, bulk-breaking point in a particular foreign market for onward transfer to other countries. The objective is to ensure that freight is transported more economically in greater bulk to a distribution point in a given foreign location and disaggregated into individual orders much closer to the other foreign markets. The transit system has similar advantages and disadvantages to the direct system.

- Classical system: the classical system is the most common system of distribution, particularly with exporters who are actively engaged in a host country. With this system, stocks are distributed to depots in each foreign market. This system offers a number of advantages. First, orders can be delivered more rapidly from the warehouse in the host market than from the factory, helping to generate additional sales. Second, freight can be dispatched to the foreign market with less urgency, permitting the use of cheaper modes of transport and offering greater scope for load consolidation. Third, as the international movement of stock is an intra-company transfer, less documentation is required and smaller import duties payable.
- Multi-country system: with a multi-country system, a single warehouse which is centrally located in close proximity to the main export markets is used as a supply point to customers in several countries. By centralizing the foreign markets' stock-holding operation in fewer locations, exporters can expect to reduce inventory costs, partially overcoming the limitations of the classical system.

Modal choice

International logistics managers have the primary responsibility of identifying and choosing the best method of distribution from four major modes of transport in their international physical distribution planning – road, rail, sea and air. The logistics manager will consider the cost and service characteristics of each mode with a view to selecting the mode or combination of modes that meet the requirements of the firm and the market. Other factors relevant in determining the appropriate choice of mode(s) include:

- transport cost;
- nature of the product;
- transit time;
- accessibility of the market;
- modes capability;
- level and quality of service;

- security of cargo;
- availability of resources.

For international physical distribution strategy to succeed, logistics managers must recognize the complex nature of this aspect of the total marketing mix. Careful attention must also be paid to the legal requirements in the host country, availability of distribution infrastructures, including facilitating agencies, and to evaluating the distribution strategies of competitors.

INTERNATIONAL PROMOTION

International promotion is used in this book to connote a range of communication tools designed to influence consumers' attitudes and behaviour towards a product or service. These tools include advertising, sales promotion, sponsorship and publicity, direct marketing and trade exhibitions. One of the main objectives of international marketing promotion is to transmit information designed to persuade the customer to take a particular action – to buy a product or service. It involves communication between a firm operating from a culture that is different from those of buyers and consumers elsewhere. The effectiveness of international promotion is based on the exploitation of cross-cultural similarities rather than differences. The marketer faces a host of problems in planning international promotion, such as differences in culture, economy, tastes and attitudes, government regulations, marketing institutions and language.

Methods of international promotion

International marketers have at their disposal a range of options for promotional activities. These tools can either be used independently or in conjunction with other tools. This section examines the various methods available for the international marketer

Advertising

Advertising is the most visible and documented form of marketing promotion and has generated most interest and attention among academics, professionals and consumers. In most marketing organizations, the bulk of promotion's budget is spent on various forms of advertising. Internationally, expenditure on advertising has been growing at an incredible rate. De Mooij and Keegan (1991) contend that worldwide expenditure on advertising has been growing faster than world gross product – the value of all goods and services produced in the world, which exceeds US$18,000 billion. Total advertising expenditure grew from US$180 billion based on sixty-six countries in 1986, to US$228 billion based on fifty-eight countries in 1988. As competition becomes more intense, this figure is certain to escalate.

As companies begin to develop their international advertising campaigns, there are a number of strategies that can be pursued in each market depending on the nature of the product, how it is used, and the company's communication objectives. According to Keegan (1970), five strategy alternatives may be considered:

- same product, same message worldwide;
- same product, different communications;
- different product, same communications;
- dual adaptation;
- new product, new message.

Keegan argues that the best strategy is one which optimizes company profits in the long term. Thus, each strategy has to be considered within the context of market needs and company objectives.

Another important aspect of international advertising relates to the media vehicles used for campaigns. These can be grouped into print (international and local newspapers and magazines, posters); or broadcast media (international broadcast media such as satellite television channels and radio stations, and local television and radio networks). The best medium is determined by its effectiveness in achieving the company objectives.

Sales promotion

Sales promotions are short-term incentives such as discounts, quantity purchase discounts, coupons, money-back guarantees, in-store consumer promotions designed to increase trials, generate sales, deepen market acceptance and increase market penetration. In international markets, these activities are of particular importance at the introductory stage of the product life cycle.

Sponsorship and publicity

Event sponsorship seeks to exploit a relationship between a firm and an event with a view to achieving specific marketing objectives such as enhancing corporate and brand image, and possibly obviating stringent controls or outright ban on advertising of certain products. Events sponsorship has become extremely important in facilitating exposure for products such as cigarettes and alcoholic beverages. Other reasons for the increasing popularity of sponsorship include the rising cost of media advertising and social responsibility. It is estimated that publicity generated through sponsorship can be more effective than straight advertising. Certainly, an effective use of a combination of these activities has made Coca-Cola the most popular trademark/brand name in the world.

Direct marketing

Direct marketing can be an effective marketing promotion tool whether used independently or in conjunction with other methods of promotion if it is carefully developed and implemented. As a result of the growing interest in customer retention instead of just customer acquisition, it has become necessary for companies to develop a system that enables them to acquire and maintain some form of database for analysis and tracking of customer behaviour, with a view to developing effective relationship marketing strategies. Direct marketing works on the principles of interaction, targeting, continuity and control. With advances in technology, it is now possible for international firms to coordinate their direct marketing activities across the world.

Trade exhibitions

Trade exhibitions are an effective tool in international marketing communication particularly for industrial products; but they remain a largely undervalued international communications technique in the literature. Trade exhibitions enable companies to come into direct contact with prospects who are either ready to buy or seriously considering a purchase. They also offers buyers the opportunity to compare different product types and designs from different countries without incurring any cost in research and international travels. Once leads and prospects have been established through trade exhibitions, direct marketing has an important role in converting prospects to buyers. Thus, there is a possible synergy between trade exhibition and direct marketing.

SUMMARY

This chapter has demonstrated that international marketing lies at the heart of international business strategy and competitiveness. Developments in international markets have elevated the profile of international marketing as the cornerstone for corporate growth, and in some cases, survival. The chapter shows that:

- expertise in international marketing management is a prerequisite for international competitiveness;
- the benefits of globalization must be put in perspective; the strategy must be pursued with due consideration for specific host country characteristics;
- marketing research is indispensable if meaningful operational strategy and tactics are to be developed;
- product and brand counterfeiting, which manifests itself in various forms, is a major problem for global brands;
- a variety of factors determine a firm's international distribution strategy;
- for international marketing promotion to be effective, it has to exploit cross-cultural similarities.

DISCUSSION QUESTIONS

1. Globalization of products is motivated by a desire for production efficiencies and economies of scale. Over the past five years, many firms have been moving away from standardized products. Discuss the causes and implications of this shift in strategy.
2. International marketing research is the cornerstone of effective marketing planning. Identify and evaluate the strengths and weaknesses of the various sources of information.
3. International pricing is a complex task for most firms. Critically examine the three approaches to international pricing.
4. Branding is vitally important in international promotion. Describe how a brand may be harnessed to maintain international competitiveness. Give examples.
5. Counterfeiting remains a major source of concern for international brand managers. Critically examine the various forms of counterfeiting. Identify and evaluate the strategies for combating counterfeiters.

REFERENCES

Albaum, G., Strandskov, J., Duerr, E. and Dowd, L. 1989: *International Marketing and Export Management*. Wokingham: Addison-Wesley.

Becker, H. 1980: 'Pricing: an international marketing challenge', in H. Thorelli and H. Becker (eds.), *International Marketing Strategy*, rev. edn. Oxford: Pergamon Press.

Bradley, F. 1991: *International Marketing Strategy*. London: Prentice-Hall.

Cateora, P. R. 1990: *International Marketing*, 7th edn. Homewood, IL: Irwin.

Cateora, P. R. and Hess, J. M. 1988: *International Marketing*. Homewood, IL: Richard D. Irwin.

De Mooij, M. K. and Keegan, W. 1991: *Advertising Worldwide*. London: Prentice-Hall.

Douglas, S. P. and Craig, C. S. 1983: *International Marketing Research*. Englewood Cliffs, NJ: Prentice-Hall.

Globerman, S. 1988: 'Addressing international product piracy', *Journal of International Business Studies*, Fall, pp. 497–504.

Griffin, T. 1993: *International Marketing Communications*. Oxford: Butterworth Heinemann.

Jain, S. C. 1990: *International Marketing Management*, 3rd edn. Boston: PWS-Kent Publishing.

Jatusripitak, S., Fahey, L. and Kotler, P. 1985: 'Strategic global marketing: a lesson from the Japanese', *Columbia Journal of World Marketing*, Spring, pp. 47–51.

Jeannet, J. P. and Hennessey, H. D. 1988: *International Marketing Management: Strategies and Cases*. Boston: Houghton Mifflin.

Kaikati, J. C. 1981: 'How multinational corporations cope with international trademark forgery', *Journal of International Marketing*, Vol. 1, No. 2, pp. 69–80.

Keegan, W. J. 1970: 'Five strategies for multinational marketing', *European Business*, January, pp. 35–40.

Keegan, W. J. 1989: *Global Marketing Management*, 4th edn. London: Prentice-Hall.

Keegan, W., Moriarty, S. and Duncan, T. 1992: *Marketing*. London: Prentice-Hall.

Kinnear, T. C. and Taylor, J. R. 1991: *Marketing Research: An Applied Approach*, 4th edn. New York: McGraw-Hill.

Kotler, P. 1988: *Marketing Management: Analysis, Planning, Implementation, and Control*, 6th edn. Englewood Cliffs, NJ: Prentice-Hall.

Larreche, J. C. 1980: 'The international product/market portfolio', in H. Thorelli and H. Becker (eds.), *International Marketing Strategy*, rev. edn. Oxford: Pergamon Press.

Levitt, T. 1983: 'The globalization of markets', *Harvard Business Review*, May/June, pp. 92–102.

McKinnon, A. C. 1989: *Physical Distribution Systems*. London: Routledge.

Monye, S. O. 1995: 'International marketing management: a separate academic discipline?', *International Marketing Review*, Vol. 12, No. 3, pp. 5–14.

Onkvisit, S. and Shaw, J. J. 1989: *International Marketing: Analysis and Strategy*. London: Merrill Publishing Company.

Phatak, A. V. 1980: 'A note on currency problems in international marketing', in H. Thorelli, and H. Becker (eds.), *International Marketing Strategy*, rev. edn. Oxford: Pergamon Press.

Robinson, R. D. 1978: *International Business Management: A Guide to Decision Making*, 2nd edn. Hinsdale, IL: The Dryden Press.

Taggart, J. and McDermott, M. 1993: *The Essence of International Business*. Hemel Hempstead: Prentice-Hall International.

Toyne, B. and Walters, P. G. P. 1993: *Global Marketing Management: A Strategic Perspective*, 2nd edn. Needham: Allyn and Bacon.

Wilson, A. 1982: *Aubrey Wilson's Marketing Audit Check Lists: A Guide to Effective Marketing Resource Realisation*. London: McGraw-Hill.

Young, S., Hamill, J., Wheeler, C. and Davies, J. R. 1989: *International Marketing Entry and Development: Strategies and Management*. Hemel Hempstead: Harvester Wheatsheaf.

6

International finance

INTRODUCTION

International finance is a subject normally associated with international business operations. The relevance of the subject to domestic businesses is increasingly being recognized and appreciated. The integrated and inter-dependent nature of the global financial markets means that events in one country, such as changes in exchange rates, inflation rates and interest rates, have a direct relevance to both domestic and international firms alike. For example, the effect of the collapse of the United Kingdom stock market in 1989 was felt around the world. Thus, a knowledge of international finance is a prerequisite for all practising and aspiring managers. Levi (1990) suggests that this is important for two reasons: it helps the financial manager to decide how international events will affect a firm and which steps can be taken to exploit positive developments and insulate the firm from the harmful ones; and it helps the manager to anticipate events and to make profitable decisions before events occur. International finance is a huge subject and it is beyond the scope of this book to cover all its highly specialized aspects. None the less, the international monetary system (macroeconomic level) and the international financial system (microeconomic level) will be covered. The purpose of this chapter is to examine the nature of international finance and the financial environments, and how the international firm can take advantage of positive developments and minimize the negative ones.

THE INTERNATIONAL MONETARY SYSTEM

Eiteman and Stonehill (1989) define the international monetary system as the structure within which exchange rates are determined, international trade and capital flows accommodated, and balance of payments adjustments made. It provides the framework for understanding the nature of global interdependence. The interdependence of the global economy is amplified by the very nature of international trade which involves exchange of goods and services for payment and establishing the nature and value of payment. It is determining the value of the currency for payment that has remained the preoccupation of governments and multilateral organizations from time immemorial. The international monetary system has evolved over the years from the gold standard to what is now known as the floating exchange rate system. This section examines the nature of the international monetary system and its evolution.

The gold standard

It is on records that before 3000 BC, the Greeks and Romans used gold coins as a medium of exchange and a store of value in transactions through informal arrangements. But as the volume of trade between nations began to increase, there was a need for a more formalized system of dealing with international trade balances. The gold standard was an attempt to established some form of value parity of national currencies in term of gold. De Grauwe (1989) notes that the main feature of the gold standard was that each participating country committed itself, with little coercion, to guaranteeing the free convertibility of its currency into gold at a fixed price. It is noteworthy that although formal multilateral agreements governing these commitments did not exist, the system was used until the outbreak of the First World War in 1914. There were, none the less, important implications for the participating nations. These included the facts that:

- residents of the participating countries had at their disposal a domestic currency which was freely convertible at a fixed price into an asset (gold) acceptable in international payment; and
- the participating countries had to accept some rules (generally known as 'the rules of the game') for this system to be workable, such as ensuring free import and export of gold and built-in mechanisms for adjusting balance of payments so that a country with a surplus would increase the volume of its money, and a country in deficit would allow the volume of its money to decrease.

Despite the commitment and desire of the participating countries to continue with the gold standard, the outbreak of the First World War meant that the pressure to finance the war campaign led to the issuing of currency without gold backing. It became impossible to respect the rules. The gold standard was thus suspended and eventually led to the total collapse of the international financial system. Some form of monetary standard for international trade had to replace the gold standard.

The Bretton Woods system

Following the collapse of the gold standard and the subsequent world-wide depression, there was considerable planning by and consultations between the governments of the United States and the United Kingdom with a view to developing a credible international monetary system that was capable of creating a genuine multilateral system of world trade. In July 1944 forty-four nations, including the United Kingdom and the United States, met in Bretton Woods, New Hampshire, in the USA, to fashion a new international monetary order. This became known as the Bretton Woods system. Under the provisions of the Bretton Woods Agreement, residents of a country were given a guarantee that their money was freely convertible at a fixed price into other currencies without gold backing. Only the US dollar remained convertible into gold at US$35 per ounce.

The Bretton Woods system was probably the most ambitious international monetary agreement between sovereign states in history (De Grauwe, 1989). It operated quite well between the 1950s and the 1960s but collapsed in the 1970s as a result of crisis of confidence in dollar, among other things. Hallwood and MacDonald (1986) suggested that the system evolved in a manner unforeseen by its designers. It was noted that the parities for currencies were changed too infrequently and the demand for additional international reserves was met not only by extra borrowing facilities at the IMF or even by gold but by vastly increased dollar holdings. The flood of dollars which engulfed the world economy in the early 1970s could not be exchanged for gold from the US reserves because there was not enough. In 1971 President Nixon declared that the dollar was no longer officially convertible into gold. This led to a series of crises which eventually wrecked the system.

Floating exchange rates

In March 1973 the major industrial nations met in Paris to attempt to salvage the Bretton Woods system. As the conference progressed, it became clear that it would be impossible to agree new parities that would seem credible to market agents. Consequently, at the end of the conference, it was decided that the fixed exchange rate regime should be abandoned and currencies allowed to float freely to determine their market value. Exchange rates became much more volatile than they had been during the fixed exchange rate regime. The volatility has been exacerbated by a number of unexpected setbacks to the world monetary order such as the oil crisis of 1973, the loss of confidence in the US dollar in 1977, the second oil crisis of 1979, wide fluctuations in the strength of the US dollar, etc.

The International Monetary Fund

One of the most notable outcomes of the Bretton Woods conference of 1944 was the creation of a new international framework with the primary aim of monitoring and regulating the international monetary system. Before the conference, the United States had spearheaded a series of consultations with the United Kingdom and other major trading nations over a considerable length of time, discussing the need to create an international regulatory body which would ensure that the experience of the 1920s and the 1930s, which had resulted in the Great Depression and the collapse of the gold standard, did not reoccur.

During the 1930s a number of countries had attempted to maintain an acceptable level of employment by engaging in trade protection – the practice of competitive currency devaluations, the use of multiple exchange rates for the same currency, and bilateral trade deals. Although these practices were intended to promote stability in the domestic markets, their overall effect was the unintended destruction of world trade and the prolongation of the depression. It is therefore not surprising that the ultimate objective of economists in both the USA and the UK was to fashion out a new international monetary framework which would prevent the disruption of foreign exchange system and the possible collapse of the monetary and credit system. The principal monetary institution created at Bretton Woods in 1944 was the International Monetary Fund (IMF).

The purposes of IMF, as stated in the Articles of Agreement, are:

1. to promote international monetary cooperation through a permanent institution which provides the machinery for consultation and collaboration on international monetary problems;
2. to facilitate the expansion and balanced growth of international trade, and to contribute thereby to the promotion and maintenance of high

levels of employment and real income and to the development of the productive resources of all members as primary objectives of economic policy;

3. to promote exchange stability, to maintain orderly exchange arrangements among members, and to avoid competitive exchange depreciation;

4. to assist in the establishment of a multilateral system of payments in respect of current transactions between members and in the elimination of foreign exchange restrictions which hamper the growth of world trade;

5. to give confidence to members by making the general resources of the Fund temporarily available to them under adequate safeguards, thus providing them with the opportunity to correct maladjustments in their balance of payments without resorting to measures destructive to national or international prosperity;

6. in accordance with the above, to shorten the duration and lessen the degree of disequilibrium in the international balances of payments of members.

The IMF commenced operation in March 1947 with 40 members but its membership has increased over the years to over 155 countries today. Only countries can be members of the Fund. The Fund is run on by a Board of Governors, which is representative of all member countries, the Council and Interim Committee, and a more manageable Executive Board, and an international staff. Although the Board of Governors is the supreme organ of the Fund with the responsibility for admitting new members, making quota increases and amendments to the Articles, etc., in practice, the Executive Board, which consists of twenty-two executive directors and a chairman, is the most important organ, responsible for the general operations of the Fund.

A number of mechanisms were put in place to facilitate the pursuit and attainment of these purposes. Edwards (1985) notes that the three most significant tools are administration of a large pool of monetary assets to which members have access to finance balance-of-payment deficits; administration of the system of 'special drawing rights'; and administration of the 'rules of special conduct' embodied in the articles, relating to exchange rate arrangements, currency controls, the system of consultations on domestic and international policies affecting economic growth, employment, and monetary and financial stability.

General Resources Account

This account is made up of national currencies, special drawing rights, and gold. The contribution of members to the account is based on subscription in the form of a quota which is determined broadly to reflect the importance of the member's currency to the global economy. A member's quota determines the size of its contribution to the Fund, drawing rights in the General Resources Account, share in the allocation of special drawing rights, and voting power. The USA controls 20 per cent of the voting power and the European nations hold about 28 per cent of the votes, while Third World nations cannot hold more than 35 per cent, although they represent nearly 75 per cent of the total population of the IMF countries (El Kahal, 1994). Consistent with the aims and objectives of IMF, the primary responsibility of the General Resources Account is for the provision of a pool of monetary assets to support members to cover short-term gaps in their balance of payments needs.

Special drawing rights

The special drawing right (SDR) is a monetary reserve asset of which the Fund is the issuer. Although this is a form of fiat money usable only by monetary authorities and other official agencies, it represents a right to obtain an equivalent amount of a freely usable national currency (Edwards, 1985). For any drawing, a member is required to prove to the Fund that the desired purchase of the currency of another member (or members) is needed for making payments in that currency (or currencies) that are consistent with the provisions of the Articles of Agreement (Tew, 1988). The Articles of Agreement specify the situations in which the rights may be exercised, and suggest circumstances under which a participant may be required to provide a freely usable currency to another participant and accept in return, special drawing rights from it (Edwards, 1985).

Code of good conduct

Part of the Articles of the Agreement to which members subscribe imposes a mandatory obligation to be of good conduct by carrying out all responsibilities as required by the Agreement. One of the implications of this part of the Agreement is that by subscribing to the code of good conduct, a member, in effect, accepts to abide by practices and requirements (such as a structural adjustment economic programme) that may be at variance with national interest and policies. Over the last ten years, most developing countries have been forced to embark on structural adjustment programmes which are clearly at variance with their national interests in compliance with this requirement of their IMF membership.

International Bank for Reconstruction and Development

The International Bank for Reconstruction and Development (IBRD), generally known as the World Bank, was created at the 1944 Bretton Woods Conference in New Hampshire to complement the activities of the IMF. The principal role of the Bank is to provide loans to member countries. In order to benefit from the loan facilities of the Bank, countries must be members of both the IMF and the Bank. But members of IMF are not obliged to belong to the Bank if they do not wish to take advantage of its facilities.

Quota subscriptions in the World Bank provide the basis upon which it floats bonds or borrow large sums in international capital markets. These funds are then loaned to member governments on governmental guarantees of repayment at prevailing market interest rates. Edwards (1985) notes that as a lender the World Bank is concerned with the general creditworthiness of the governments in countries where it makes loans. But the criteria for assessing a country's creditworthiness are different from those used in assessing individuals. The application of these criteria gives the World Bank a great deal of latitude and power over borrowing nations, such as insisting that the borrowing nations embark on structural adjustments, devaluation of currency, elimination of trade control measures, etc.

THE INTERNATIONAL FINANCIAL SYSTEM

The international financial system deals with the international payment system, the foreign exchange market, and the role of the international banks. This aspect of international finance is of particular interest to all international business operators as every international transaction involves a payment. In this section, the organization of the international payment system and its impact on the foreign exchange market are examined.

Foreign exchange systems

An exporter in country X who sells goods to an overseas customer in country Y would naturally expect to receive payment in the form that can be used in country X. As country Y does not use country X's currency, the exporter must convert the foreign currency to his local currency through the exchange rate system. The system facilitates the purchase and sale of international currencies at rates determined by the market forces through the exchange rate markets. Currencies are bought and sold in exchange for one another in a twenty-four hour over-the-telephone market by individuals, companies, securities firms, and central banks, all of which deal with the foreign exchange traders at commercial banks (Giddy, 1994). Thus, the exchange rate market may be defined as one of several markets in financial assets, the asset to be traded in this case being two or more currencies simultaneously. The rates at which foreign currencies are exchanged are determined by the forces of demand and supply prevailing in the market at any given point in time. The operations of the exchange rate markets may be classified into the spot market and forward market.

Spot markets

A spot market may be described as a market-clearing process where foreign currencies can be purchased for immediate delivery, normally within three days. The spot exchange rate is the domestic currency price of a unit of foreign currency. The term 'spot' rate denotes the immediacy of the transaction compared with the forward rate. Exchange rates are determined daily in the foreign exchange markets, which are formed by banks in various countries in instantaneous communication with each other (Hallwood and MacDonald, 1989). Honeygold (1989) notes that quotations of most currencies are based on their value in terms of one US dollar unit, and are known as direct quotations. The exception to this rule concerns the quotation for some prime currencies such as the pound sterling and the Irish punt, whose values are considerably higher than the US dollar and are often expressed in terms of the number of US dollar units which they constitute. This is known as indirect quotation.

Forward markets

A forward market involves forward exchange contracts and it is distinguished by default risk, which may arise as a result of the inability or unwillingness of one of the parties to a contract to honour a commitment. Giddy (1994) defines a forward exchange contract as a fixed-price contract made today for delivery of a certain amount of a currency at a specified future date, usually 30, 60 or 90 days ahead. The specified date is the settlement date and the agreed price is termed the forward rate. According to Hallwood and MacDonald (1994), the forward rate is often interpreted as the market's consensus, or mean measure of the expected spot rate. The rate is determined either by adding a premium to a prevailing spot rate between two currencies, thereby making it more expensive, or by sub-tracting a discount from a prevailing spot rate between the two currencies, and making it cheaper (Honeygold, 1989). Forward market operators are the international traders (traders of goods and services seeking to divest risks by hedging assets or liabilities denominated in foreign currencies), the arbitrageurs (dealers seeking a riskless profit from the configuration of interest rates and spot and forward exchange rates) and speculators (who accept risks, taking open positions in forward exchange in anticipation of exchange rate changes). Hedging foreign exchange risk entails taking all the necessary actions that will ensure that risk of loss from currency fluc-tuations is minimized. Giddy (1994) identifies three situations when hedg-ing may be used:

1. Hedging transaction exposure: this entails buying or selling foreign exchange for future delivery to match a known foreign currency pay-ment or receipt. This is usually known as monetary or contractual hedging.
2. Hedging balance-sheet exposure: this means using short-term forward contracts to offset 'paper' gains and losses on the long-term assets and liabilities of foreign subsidiaries.
3. Hedging economic exposure: this entails estimating neither immedi-ate transactions nor the accounting exposure but rather the effect of an exchange rate change on the firm's overall profitability.

Futures and options markets

Financial derivatives are a variant of financial instruments which take two basic forms. These may be contracts which commit the parties to buy or sell financial instruments, such as long-dated gilts, at set prices on some agreed future date. These are known as futures contract. Alternatively, they may be options contracts which give one party the right, but not the obligation to buy or sell at a set price on an agreed future date, while the

---

EXHIBIT 6.1

Weak yen boosts Sony profits

Strong sales in all regions and a weaker yen helped Japan's Sony Corporation post a near 50 per cent jump in first-quarter group profit. On Wednesday, 31 July, 1996 Sony said in a statement that consolidated pre-tax profit rose 48.9 per cent from a year earlier to 43.76 billion yen (US$401 million) in the three months to June.

The consumer electronics maker said first quarter revenue rose 30.9 per cent to 1,172.2 billion yen due to higher sales in each geographic area and the depreciation of the yen. The company noted that during the quarter the yen depreciated by about 22 per cent against the dollar, 18 per cent against the pound, and 15 per cent against the mark.

It said sales in its electronics business rose 29.2 per cent on a year earlier to 883.95 billion yen, entertainment business sales increased 36.5 per cent to 229.7 billion yen, and insurance and financing rose 35.5 per cent to 58.5 billion. Sony forecast a group pre-tax profit of 195 billion yen for the year to March on revenue of 5,000 billion yen, on the basis of the yen averaging 105 to the dollar for the year.

Had the value of the yen remained at the same average level as a year earlier, consolidated sales would have been about 170 billion yen less than reported, Sony said.

Discussion questions

1. Explain why it is believed that consolidated sales would have been less than reported if the value of yen had remained at the same average level as a year earlier.
2. What strategies should the company adopt in order to protect itself from the effect of foreign exchange fluctuations?

---

other party takes on the obligation to sell or buy if the first party chooses to exercise his option (Bain, 1992). The contract may be on financial instruments themselves or even on other financial derivatives such as interest rate futures. The financial futures and options markets are inherently volatile and very risky, as shown by the collapse of Barings merchant bank in February 1995. Honeygold (1989) notes that the futures and options markets attract two basic types of user: hedgers who are risk averse and use such contracts to 'insure' against the more extreme changes in foreign exchange and interest rates or stock market prices; and traders who use them as a means of gearing up their exposures at low cost with a view to profit.

Honeygold argues that futures trading offers at least four advantages over dealing in cash or forward markets:

- Instruments which trade on the floors of commodity exchanges are not assets which confer an instant ownership in return for payment of the purchase price; instead they are binding contracts which, in return for a deposit of a fraction of the nominal value of that contract, call for the future delivery of an asset.
- They entitle their holders to buy or sell at some specific date in the future, at a price fixed at the time of contracting on the floor of the exchange, a multiple of a defined commodity which is standardized as to the amount and deliverable grade. Because one can go long (buy) or go short (sell) in any market with equal facility, this makes it far easier to establish and liquidate an open position.
- Because all trading is effected 'on the margin', dealing is effectively cheap and simple, and investors are enabled to make large profits on small outlays.
- There is no obligation on the buyer or seller in a futures market to sustain a contract, or 'leave the position open' through to its maturity date, which would entail the making or taking of actual physical delivery. He can merely cancel or 'close' his position by reversing the deal. That is to say, he will sell or buy the same number of contracts at any time before maturity.

PAYMENT FOR INTERNATIONAL BUSINESS

International payment is an integral part of international business management that is rather complex. Its complexity stems from the very nature of international transactions:

- different legal systems within which the international marketer has to decide his payment policy and issues relating to recovery of goods;
- fluctuating rates of exchange;
- intense competition resulting to a greater demand by buyers for discounts and longer credit period; and
- political risks.

This section examines the nature of international payments under two separate but related themes, namely the financing of international trade, and accounts receivable.

Financing international trade

Firms engaged in international business have access to a wide range of financing options which can be utilized to achieve maximum benefits. These options may be classified into:

- non-financial institution sources;
- financial institution sources; and
- government agencies.

Non-financial institution sources

The consideration for export financing would normally commence with an evaluation of the internal sources. Multinational enterprises are known to favour the financing of their international operations with internally generated funds. Thus, exports may be financed through any of the following internal sources:

- The exporter may choose to utilize surplus funds if these are sufficient to cover the entire cost of the transaction.
- Dividends may be withheld in order to plough back profit into the business and use it for international expansion.
- Subsidiaries of multinational firms may borrow from either the parent company or those affiliated to the parent company on very favourable terms.
- Public companies may raise capital by offering stock of shares for sale in the capital market.

These internal sources are generally known as supplier credit.

Financial institutions

International firms have at their disposal a number of financial institutions, both locally and internationally, and may choose to meet their financing needs from a host of financial instruments and techniques such as direct loans, or indirect methods such as factoring (discounting of trade invoices). The usual criteria for assessing the viability of business proposals apply to applications for financing international transactions, and will not be discussed here.

The more recent development in international trade financing is the use of the eurocurrency market, which has become a very popular and important external source of finance for the international operators. The eurocurrency market may be described as a market in which banks accept time and other interest earning deposits and make loans in a currency other than those of the country in which they are located (Hallwood and MacDonald, 1989). Hence, eurodollars are dollar deposits in commercial banks situated outside the USA, and eurosterling is sterling deposits in banks located outside the UK. These markets are commonly known as external or offshore markets.

It is worth noting that any convertible currency can become a eurocurrency simply by being deposited in an offshore bank, not necessarily based in Europe, where the creditor has no intention of utilizing the deposit. The eurocurrency market enables lenders and borrowers to avoid national controls. In addition, the rate of interest is usually lower than those of the domestic currency markets, which constitutes one of the market's major attractions for borrowers.

Government agencies

Government agencies provide a considerable amount of support for exporters through various schemes ranging from concessionary financing to export credit insurance. Where loans are provided, rates of interest are normally lower than the market rates. Similarly, the terms and conditions of such loans are more favourable than those of the financial institutions.

Government agencies which provide support for international trade and investment include:

- the Small Business Administration (USA), which offers assistance to small firms through its revolving lines of credit loan;
- the Overseas Private Investment Corporation (USA), which provides political risk insurance as well as loans for investment rather than export;
- the Export/Import (EXIM) Bank (USA), which offers direct loans and protective guarantees for other banks' loans;

- the Export Credit Guarantee Schemes (UK), which offer different types of insurance policies for the UK exporters;
- the European Community Export Financing Arrangements (EU) offer insurance against political risks associated with exporting to the developing world.

Accounts receivable

On completion of international business transactions, firms expect to be paid. However, one of the greatest risks associated with international business is that of payment difficulties. A transaction is incomplete until payments are effected. On the one hand, an exporter needs to ensure that payment will be made for goods shipped by insisting on payment in advance. On the other hand, the importer will need to be assured that the exporter will deliver the quantity and quality of goods ordered on time. These uncertainties may be minimized by using a number of payment methods available from commercial banks. These methods include:

- prepayment
- open account
- documentary credit
- factoring
- countertrade

Prepayment

Prepayment, undoubtedly, represents the best payment option for the international marketer. It enables the exporter to receive payment before goods are either made to order or shipped to the buyer. This method of payment can also be used as a source of finance by smaller exporters with limited capital. The exporter will normally insist on this method of payment for new buyers whose creditworthiness has not been established. Similarly, buyers from countries where there are foreign exchange difficulties may be requested to prepay an order as a way of ensuring that payments are made even by well-known buyers. The limitation of this method of payment is that buyers are often reluctant to make payment for an uncertain shipment. With increasing international competition, insisting on prepayment may lead to loss of orders.

Open account

This is sometimes known as sale of unsecured credit. It is a very common method of payment for well established customers, and it is extensively used in international marketing. It is suggested that over 60 per cent of British export trade is conducted on open account basis. The mechanism for payment is quite simple – the exporter dispatches his goods together with the accompanying documentation such as the bills of lading and invoices. It is expected that, all things being equal, payment will follow thereafter. The main advantage with this method of conducting export business is its simplicity. It minimizes procedural difficulties. Its main limitation is that it offers the least security to the exporter. For example, where there are disputes arising from such sales, it is very difficult to recover the goods.

Documentary credit

This may be described as a documentary authorization which enables a bank, acting at the request and instruction of a customer, to make payment or accept bills of exchange drawn by the beneficiary or to authorize another bank to effect such payments or negotiate such bills of exchange against stipulated documents, provided that the terms and conditions of the credit have been met. There are two basic types of documentary credit:

- draft
- letter of credit

A draft, which is also known as a bill of exchange, is an unconditional promise drawn by one party, usually the exporter, on the importer's bank (drawee) requesting the drawee to pay the face amount of the draft at sight or at a specified future date (Madura, 1992). The distinction between sight and time drafts is as follows. If the draft requests payment at sight, it simply means that payment would normally be expected to be effected upon the presentation of the necessary documents. If payment is requested at a specified future date, it is known as a time draft.

A time draft directed to a bank can become a banker's acceptance if the bank accepts the draft as a valid claim of payment for goods sold to the importer. The endorsement of the draft by the bank makes it a negotiable instrument and may be discounted before its maturity date (time draft).

Madura (1992) defines a letter of credit as an undertaking by a bank to make payment on behalf of a specified party to a beneficiary under specified conditions. A letter of credit may be revocable, irrevocable or confirmed irrevocable:

- A revocable letter of credit enables to importer to amend or cancel the credit without prior notification or agreement of the exporter. This type of letter of credit exposes the exporter to the mercy of the importer who can exercise the right to amend or cancel the credit after the goods have been shipped. Consequently, it is not often used.
- An irrevocable letter of credit is a credit that can be amended or cancelled only with the knowledge and agreement of all parties to the credit – the buyer, issuing bank, advising bank and exporter. It offers a considerable degree of protection to the exporter. Provided that the exporter complies with the terms and conditions of the credit, the issuing bank will continue to guarantee payment, even if the importer changes his mind. With a confirmed letter of credit, it is the integrity of the issuing bank that is at stake rather than that of the importer. It is noteworthy that the advising bank located in the exporter's country undertakes no responsibility to pay the exporter.
- A confirmed irrevocable letter of credit may be confirmed by the exporter's bank where it is confident of the confirmation and integrity of the exporter's bank or where the value of the credit has been deposited with it. The exporter's banker's confirmation virtually assures payment. The confirmation changes the status of the exporter's bank from being an advising bank to a confirming bank, thus guaranteeing payment to the exporter, so long as the terms and conditions of the credit are complied with.

Factoring

A time draft which is issued to an importer with a specified future date may be cashed before its maturity date by selling the accounts receivable to specialized financing agencies at a discount. This arrangement is generally referred to as factoring – the factor being the financing agent. The factor has no recourse to the seller, and assumes the entire risk, so long as the exporter adheres to the terms of the credit, such as delivery time and the quality of the goods. The main benefit of factoring is that it provides instant payment opportunity for the exporter, thus minimizing cash flow difficulties.

Countertrade

Countertrade is a generic term which covers a range of payment arrangements for international trade. Its principle is that payment for goods and services are made in kind rather than in cash. It is the oldest method of settlement for international transactions and remains widely used today. The popularity of countertrade peaked in the 1980s when foreign exchange shortages compelled most of the poorer countries of Asia, Latin America, Africa and Eastern Europe to seek alternative methods of payment for the much needed foreign produced goods. Multinational firms responded to these payment challenges by developing sophisticated forms of countertrade arrangements in order to continue trading with these countries. Today, it is estimated that countertrade accounts for up to 25 per cent of the global trading arrangements. The main variants of countertrade are discussed below:

- Barter is the oldest form of countertrade and represents a simple exchange of goods for goods of equal value. It is very prevalent at macro level. For example, between 1985 and 1989, Nigeria agreed to supply over US$10 billion worth of crude oil to Brazil in exchange for both food and industrial products.
- Switch trading is a tripartite arrangement which enables either the buyer or the seller to introduce a third party, normally a specialist trading company, to buy the goods being exchanged if they are unwanted by the receiver at a discount. The third party has no recourse either to the buyer or seller as long as the terms of the contract are complied with.
- Counterpurchase is a sophisticated form of payment arrangement where two or more unrelated contracts are made simultaneously, which enables the original buyer to receive back his money. Technically, no money changes hands. For example, Julius Berger Gmb, a German construction firm, won a contract of U$2 billion to build a number of facilities in Nigeria's new capital city, Abuja, only after it had agreed to buy Nigeria's crude oil worth US$2 billion over a specified period of time.
- Compensation trade, sometimes known as a buy-back arrangement, may be described as a part cash and part product exchange arrangement which enables the supply of industrial equipment to be paid partly with the goods made from the equipment supplied. Unlike counterpurchase, the sale and product buy-back contracts are inextricably linked. For example, in 1993, a British company supplied gold

mining equipments to De Beer, a South African mining company with the contract specifying that part of the payment was to be made with gold mined with the equipments supplied.

MANAGEMENT OF INTERNATIONAL FINANCE

The performance of the international firm with a network of subsidiaries across the world depends largely on how well it is able to deal with the management of its international financial transactions. This includes developing effective strategy and management of exchange rate and political risks.

Exchange rate risk management

The management of exchange rate exposure is central to the management of finance by the multinational firm. There are three types of exposure: transaction, economic and translation exposure. Accurate exchange rate forecasting is essential for such important decisions as hedging, financing and sources of finance, budgeting and earnings projection. Over the last twenty years, sophisticated techniques have been developed and perfected for minimizing the risks of exposure.

Political risks

Political risks represent a real source of uncertainty in the management of a firm's international finance. Technically, political risks are unexpected risks which may manifest themselves as a result of sudden change of government by military *coup d'état* or changes in government policies on issues such as nationalization, expropriation and indigenization or domestication. Risks that are predictable or expected cannot be described as political risks. Thus, most developing countries being ruled by dictators are prone to irrationality in policy matters and may not constitute unexpected risks. Political risks are known to have arisen in developed countries. For example, following the election of President François Mitterrand, there was a spate of nationalization in France in 1982.

A number of indicators are pertinent in the assessment of political risks in the international business environment. These would include attitudes of nationals to international businesses, social unrest and antecedents of the government or its predecessors.

Onkvisit and Shaw (1989) suggest that in managing political risks, there are four policies that a multinational firm can pursue: (1) avoidance of politically uncertain counties; (2) insurance against losses due to political reasons; (3) negotiating the environment by defining the rights and responsibilities of the international firm, local partners and the host country government before the investments are made; and (4) structuring the investment by adjusting the firm's operating and financial policies in order to minimize threats.

SUMMARY

In this chapter, it has been shown that international financial management is normally associated with international business but its impact is felt by both domestic and international firms alike because of the integrated and interdependent nature of the global financial markets. The chapter has also examined the nature of the international monetary systems, international financial systems, ways of financing international trade and methods of payment for export activities. It has been shown that:

- The international monetary system has evolved from the earliest attempts to use the gold standard as the basis of settlement for international transactions to what is now known as the floating exchange rate system.
- The objective of the IMF was to provide an international body with the primary aim of monitoring and regulating the international monetary system.
- The management of the international financial systems affects the day-to-day operation of multinational businesses.
- Exports and other international business activities may be financed by both internal and external sources.
- The eurocurrency market is one of the more recent developments in business financing that is growing in acceptance and popularity.
- The range of methods of receiving payments for international transactions must be evaluated carefully before a choice is made.
- There are political risks in both developed and developing countries.

These can be avoided or minimized by predicting host country behaviour on the basis of history and antecedents.

DISCUSSION QUESTIONS

1. Explain the term 'options'. To what extent can the options market be used to hedge against exposures?
2. Identify and discuss the key characteristics of a successful exchange rate system.
3. With reference to two countries of your choice, compare and contrast the operation of two different exchange rate systems, and discuss the extent to which they meet the criteria in (2) above.
4. Discuss the relationship between interest rates and foreign exchange rates.
5. In the context of international lending, discuss the nature of country risk and various approaches used to quantify it.

REFERENCES

Bain, A. D. 1992: *The Economics of the Financial System*. Oxford: Blackwell Publishers.

De Grauwe, P. 1989: *International Money: Post-War Trends and Theories*. Oxford: Clarendon Press.

Edwards, R. W., Jr. 1985: *International Monetary Collaboration*. New York: Transnational Publishers.

Eiteman, D. K. and Stonehill, A. I. 1989: *Multinational Business Finance*, 5th edn. Reading, MA: Addison-Wesley.

El Kahal, S. 1994: *Introduction to International Business*. London: McGraw-Hill.

Giddy, I. H. 1994: *Global Financial Markets*. Lexington, MA: D. C. Heath.

Hallwood, P. and MacDonald, R. 1986: *International Money: Theory, Evidence and Institutions*. Oxford: Basil Blackwell.

Hallwood, P. and MacDonald, R. 1989: *International Money and Finance*; Oxford: Blackwell Publishers.

Hallwood, P. and MacDonald, R. 1994: *International Money and Finance*, 2nd edn. Oxford: Blackwell Publishers.

Honeygold, D. 1989: *International Financial Markets*. New York: Woodhead-Faulkner.

Levi, M. D. 1990: *International Finance: The Markets and Financial Management of Multinational Business*, 2nd edn. New York: McGraw-Hill.

Madura, J. 1992: *International Financial Management*, 3rd edn. New York: West Publishing.

Onkvisit, S. and Shaw, J. J. 1989: *International Marketing: Analysis and Strategy*. London: Merrill Publishing.

Tew, B. 1988: *The Evolution of the International Monetary System 1945–88*. London: Hutchinson.

7

International production

INTRODUCTION

International production decisions involve a complex set of trade offs between own production facilities abroad and international subcontracting; new plant on a greenfield site or acquisition of an existing facility; sources of material input; and the location of R&D and production site(s). In making these decisions, it is noteworthy that recently the political significance of product nationality has been effectively regarded as a determinant factor in decisions concerning the choice of international production locations. The aim of this chapter is to examine the nature and characteristics of international production.

INTERNATIONAL PRODUCTION THEORY

Over the years there have been attempts to explain the phenomenon known as international production. The contending explanations seek to provide a theoretical framework underpinning various aspects of international investment and production. The traditional explanation of international portfolio investment derives from the understanding that the key determinant of the flow of capital from home to foreign markets is the difference in interest rates. All things being equal, interest rates will be higher in markets where capital is scarce. Consequently, capital will flow from countries with abundant supply to where it is scarce. These theories, however, do not explain why capital flows should take the form of foreign direct investment (FDI) instead of portfolio investment. Hood and Young (1979) suggest that the search for a theoretical explanation for international business stems from the fact that the 'pure' orthodox theory of the firm cannot be applied to foreign direct investment. The various theories of international production are examined in the subsequent sections.

Hymer and Kindleberger's industrial organization approach

In his dissertation of 1960, Stephen Hymer attempted to provide some explanations to the intriguing question of FDI. Hymer's work was a major departure from the orthodox theoretical explanations, dismissing the issue of interest rate differentials as an explanation for direct investment. He explains that the unique feature of FDI is the control which the investor exercises over the investment in order to safeguard it. Subsequently, Kindleberger (1969) – who supervised Hymer's dissertation – insisted that portfolio investment was not to be confused with FDI. He argued that:

1. direct investment may not always involve capital flow as this can be financed from host country sources;
2. direct investment may originate from any country, including countries with scarce capital;
3. direct investments tend to be concentrated in certain industries across the world.

This suggests, therefore, that while capital flow is important in the process, it is not necessarily the entire determinant of FDI. Hymer recognized that a firm operating in a foreign country will be faced with additional costs arising from culture, legal, institutional and linguistic differences, lack of knowledge of market conditions, and the increased expense in terms of communications and misunderstanding of the limitations of operating at a distance. He contended that such a firm must have some advantages not available to the competitors in the host country in order for a direct investment to be profitable. These advantages must be firm specific and readily transferable. Not surprisingly, Hymer's work has generated many follow-up studies, primarily to correct the weaknesses in this theory.

Dunning (1977) argues that the advantages which Hymer talked about are a necessary but not a sufficient condition for FDI. Hood and Young (1979) point out that a foreign firm possesses some monopolistic or oligopolistic advantage over indigenous competitors which gives the MNE its unique character; but they did not explain why the production process needed to be located abroad. They suggested that the foreign firm could exploit its advantage through producing at home and exporting or by licensing a foreign producer. Ietto-Gillies (1992) argued that by concentrating on why multinational corporations invest abroad rather than at home,

Hymer and, subsequently, Kindleberger overlooked the issue of many big multinational corporations competing to get into a particular host country.

Hymer's theory of international production has led to a lot of theoretical postulations. Some of the later theories include Raymond Vernon's international product lifecycle, Robert Aliber's currency and customs area theory and Dunning's eclectic paradigm/model.

The international product life cycle

Vernon (1966) developed a theory of international production based on international differences in innovation in technology. He used the analogy of the life cycle of a product to illustrate possible patterns in international production and consumption of products. This theory features as the technological gap theory of international trade. In fact, it has been suggested that Vernon's work is rooted in the technological gap school of thought, which is well developed in Posner (1961) and Hufbauer (1966). While the main plank of Posner's thesis was the cumulative advantages associated with innovation, Hufbauer identified the motivation for spreading the manufacture of new products. However, the main thrust of Vernon's theory is on the motivating force behind innovation. Deriving from this are the following key elements of the theory:

- the origins of ideas for innovation;
- the initial location of production of new products based on the innovation;
- the motivation for subsequent foreign production; and
- the effect of this motivation on the flow of FDI and international trade.

The international product life cycle is based on the principle of imperfect markets: lack of adequate flow of information between markets; differences in market characteristics and tastes; the evolutionary nature of the production and marketing techniques in the course of the lifespan of a product; and economies of scale in production. Vernon recognized that while technological innovations could take place anywhere in the world, they were more likely to occur in advanced countries. Furthermore, he distinguished between knowledge of a scientific principle and the application of that knowledge for the production of marketable products influenced by market characteristics. For example, new product ideas are normally determined by perceived need. Vernon illustrated this point with the production of labour-saving devices such as washing machines in the USA because of the high cost of labour.

It is argued that while the product remains a 'novelty' item, costs of production will be relatively unimportant as these are passed on to the consumers. With a maturing product and imminent competition from producers with similar products at cheaper prices, costs become highly significant. As the product continues to enjoy market penetration at home, it is likely that demand for it will begin to spread to other advanced countries with similar tastes and standard of living. Overseas demand will be met, in the short term, by exports from the home market. It is thought that, with the passage of time, questions about the alternative lower costs of international production locations become important and leads to international production. The dynamics of the process will continue until the least costly global locations are found to support market demand for standardized and cheaper versions of the product around the world.

Despite its explanatory power, the international product lifecycle theory has not gained general acceptance. In subsequently papers, Vernon (1977, 1979), has responded to the criticisms by modifying the original product life cycle to strengthen its application. He has also listed circumstances in which the product life cycle is still relevant. It is worth noting that other researchers such as Wells (1972) and Onkvisit and Shaw (1983) have developed extensive arguments for the relevance of the product lifecycle theory. Hood and Young (1979) note that the major importance of the product life cycle approach lies in its appreciation of the close links between trade, FDI and the growth of the firm.

The currency area or customs area phenomenon

Aliber (1970) contends that a theory of direct investment must answer several questions in order to be complete. He explains that firms engaged in direct foreign investment operate at a disadvantage relative to their host country competitors – they incur additional costs associated with management of an enterprise at some distance, and political risks. Thus, source-country firms need an advantage to overcome these costs. Aliber suggests that a theory of foreign investment must answer the following questions:

1. What is the primary source of advantages?
2. Why has there been substantial FDI between 1945 and 1970 by US firms?

3. Why does the pattern of direct investment differ substantially by industry?
4. What is the explanation why foreign investments differ substantially by industry?
5. What are the explanations for cross-hauling – i.e. why foreign firms invest in the United States at the same time as US firms invest abroad?

Aliber contends that:

> Theories of direct foreign investment derived from the theory of industrial organisation have limited explanatory power – while they may explain the advantage of source-country firms, they cannot predict the country pattern of foreign investment or its industrial pattern. Nor can they explain adequately foreign investment through takeovers. These theories are not integrated with alternative ways – exports and licensing – that the source-country firms might exploit the market in the host country. Finally, these explanations derived from industrial organisations lack the element of 'foreignness' in the sense that the explanatory variables do not include any of the factors that distinguish national economies, including participation in different custom areas, and tax jurisdictions. These explanations are not theories of direct foreign investment but rather theories of the growth of the firms applied to an international economy on much the same terms as to a national economy.

He goes on to argue that the key factors in explaining the pattern of FDI involve capital market relationships, exchange risks, and the market preferences for holding assets denominated in selected countries. Aliber argues that these relationships have explanatory power for the pattern of direct investment by industry. Furthermore, these factors have a unique international element and are based on the existence of different currency areas – FDI is a currency-area or customs-area phenomenon.

At the heart of this contention is the fact that FDI involves the acquisition of plant and equipment for production in a customs area or a currency area other than that area in which the firm is domiciled. Thus, the 'foreignness' of the investment reflects the movement across the boundaries between currency areas. In the absence of such boundaries, the distinction between foreign investment and domestic investment disappears. To address the question of why firms may engage in FDI rather than export or license out, Aliber suggests that a firm that licenses a patent must police its use and prevent infringements, and the firm may find that the information feedback is less comprehensive than when the patent is exploited internally. Furthermore, the existence of several customs areas means that firms may forgo economies of scale available from concentrating production; and to avoid the tariff, they may produce with smaller than optimal plants in each of several customs areas.

Finally, Aliber suggests that the geographic pattern of FDI reflects the dispersion in capitalization rates for equities denominated in different currencies. He explains that in 1970 the United States was the largest net source of foreign investment because the capitalization rates for US firms were higher than those of foreign firms. Thus, national differences in capitalization rates are the major factors that explain the country pattern of direct investment; otherwise the pattern would be random. The differences in the pattern of FDI reflect the size of the host country, the value of the patents, the height of tariffs, the cost of doing business abroad in a particular country and the dispersion in capitalization rates, both by country and by industry within countries.

Aliber's work was ambitious and thought provoking, and included a considerable number of variables in the analytical framework. He provides a series of analyses to answer those questions which he believes are fundamental to any theory of international production. However, his work has been criticized for being superficial in predicting the pattern of FDI. Similarly, there has been uneasiness about the capitalization argument as an explanation for FDI.

The eclectic model

Dunning (1977) attempted to develop a comprehensive explanation for international production by accommodating both the trade and FDI theories. He drew on the theory of intellectual property or patents rights, trade theories and the theory of industrial organization to formulate the eclectic model of international production. The model is seen as an attempt to harmonize the various contending theoretical explanations for international production under three main themes: why firms produce abroad (internalization advantages); how they are able successfully to compete with host country firms (ownership advantages); and why MNEs of a particular nationality produce in particular host countries (locational advantages). Dunning identified three set of conditions that would motivate a firm to engage in international production:

1. Ownership-specific factors: these factors should be a source of competitive advantage, albeit temporarily, and include elements such as

trademarks or brand names, technology, marketing expertise, resources and other intangible assets.

2. Location-specific factors: for foreign markets to be attractive for investment, they must offer certain unique advantages. Significantly, such an advantage or advantages would have to be exploited in the host market – natural resources, available skilled and cheap labour, proximity to a third market.

3. Internalization: for a firm to invest abroad, it must want to take advantage of its competitive factors to exploit the location-specific factors itself rather than externalize them through licensing.

Thus, in order for a firm to become multinational, it must satisfy each of the prerequisites mentioned above. Dunning's eclectic model was anticipated by Hirsch (1976), who formulated a model in which he defined various circumstances under which different methods might be applied in servicing overseas markets. His work was the first attempt to integrate many theories into a model which can show conditions under which markets will be serviced by export or direct investment. Hirsch identified these factors as comparative input costs, firm-specific revenue-generating factors, and information and transaction costs.

With further development and refinement of this concept of an integrative model, Dunning developed the eclectic model which suggests that a firm with ownership-specific advantages will engage in international production to exploit location-specific advantages, all things being equal. Although it is a useful explanatory framework for international production, the eclectic theory does not seem to provide a satisfactory explanation for international acquisition of technology for production in a host market, or even cross-hauling, which Robert Aliber mentioned in his work. Cantwell (1991) argues that the eclectic paradigm is not an alternative analytical framework but, rather, an overall organizing paradigm for identifying the elements from each approach which are most relevant in explaining a wide range of various kinds of international production, and the different environments in which international production has been established.

Kojima's hypothesis also raised doubts over the universal application of the eclectic model. In his book Kojima (1978) distinguished between what he called 'trade-oriented' foreign direct investment and 'anti-trade-oriented' investment. He contends that the objective of Japanese firms investing abroad was to complement their limited resources at home such as labour and natural resources and, therefore, that such investments were

---

EXHIBIT 7.1

Foreign firms blocked from Indian market

On Monday, 12 August 1996, the Indian government ruled out the entry of foreign print media into India and said it would not allow foreign television networks to broadcast from India. 'There will be no entry in the country of foreign media, no uplinking (broadcast) of foreign networks also,' a government spokeswoman said on Monday, quoting Information and Broadcasting Minister, C.M. Ibrahim as talking to reporters in New Delhi.

The decision came after speculation that India, which began opening up its economy to the world under a liberalization programme started in 1991, might allow foreign and domestic firms to end a state monopoly over broadcast stations. The announcement confirms that India has decided not to reverse a decision by the cabinet in 1955 to bar foreign media firms from publishing in India.

Foreign networks currently beam to India from abroad and publishers sell to India editions printed abroad. The government's decision blocks an attempt by Britain's *Financial Times*, owned by Pearson plc, to acquire a stake in an Indian company that publishes a business daily, *Business Standard*. The Pearson proposal caused a raging debate after newspapers said the Foreign Investment Promotion Board (FIPB) recommended to Prime Minister H. D. Deve Gowda's cabinet that Pearson may be allowed to buy an unspecified stake. But a government spokesman denied that such recommendation was made. The government has been accused of protecting the interests of local media owners.

Two of India's leading communist parties in the coalition government insist that domestic media, cultural and economic interests would be hit if foreign media were allowed in.

Discussion questions

1. Examine the factors which may have affected the government's decision to block foreign media from India.
2. Discuss the likely impact of this decision on advertising and competition.

---

made to enhance trade. On the other hand, he suggests that investments by US, Canadian and West European firms are anti-trade-orientated as they are made to defend an oligopolistic position in a market or respond to trade barriers. Kojima argues that the eclectic model is not applicable to

Japanese multinational enterprises. Dunning has tried to respond to this and other criticisms of the eclectic paradigm in some of his subsequent works.

Although the contending theories of international production are important in understanding the behaviour and conduct of multinational enterprises, it needs to be recognized that these theories are rooted either in the neoclassical trade theories or industrial organization theories (theories of the firm). Indeed, Cantwell (1991) suggests that the various theories of international production may be grouped into four theoretical frameworks: the Hymer framework, based on the view of the firm as an agent of market power and collusion; the internalization approach, which views the firm as a device for raising efficiency by replacing markets; the third approach, encompassing the various paradigms for analysing competitive interaction in international industries (exemplified by Vernon's product life cycle and Jenkins's internationalization of capital approach); and the macroeconomic development approaches, which include work by Hirsch and Kojima.

THE NEW PRODUCTION ENVIRONMENT

The historical evolution of the political environment for FDI has been quite interesting and remarkable. The climate for foreign investment has oscillated between outright hostility and one of red-carpet reception. Host governments have often had to deal with the difficulty of balancing the need for the benefits that accompany foreign investments and the costs of such activities. While the benefits are believed to include capital, technology and possibly access to overseas markets, the misgivings over foreign investments arise from the perceived long-term effects of such activities on national enterprises, balance of payment, and the political independence of host countries. These reservations, which have frequently led to extensive controls over the activities of foreign-owned firms, are discussed in the following section.

Transfer of capital

Transfer of capital assets to host countries is often mentioned as one of the key benefits of FDI. However, the extent to which capital assets are actually transferred to host countries remains contentious. On the positive side, it is believed that capital transfers by foreign investors supplement resources that can be mobilized from domestic sources, and therefore assist in alleviating balance of payment and foreign exchange difficulties. Furthermore, it is suggested that international firms have at their disposal a range of international sources from which to raise funds to support investments in host countries. Critics, on the other hand, argue that the actual capital transfer associated with any foreign direct investment is very negligible. Vernon and Wells (1991) contend that most governments are aware that FDI rarely accounts for more than a minor part of the capital formation of any national economy. Hood and Young (1979) point to the fact that the contribution of foreign capital to worldwide capital formation has been small. In specific terms, Vernon and Wells suggest that in countries where direct investment has played a major role such as Australia and Spain, the proportion of FDI to gross capital formation has not been much over 5 per cent.

Furthermore, host governments often express concerns about the possibility of capital drain as a consequence of FDI. It is recognized that foreign investors often mobilize the bulk of their capital requirements from local investors and banks rather than from foreign sources. The size and reputation of the big multinationals undermine the ability of indigenous firms to compete effectively in the domestic capital market to raise funds. Therefore, in addition to the prospect of capital drain through repatriation of profits, indigenous firms may be denied easy access to domestic sources for funds.

Transfer of technology

The important role of technology in any economy is unquestionable and, for developing countries, constitutes the most desirable attribute of FDI by multinational enterprises. Vernon and Wells (1991) believe that the international market for technology and management can be highly inefficient, and as a consequence, the channels that exist between a foreign-owned subsidiary and the rest of the multinational network to which it in some cases belongs, may represent the most efficient means by which a country can acquire such assets. While the technology transfer component of FDI is acknowledged, host governments harbour latent fear of perpetual dependency on foreign companies for their technological development. Other problems include the appropriateness of transferred technology and the cost of such transfers. It is believed that technology transfers through intra-company channels have limited scope for diffusion in an economy.

Access to overseas markets

One of the factors influencing the location of FDI is the availability of raw materials which can be converted into intermediate material inputs for the parent companies in their home countries and elsewhere. Indeed, with the growing intensity of price-based competition, there is a clear trend in international production towards least-cost global locations. Deriving from this is the potential of improved balance of trade and balance of payments which may arise from the additional export activities of these subsidiaries. But doubts persist about the contribution of the subsidiaries of multinational firms to the balance of trade and balance of payments. In fact, such concerns have led the European Union to impose performance requirements on foreign investors, whether already established or planning to enter a Union country.

Despite these arguments, recipients of FDI remain sceptical about their net impact on their economy. For example, before the mid-1980s, the United States stood out as a nation with an outstanding record of not only encouraging FDI on its shores and elsewhere but also vigorously campaigned to persuade other countries to eliminate restrictions on foreign investors. In the 1980s many developing nations threw caution to the wind and abandoned their misgivings about giving unrestrained access to foreign firms to their markets under the misguided concept of the structural adjustment programme. Instead, they began to encourage foreign investment with various incentive schemes. Similarly, West European countries began to offer huge inducements to attract inward investments to offset the effects of outward investment flows.

Vernon and Wells (1991) observe that by the end of the 1980s, FDI in the United States was growing at the rate of over US$50 billion annually. Most of the increased flow was coming from Western Europe, but Japan's contribution was growing fast. They note that, abruptly, members of the Congress and the public press began to explore the pros and cons of FDI, raising serious questions for the first time in a century over its effect on host countries. Eventually, acting under the Omnibus Trade and Competitiveness Act of 1988, the US government set up an inter-agency committee with the responsibility to review certain investments of foreigners for their bearing on *national security*. It is a remarkable turnaround for a country which has, for a very long time, encouraged other countries to eliminate restrictions on foreign investors, to begin to raise questions of national security simply because the flow of FDI was in the 'wrong direction'. Is this a case of the United States having a taste of its own medicine?

SITE SELECTION AND PLANT DESIGN

Once the decision is taken by management to undertake overseas production on a greenfield site in a particular country, there are a number of operational questions that need to be addressed before the construction of the plant can commence. For example, where will the plant be located in the host country? What types of plant design would be appropriate for the location? What mix of technology and labour is necessary and suitable for a particular site? Surprisingly, firms are known to spend more time and effort in selecting a site within a country than in selecting the country. Evidence from Japanese firms that have invested in Europe between 1980 and 1996 show that while over 70 per cent of these firms have no hesitation in choosing the UK as the country in which to invest in Europe, deciding on specific sites within the UK tended to be a more difficult decision. Part of the difficulty arises from the apparent lack of economic rationale for site selection. It is known that firms did not select the location promising the highest net present value but, rather, the site which was likely to create fewest problems. Certainly, the fact that the UK is preferred to countries such as Portugal and Spain – which offer cheaper sources of skilled labour and the same access to the European Union market – as an investment location, give credence to the fewest problems hypothesis.

Although there are standard checklists of site selection factors which may be considered in making decisions, most firms do not apply any structured evaluative criteria. Consequently, the evaluation of sites in a country is often subjective. Traditionally, plants were located near sources of raw materials, at locations with easy access to air and sea ports, and free trade zones. Although such sites remain important to foreign investors, host government's sweeteners such as the provision of infrastructural support, tax holidays and investment grants play a more decisive role in such decisions. Incentives are normally provided to encourage the location of plants in run-down areas that require economic regeneration by creating employment opportunities. Regional development agencies in the UK have been very successful in attracting inward investments.

Allied to the question of site selection is the issue of appropriate plant design for the new site. Plant design has to do with seeking a balance between automation and manualization on the basis of the relative capital and labour costs. In other words, how much skill should be built into the machine? How much into labour? Ideally, the emphasis will be on greater automation in a country where skilled labour is scarce and costly and vice versa. Baranson (1971) observes that in developing countries, plant designs are subject to further constraints and rest upon several inter-related criteria such as:

- the scale of production;
- precision or quality requirements;
- the stage of development of supplier industries;
- the availability of management and technical skills;
- wage rates relative to capital costs;
- the supply of factory labour; and
- national employment goals.

Thus, for developing countries, it is not an either/or choice between automation and handicraft technology. Technology should be viewed as a continuum of production techniques, with choices depending on the one hand, on the scale and precision of production, and on the other hand, on the wage rates relative to capital costs – within the emerging framework of manpower skills and industrial capabilities.

Degree of plant integration

In setting up a foreign production facility, a decision has to be made about the relationship between the new plant and the company's facilities else-where. Should the company depend on a single plant for the benefits of economies of scale? Or would a multi-plant arrangement achieve opti-mum results? These decisions are usually very tricky, particularly within a large customs union area or common markets such the European Union. The principal limitation of the single plant approach is that there is a cer-tain belief that the concentration of productive facilities in one market or country creates uneasiness about the risks of overdependency on such a single location.

Often, the solution for the bigger multinationals is the adoption of a multi-plant set up which enables them to have a diverse but integrated operation. In terms of design of facilities for optimum result, the choice ranges from plant specialization (by product or process) to the absence of any specialization. With a multi-plant arrangement, there is now a trend towards manufacturing interchange between facilities. This enables each plant to specialize in the production of specific components: all exchange with one another, and all assemble the same products. Ford of Europe is an excellent example of a company with such a highly integrated opera-tion across Europe. It has to be noted that the main limitation of the manufacturing interchange relates to the issue of interdependence between facilities. It is expected that any disruption through, for example, mechanical failure or labour unrest in one plant, will inevitably and automatically affect operations in other facilities. Ultimately, the choice between a single- or multi-plant operation depends on factors such as economies of scale in production of components, costs of transport between plants, and logistical and inventory control issues.

LOCATING R&D FACILITIES

The importance of R&D for long-term competitiveness is well documented in technology literature and this is partly reflected by the increased emphasis and expenditure on R&D around the world. Indeed R&D expenditure by US, Japanese and European corporations has been increasing faster since 1983 than at any other period since 1945. The growth of R&D expenditure is seen as a reaction of corporations faced with the quickening pace of competition (Dussuage *et al.*, 1992). Similarly, the geographic location of R&D facilities has become a central issue in strategic planning by these corporation. Whereas in the past there was a certain inflexibility in decisions concerning the location of R&D facilities, strategic planners in recent years have come to accept the need to globalize this important activity as a way of responding to the needs of customers in overseas markets.

The globalization of MNEs' R&D facilities is, thus, a relatively new phenomenon. While FDI continues to broaden in geographical spread, internationalization of R&D facilities has been rather slow, with large companies keeping most of their technological activities at home. Surprisingly, it is acknowledged that locating an R&D facility in a home market limits the capacity of the firm to be responsive to the needs of foreign markets. Robinson (1978) writes that a research and development division embedded in a domestic operation, that is, one in which foreign markets are only a peripheral vision of management, is unlikely to develop the interest and skills necessary for devising optimum solutions to meet specific host country requirements. With the increasing popularity of the concept of globalization of business, it is remarkable that multinational enterprises show considerable reluctance to globalize their R&D facilities. This reluctance is not unconnected with the orientation of management towards international production. Heenan and Perlmutter (1979) describe these orientations as ethnocentric, polycentric, regiocentric and geocentric, and they are discussed in chapter 9. By implication, geocentric-orientated firms (those that seek to integrate diverse subsidiaries through a global systems approach to decision-making) are more susceptible to the idea of decentralized R&D facilities. This is by no means the most important determinant of overseas location of R&D laboratory. Other factors are just as significant. Howells and Wood (1993) note that location of R&D facilities is influenced by certain parameters, be they domestic or overseas. They suggest that the following factors are particularly important:

- Organizational framework: the structure and functioning of R&D within large corporations is influenced by the evolution of the overall corporate structure of the enterprise. This was associated with the trend away from single product, unitary enterprises, with their functional structure based upon specialized departments, and into a multi-divisional form composed of a series of semi-autonomous divisions, responsible for administering a particular product or geographical market sector. It is suggested that the evolution of many large enterprises into multi-form type structures had important implications for the organization of research, in that R&D was no longer necessarily a corporate-wide task. Thus, even if a firm did maintain a centralized corporate establishment, it would find it increasingly necessary to have specialized research departments to cope with the particular needs of the different product divisions.
- Locational rigidity: existing research facilities have been extremely rigid and inflexible in their locational structures. As such, much of the existing spatial pattern of R&D in industry has changed very little since its initial establishment and this has resulted in an almost static spatial pattern of existing research laboratories. It is argued that the possible factors behind the low locational mobility include fear of losing key research staff and the high cost of setting up new research facilities. The geographical rigidity in R&D location is heightened by the fact that in existing companies, new R&D units are frequently sited at, or near to, existing corporate research establishments in order to maintain a good research communication flow.
- Type of R&D activity: three types of R&D activity can be identified. These are basic research, applied research and development work. The characteristics and orientation of these R&D activities will in turn influence their location. Thus it is unlikely that if a company decides it needs to expand work in process-related development activities, it will decide to locate in a stand-alone facility away from any production facilities.

Although there was an overwhelming concentration of MNEs' R&D facilities at home some twenty years ago, there is increasing evidence to believe that the situation is changing. Robinson (1978) suggests that the following factors are influential in this trend:

- growing aggregate R&D expenditure by Europe and Japan;
- the increasing cost advantage of doing R&D outside the home market;
- increasing awareness of the tax advantages in a low tax country so that the subsequent patents may be owned by a subsidiary in that country;
- improvement of the protection of patents and commercial secrets in many countries;
- increasing host government pressure to undertake local R&D ; and
- an unwillingness by some LDC governments to permit subsidiaries to pay related companies for technology either through royalties, fees or assumption of a general overhead burden.

In addition to these considerations, the on-going debate about the advantages and disadvantages of centralization versus decentralization is useful in comprehending the behaviour of the MNEs towards the location R&D facilities. Howells and Wood (1993) have summarized the advantages of centralization as:

- benefits of economies of scale and scope associated with larger R&D operations;
- minimum efficient size associated with the indivisibility of certain scientific instruments, facilities or specialist staff;
- good internal communication links within the R&D function;
- research can concentrate on producing original ideas and not be involved in short-term operational problems;
- increased security over in-house research, reducing the risk of competitor copying or 'leapfrogging' in key research fields; and
- ability to create a well-established dense local innovation network with higher-education institutes, contract research companies and other support agencies and related institutions.

The establishment of R&D facilities abroad may occur either as a part of the developmental process of internationalization of the firm to support overseas production activities or through the acquisition of a firm with a well-established and functioning R&D laboratory. In either case, the advantages of decentralization, which are well developed in the literature, are also summarized in Howells and Wood (1993), as follows:

- more effective and pertinent R&D effort focused on the actual needs of the business and operational units;
- improved communication or 'coupling' between R&D and other key corporate functions, particularly productions and sales and marketing;
- related to this, fewer problems of 'programme dislocation' when a project is transferred from R&D to production;
- ability to tap pools of scarce scientific and technical talent;
- monitoring of, and linkage with, localities that have a lead in a particular technology;
- access to key lead suppliers or customers in a particular technology or product field;
- better responsiveness to various local market needs;
- overcoming problems of perceived optimum efficient size for single research laboratories; and
- ability to tap into government aid or tax incentives for establishing R&D units in selected areas.

The decision concerning the location of R&D facilities is made on the basis of a considered assessment of the benefits and disadvantages of such a move. The indications are that the increased globalization of business activities is inducing the overseas location of R&D facilities. Although there are no global statistics, expenditure on overseas R&D activities of the US, European and Japanese multinationals, as a percentage of their total R&D budget, has been increasing rapidly over the last ten years. With the intensification of global competition, it is expected that this trend will continue in the future.

SUMMARY

International production is a huge area which cannot be adequately covered in this book. However, this chapter has covered some of the basic issues in international production. The theories of international production, the environment for FDI, operational issues such as location, design and integration of plants have been examined. The chapter has shown that international production decisions involve an array of interrelated factors, and that each situation is unique. In particular, it has shown that:

- The economic environment for international production is dynamic.
- Site selection in a host country is a more difficult process than the country selection.

- Plant designs must take into account the pros and cons of international manufacturing interchange.
- Cross-border acquisitions, if not properly conceived and managed, can turn out to be costly mistakes. In most cases, apparent compatibilities are concealed by major dissimilarities.
- The pace of the globalization of research and development facilities by multinational companies is still very slow.

DISCUSSION QUESTIONS

1. Examine the argument that all neoclassical theories of international production are rooted in the industrial organization theories.
2. To what extent did Aliber succeed in shifting the debate on international production away from the traditional industrial organization approach?
3. Identify and discuss the various types of R&D activity.
4. Critically examine the factors responsible for the slow pace of the globalization of the R&D facilities of global firms.
5. What are the determinants of the choice of location for foreign R&D facilities?
6. Critically evaluate the pros and cons of foreign direct investment in a host country.
7. What factors influence plant designs for overseas production?
8. Outline and discuss the factors encouraging cross-border acquisitions. To what extent do think that the recent upsurge in cross-border acquisition will be sustained?

REFERENCES

Aliber, R. Z. 1970: 'A theory of direct foreign investment', in C. P. Kindleberger (ed.), *The International Corporation*. Cambridge, MA: MIT Press, pp. 17–34.

Baranson, J. 1971: 'Automated manufacturing in developing economies', *Finance and Development*, Vol. 8, No. 4, pp. 10–28.

Bengtsson, A. M. 1992: *Managing Mergers and Acquisitions: A European Perspective*. Aldershot: Gower Publishing.

Cantwell, J. 1991: 'A survey of theories of international production', in C. N. Patelis and R. Sudgen (eds.), *The Nature of the International Firm*. London: Longman.

Dunning, J. H. 1977: 'Trade, location of economic activity and the MNE: a search for an eclectic approach', in B. Ohlin, P. O. Hesselborn and P. M. Wijkman (eds.), *The International Allocation of Economic Activity*. London: Macmillan.

Dussuage, P., Hart, S. and Ramanantsao 1992: *Strategic Technology Management*. Chichester: John Wiley.

Heenan, D. A. and Perlmutter, H. V. 1979: *Multinational Organisational Development: A Social Architecture Perspective*. Reading, MA: Addison Wesley.

Hirsch, S. 1976 'An international trade and investment theory of the firm', *Oxford Economic Papers*, Vol. 28, pp. 258–70.

Hood, N. and Young, S. 1979: *The Economics of Multinational Enterprise*. London: Longman.

Howells, J. and Wood, M. 1993 *The Globalisation of Production and Technology*. London: Belhaven Press.

Hufbuaer, G. C. 1966: *Synthetic Material and the Theory of International Trade*. London: Duckworth.

Hymer, S. 1976: *The International Operations of National Firms: A Study of Direct Foreign Investment*. Cambridge, MA: MIT Press. [This is Hymer's 1960 dissertation published after his death.]

Ietto-Gillies, G. 1992: *International Production: Trends, Theories, Effects*. Cambridge: Polity Press.

Kindleberger, C. P. 1969: *American Business Abroad*. New Haven, CT: Yale University Press.

Kojima, K. 1978: *Direct Foreign Investment: A Japanese Model of Multinational Business Operations*. London: Croom Helm.

Onkvisit, S. and Shaw, J. J. 1983: 'An examination of the international product life cycle and its application within marketing', *Columbia Journal of World Business*, Vol. 18, pp. 74–87.

Posner, M. V. 1961: 'International trade and technical change', *Oxford Economic Papers*. Vol. 13, pp. 323–41.

Robinson, R. D. 1978: *International Business Management: A Guide to Decision Making*, 2nd edn. Hinsdale: The Dryden Press.

Vernon, R. 1966: 'International investment and international trade in the product cycle', *Quarterly Journal of Economics*, Vol. 80, pp. 190–207.

Vernon, R. 1977: *Storm Over the Multinationals: The Real Issues*. Cambridge, MA: Harvard University Press.

Vernon, R. 1979: 'The product cycle hypothesis in a new international environment', *Oxford Bulletin of Economics and Statistics*, Vol. 41, pp. 255–67.

Vernon, R. and Wells Jr, L. T. 1991: *The Economic Environment of International Business*, 5th edn. Englewood Cliffs, NJ: Prentice-Hall.

Wells, L. T. 1972: *The Product Life Cycle and International Trade*. Cambridge, MA: Harvard University Press.

8

International human resource management

NATURE OF INTERNATIONAL HUMAN RESOURCE MANAGEMENT

The pivotal role of human resource management (HRM) in the process of organizational development cannot be overstated. As is frequently emphasized, human resources are the most valuable asset of any organization. The management of human resources is a complex and challenging task which extends beyond the traditional role of personnel management (recruitment and selection, performance appraisal, pay bargaining, training and development). It involves the integration of 'people management' issues into the strategic planning process. Sparrow and Hiltrop (1994) define human resource management as the strategic process of managing the organizational culture, designing the structure, and resourcing the organization with an appropriate set of competencies. A well-conceived human resource management strategy will facilitate the effectiveness of the international firm in achieving and maintaining competitiveness in all areas of operation such as R&D, production and marketing. The term human resource management may be described as generic, incorporating but not synonymous with personnel management; the two terms cannot be used interchangeably.

What is international human resource management?

Torrington (1994) contends that international human resource management is neither about copying practices from other countries nor a process of managers learning the cultures of every country in which they have to deal and suitably modifying their behaviour when dealing with foreign nationals. In many ways, international human resource management is simply human resource management on a larger scale. Academics suggest that the strategic considerations in international human resource management are more complex and that the operational units are more varied, needing coordination across more barriers. The effectiveness of this process influences both the shaping of the strategy of the multinational firm and represents a vital component in its successful implementation. It is arguable that the task of internationalizing the practical issues of human resource management such as industrial relations, ethics and standards, pay and reward, and social responsibility may be difficult to achieve because of national and cultural differences that exist between nations. It therefore raises a number of important questions concerning the feasibility of the globalization of human resource management practices. The key question is the extent to which multinational firms can maintain a consistent approach in dealing with both developed and developing country markets on issues such as conditions of employment and social responsibility.

Although it has become fashionable to suggest that practices in all functional areas of business operation can be globalized, practical issues in areas such as human resource management would indicate otherwise. However, it is fair to say that multinational firms committed to raising ethical standards and good practices in markets where they operate can do so within the context of the environmental and regulatory constraints in those markets. It is also noteworthy that for the MNE to be effective with its HRM policy and strategy, there is a need for a comparative awareness of HRM practices in both the home and foreign markets. Host country practices must be accommodated within the broad framework of the firm's overall policy.

ORGANIZATIONAL STRUCTURE OF THE MNE

The organization's structure is the basic arrangement for coordinating the firm's activities. The nature and design of the structure of an organization is largely determined by its size. As domestic firms become multinational in their operation, organizational designs change dramatically. Chandler (1962) argues that when a firm pursues growth strategies, it will evolve from a simple uni-functional organization to a multi-functional, single-product form and from that to a multi-divisional form capable of dealing with the problems of multiple products. At a simple level in a domestic operation, firms will be content with a simple organizational design which may be described as the entrepreneurial organization. This is ideal for a single product or service. Normally, functional responsibilities are shared and departmentalization is minimal. But with increase in activities, there is a corresponding need for specialization and departmentalization. Dittrich (1988) suggests that as the volume of business increases, adminis-

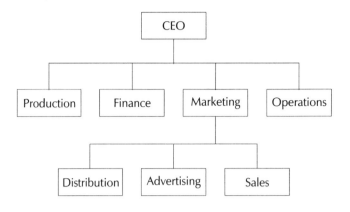

Figure 8.1 A simple functional structure

Figure 8.2 A divisionalized structure

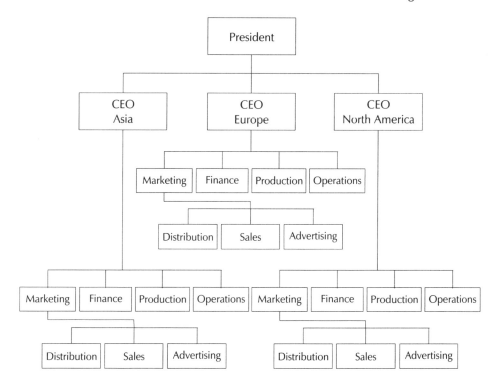

Figure 8.3 A multinational structure

trative responsibilities are separated from operations, and functional assignments are made to clarify roles and responsibilities. For example, much of the responsibility for coordination would shift to the formally defined administrator.

As a firm grows either through internal development or by acquisition, the coordinating mechanisms change in order to cope with a large-scale operation. This may include redefining coordinating responsibilities along functional or geographic lines, and for very large operations, sub-specialisms such as marketing research, advertising and promotion, product management, public relations, and sales. Figures 8.1– 8.3 show variations in organizational designs. Figure 8.1 shows a simple functional organizational structure; figure 8.2 illustrates a divisionalized structure while figure 8.3 shows a typical structure of a multinational firm.

As stated earlier, the organizational structures of multinational firms are determined by the requirements of size and the need to respond adequately to the operational and strategic objectives of the firm. Dittrich

(1988) contends that organizational considerations in the multinational firm follow many of the dynamics as in the domestic markets. He suggests a theoretical framework which should form the basis for developing an organizational structure for the multinational firm. It incorporates four broad classes of strategy, as illustrated in table 8.1 and described below.

- Volume expansion: this involves the export of finished goods to markets remote from the production sites in the home country. It may be limited initially to the employment of sales agents or locally owned outlets. Carried out more extensively, this strategy may involve a large-scale sales and distribution effort designed to support an intensive marketing campaign.
- Resource acquisition: this is an adaptation of vertical integration and is used to secure low-cost material. The foreign operation is characterized by its extractive, labour-intensive nature. The operation is managed by a limited number of expatriate managers.
- Reciprocity: this involves two countries and an exchange of goods and services between the two. In a complex reciprocal arrangement, goods acquired in one country may be shipped to another for processing and then on to a third country for use or for further conversion. In the reciprocity strategy, the production of local administrative and management to operations personnel will be higher than in either of the two strategies described earlier. Communications will tend to be multidirectional. As the reciprocal network becomes more complex, greater decision-making autonomy is needed in the local office.
- Integrated operations: this is a strategy in which local organizations serve as profit centres. Foreign and domestic markets are given equal weight in decision-making. Products and services are adapted to meet the needs of local or regional markets. The organization is staffed with a large proportion of local management personnel. A high degree of autonomy exists within broad parameters established by the home office. The local organization structure is fully developed, with the full range of business functions represented.

MANAGEMENT STAFF: PARENT COUNTRY VERSUS HOST COUNTRY NATIONALS

Decisions concerning the selection of staff to manage overseas operations can be tricky and sometimes an emotive issue for the host nation. In taking

Table 8.1 Home/local structural implications of strategy

Local structural implications	Strategy			
	Volume expansion	Resource acquisition	Reciprocity	Integrated operations
Structure type	Functional line	Functional line; wide span of control	Functional/ product; line-and-staff	Functional/ divisional
Formalization	Bureaucratic	Bureaucratic	Somewhat less bureaucratic	Less bureaucratic
Decision locus	Home	Home	Policy – home; operations – local	Local
Staff locus	Home	Home	Small local staff	Local
Communication	One-way	One-way	Two-way, lateral	Two-way
Control	Tight; loose local operations	Tight	Looser	General
Performance measures	Quantitative, cost	Quantitative, cost centre	Profit or cost centre; somewhat less rigid or quantitative	Profit centre; ROI
Managerial personnel	Few; most locals	Expatriates	Larger administrative component; expatriate/local mix	Locals
Home office relationship	Close control by home office	Close control by home office	Less close control by home office	Loose; autonomous operations within policy
Output	Limited product line	Limited product line	Limited product line	Full line
Investment/profits policy	Bare bones investment; repatriation of profits	Bare bones investment; repatriation of profits	Greater investment; local investment of profits	Local investment and capital sources

Source: Dittrich, J. E. (1988) *The General Manager and Strategy Formulation*. Copyright © 1988 John Wiley. Reprinted by permission of John Wiley & Sons, Inc.

EXHIBIT 8.1

Tools of the team

Many big companies in recent years have tried to reduce the vertical and horizontal barriers in their management structures that hold up the flow of ideas. In large part, the aim has been to increase responsiveness to consumer demands, improve product quality, and speed up the product development cycle. Few, however, have gone as far as the main European manufacturing division of Black and Decker in changing its organizational structure in both directions at once. The US-owned maker of household and professional tools has been intent on allowing new technological concepts to flow more easily between product development engineers and the shopfloor, and also on facilitating better communication between managers and operators.

The changes can be glimpsed at the company's biggest European factory at Spennymoor, County Durham, one of the world's largest power tool factories. This employs 2,000 people and in 1995, will have made some US$500 million worth of handheld tools and related consumer items including lawnmowers – equivalent to roughly a tenth of Black and Decker's worldwide sales.

According to Charles Pettican, Black and Decker's European Vice President in charge of consumer products, the changes are part of the company's overall interest in breaking down 'functional barriers' between areas such as manufacturing, marketing and product development to enable quicker and better-informed decision-making over getting products to the market. The most visible embodiment of these changes is Bob Bowlam, formally the Spennymoor plant's manufacturing director: since the summer he has taken on a new role as technical director for the company's European consumer product business. Bowlam can be thought of as having three simultaneous jobs. He has a responsibility for product development and manufacturing within his branch of Black and Decker business within Europe, while also linking up with other Black and Decker people around the world working on technology developments related to all its various product areas.

With his manufacturing responsibilities, he also talks to Black and Decker's 'technical coaches' – a relatively new breed of shopfloor worker which has appeared at the Spennymoor factory in the past eighteen months to facilitate changes needed to improve quality and production flow. In addition to Bowlam's technology and product interests in the European dimension, he is one of about nine people worldwide involved in a number of countries and product business units who report to Chris Hughes, Black and Decker's global vice president in charge of technology. *cont.*

'Bob's role is a recognition by the company that technology is a process and a skill that sits neither solely with boffins at a research centre or just on the shop floor, but is something endemic to the organization' says Chris Gill, Black and Decker's European finance director in charge of consumer products. A broad area of organizational innovation at the Spennymoor plant in which Bowlam has a key role – a horizontal initiative – concerns the factory's squad of twenty 'technical coaches'. These were set up last year who work alongside plant operators to encourage new thinking.

Source: Peter Marsh, *Financial Times*, 6 December 1995. Reprinted by permission.

a position on the subject, two factors are of consequence: (1) the prerequisites for holding key management positions, and (2) the extent to which local nationals could be relied upon to perform the necessary tasks satisfactorily. Ultimately, these decisions are made on the basis of the previous experience of the firm. It is expected that where there is an experience of successful utilization of local nationals in the past, MNEs are likely to use a high proportion of local managers in the subsidiary. Similarly, where a firm has no previous or less than satisfactory experience in the employment of local nationals in management positions in overseas subsidiaries, it is likely to have a high percentage of expatriate managers in overseas operation. Furthermore, Franko (1973) suggests that the number of expatriate managers in the subsidiary operation can be related to the stage of internationalization of the firm.

Franko described these stages as: (1) export, (2) initial manufacture, (3) foreign growth, (4) foreign maturity, (5) stable growth, and (6) political and competitive threats. Between stages (1) and (3), headquarters technology needs introduction in foreign manufacture and calls for a high proportion of expatriate managers. Between stages (4) and (6), it is expected that the technology will now be widely diffused and that marketing programmes will be very transferable, thereby minimizing the need for expatriate managers.

However, it is highly unlikely that the availability of qualified and experienced local nationals will obviate the need for expatriate managers in foreign subsidiaries. According to Robinson (1978), it may be that some of the mature multinational and transnational corporations actually plan on maintaining between 5 and 10 per cent expatriates or third country nationals in local subsidiary management on the assumption that there are benefits in mixed management, such as providing multinational experience and intensifying corporate socialization for all parties.

The benefits of employing local managers include a lower wage bill. This has to be seen within the context of the country of origin of the multinational firm. It is doubtful whether a European multinational firm will benefit from a lower wage bill if it operates and employs local managers in the USA. A second benefit is intimate knowledge of local politics, culture and business practices. In some markets such as Japan and number of developing countries, it is extremely difficult to use expatriate managers effectively. Therefore, recruiting local managers should constitute a source competitive advantage for the MNE if the benefits are properly developed. The limitations of employing local managers stem from their lack of international mobility. The skills and expertise of local managers are seldom transferable. It is not very common to find MNEs using third country nationals purely on the basis of managerial effectiveness without regard to nationality.

COMPENSATION

Compensation may be described as reward for services rendered to an employer. The economics of compensation is based on the principle that such rewards should be sufficiently attractive to secure the employment and commitment of the right calibre of staff to enable a firm to achieve its objectives. The management of pay and reward is a rather complex subject because of the difficulty in establishing a pay structure that will be satisfactory and acceptable to all staff. The complexity is perhaps more pronounced in the international management of human resources. For example, what factors should be considered in determining a decent pay structure in multiple markets with varying levels of standard of living and economic development? It is arguable that multinational firms face moral and ethical dilemmas in determining an appropriate pay structure where the host market is classified as a low wage economy. Sparrow and Hiltrop (1994) contend that the challenge to multinational organizations is not to take advantage of low wage opportunities but to design compensation strategies that are most appropriate for the specific cultural traditions.

Furthermore, the move towards transnational organizations has brought a requirement to remunerate more expatriate managers, and to reward a flexible, mobile cadre of international managers (Sparrow and Hiltrop, 1994). According to Robinson (1978), compensating expatriate managers raises a number of problems as a result of the need to: (1) pro-

Table 8.2 Employment of parent country, third country or host country nationals: determinants of optimum strategy

Variables	Strategy
Stage of internationalization	High proportion of expatriates at the introduction and growth stages; low proportion of expatriates at the maturity stage
Previous experience	High proportion of expatriates where previous experiences have not been satisfactory; and vice versa
Availability of suitable local expertise	Low proportion of expatriate managers
Lack of familiarity with local markets	Low proportion of expatriate managers
High degree of centralization	High proportion of expatriate managers; and vice versa
Need to maintain a foreign image	High proportion of expatriate managers
Multi-racial or multi-religious society	A local manager of either racial origin or religion would make the firm politically vulnerable. Expatriate managers would make it less vulnerable

vide inducement to leave the home country, (2) maintain a home country standard of living, (3) facilitate re-entry into the home country through maintenance of a home and professional updating, (4) meet the requirements of children's education, and (5) maintain social obligations *vis-à-vis* friends and family.

Although there is a host of alternative methods of dealing with the issue of pay and reward in international management, Robinson argues that the choice of basic strategies relating to remuneration is limited to two:

- multiples (that is, parent country personnel on a parent country salary scale, all others on the relevant local scales); or
- an international base plus a variety of extras (such as a cost of living differential, an expatriate bonus to compensate for being away from home, and a number of personal adjustment payments – moving allowance, children's education, entertainment, special health and accident insurance).

In practice, the issue of compensation in a globalized firm is neither straight forward nor clear cut. A special kind of difficulty relates to the harmonization of local and expatriate staff pay structure. For example, how would a multinational firm deal with the question of compensation for two managers – one expatriate and the other local – doing the same job at the subsidiary level? In recent years, a growing number of multinational firms have developed a variety of compensation schemes designed to maintain fairness and consistency. Performance-related payment schemes are growing in popularity as a mechanism which recognizes the need for variable pay structure based on contribution rather than status or labels (local or expatriate staff) within the organization. Other incentive schemes include bonus, share option, and profit-sharing.

NATIONAL VERSUS CORPORATE CULTURE

The term 'organizational culture' refers to the sum of perceptions that develop within an organization – perceptions that develop through the employees' own experience and perceptions deliberately manipulated by top management to provide employees with a sense of identity and source of commitment to an organizational reality which is greater than that of an individual (Mead, 1994). Furthermore, Mead suggests that these may be achieved through the systematic development of the following:

- organizational beliefs: conscious certainty that something exists, or is good, in the organization;
- organizational attitudes: conscious stances about how things are, or ought to be, in the organization; these are expressed in rituals, mission statements, etc.;
- organizational values: which are preconscious assumptions about 'how things ought to be' in the organization, and are acquired there.

In these respects, the definitional parameters of culture remain the same whether it relates to an organization or a nation. However, it is suggested that the most significant disparity occurs in the notions of national cultural values and organizational values. National culture is acquired unconsciously from an early age whereas organizational culture is learned in the workplace consciously as a subculture. The fundamental questions which international managers need to consider are:

- Which cultural values should be of overriding importance – national or corporate?
- To what extent can successful organizational cultures vary within any one national culture?

As multinational firms embrace wholesale globalization both in strategy and structure, the global managers are expected to deal with the important issues of cultural diversity between headquarters and their overseas subsidiaries. Although it is recognized that the culture and practices at headquarters tend to shape the managerial behaviour of global managers, elements of the culture of the host-country environment must be recognized and accommodated within the overall framework of a firm's operating strategy. Vernon-Wortzel and Wortzel (1991) argue that managerial skills, attitudes and commitment should fit the firm's global strategy. Thus, global managers should seek to maximize the positive interaction of national and corporate cultural elements. But even with the best of intentions, certain difficulties must be anticipated and planned for. For example, where there is a strong national culture, it is likely that the local employees will primarily be influenced by such a culture.

WOMEN AS INTERNATIONAL MANAGERS

The role of women as international managers is an area that remains contentious. Discussions on the deployment of expatriate managers to overseas assignments presuppose that men and women are given equal consideration in the process. In practice, this is seldom the case. Mead (1994) contends that many companies hobble their chances of selecting the best candidate for an overseas assignment by unnecessarily restricting the candidate pool. They do not seriously consider posting their women managers because of very deep-seated views that

- women do not want to be international managers;
- foreigners' prejudices against women render them ineffective.

The first point is just a counterfactual argument. Women are as committed and interested in international management as their male counterparts. The problem is simply that the MNEs are prejudiced against the deployment of women managers to overseas assignments. There are indications that the attitude of the male-dominated corporate boards towards women managers has not changed significantly over the last twenty years. With regards to the issue of foreigners' prejudices against women managers, this is limited to a number of developing countries with strong religious beliefs about the role of women in the society. None the less, this cannot be used to justify the lack of or limited deployment of women managers to overseas assignments.

Adler (1984) argues that the conventional myths about the so-called disadvantages of sending women overseas cannot be substantiated. Evidence from Adler's studies suggest that women would welcome the chance of taking on expatriate posts. Other considerations which the MNEs have had to deal with in the past over the deployment of women managers to overseas assignment include the treatment of married women with dependants. For example:

- Is it ethically right to deploy a married woman with pre-school-age children to an overseas job?
- Would she have the option of rejecting such a posting without prejudicing her managerial career?
- If she has a dependent husband, would he be taken care of?

These questions are important and would probably have wider implications both for the firm and the individual manager concerned. It has to be stressed that the issues of overseas deployment of women managers (whether married or single) should be dealt with purely on the basis of the competencies required for the job. Similarly, it is wrong to suggest that the chances of success for male expatriate managers would be higher than for female expatriates. MNEs' expectations for expatriate managers, the success criteria and the available support facilities (such as relocation training and support) for an overseas assignment must be clearly stated and communicated to all managers. This will enable managers to decide whether they are suitable for overseas postings and increase the transparency of the decision-making process.

INTERNATIONAL LABOUR ISSUES

The intense competition among nations over the last fifteen years to attract foreign investments has effectively changed the environment for industrial relations practices across the world. The traditional militant approach of trade unions has given way to a more cooperative but equally effective style in their relationship with management. At the same time, there is a growing sense of responsibility towards the employees by management with the corresponding recognition of the rights of the workers to participate in important decisions affecting their welfare, and the growth of the firm. These developments are partly due to the acceptance of the Japanese management style, which is based on the principle that the workers and managers identify with the goals and activities of the firm, and partly due to more effective legislative control of the powers of the trade union. However, the emphasis is on the globalization of the Japanese management style, which has given rise to talks of the japanization of management.

While the merits of worker participation in management are acknowledged, the real questions that must be addressed include:

- Would worker participation lead to the loss of management's right to manage?
- To what extent should workers influence the decision-making process in the firm?
- Is it culturally feasible or right to globalize the Japanese management style?

SUMMARY

Chapter 8 has explained the international dimensions of human resource management, emphasizing the importance of organizational design and effective strategy. It started by examining the distinction between HRM and IHRM and the factors which are important in the effective management of HRM issues in MNEs. In staffing overseas subsidiaries, the MNE has to consider both the merits and limitations of using either home country or host country nationals within the constraints of its previous experience, stage of internationalization, policy and strategy. Regardless of the option chosen, there are wider issues of compensation, the deployment of women managers and industrial relations to be considered.

REFERENCES

Adler, N. J. 1984: 'Women in international management: where are they?', *California Management Review*, Vol. 26, No. 4, pp. 78–89.

Chandler, A. D. 1962: *Strategy and Structure*. Cambridge, MA: MIT Press.

Dittrich, J. E. 1988: *The General Manager and Strategy Formulation*. New York: John Wiley.

Franko, L. G. 1973: 'Who manages multinational enterprises?' *Columbia Journal of World Business*, Summer, pp. 33–49.

Mead, R. 1994: *International Management: Cross Cultural Dimensions*. Oxford: Blackwell Publishers.

Marsh, Peter 1995: 'Management: tool of the team', *Financial Times*, 6 December, p. 14.

Robinson, R. D. 1978: *International Business Management: A Guide to Decision Making*, 2nd edn. Hinsdale, IL: The Dryden Press.

Rugman, A. M., Lecraw, D. J. and Booth, L. D. 1985: *International Business: Firm and Environment*. New York: McGraw-Hill.

Sparrow, P. and Hiltrop, J. M. 1994: *European Human Resource Management in Transition*. London: Prentice-Hall.

Torrington, D. 1994: *International Human Resource Management*. London: Prentice-Hall.

Vernon-Wortzel, H. and Wortzel, L. H. 1991: *Global Strategic Management: The Essentials*, 2nd edn. New York: John Wiley.

PART III
Managing international business

9
Global strategic management

INTRODUCTION

The concept of global strategy has received considerable attention in international management literature in recent years. A powerful force which is shaping the debate on global strategy derives from the influential globalization school of thought, boasting academics such as Theodore Levitt, Kinichi Ohmae and Michael Porter. In what is increasingly becoming a borderless world, there is a realization that competitive success in this global setting requires a strategy which takes into account the economic, political and socio-cultural imperatives of international business management.

The term 'strategy' evokes different interpretations and can sometimes be equated with a simple programme of action. In this book, we take a broad view of the term, defining strategy as the long-term direction and level of an organization's activities. In other words, strategy deals with the question of defining the business of the organization and establishing how to synchronize the internal strengths and weaknesses of the firm with the external opportunities and threats to justify its existence. Simply put, a strategy is an all-encompassing plan which enables a firm to achieve its goals. Although the elements of strategy are the same in domestic and multinational business, the operational matters facing multinational firms are substantially different from those encountered by firms operating in a purely uni-national market setting. These differences emanate from socio-cultural and economic environments in which international businesses are conducted. These differences are well developed in table 9.1.

The most important challenge which an international manager faces is that of establishing the overall strategic direction of the firm, and then designing and implementing a strategy which will ensure that goals are achieved. According to Taggart and McDermott (1993), putting together such a corporate strategy involves planning future activities, together with their timing and location; allocating the firm's resources of time,

Table 9.1 Difference between domestic and international planning

Domestic planning	International planning
1. Single language and nationality	1. Multi-lingual/multinational/multi-cultural factors
2. Relatively homogeneous market	2. Fragmented and diverse markets
3. Data available, usually accurate and collection easy	3. Data collection a formidable task, requiring significantly higher budgets and personnel allocation
4. Political factors relatively unimportant	4. Political factors frequently vital
5. Relative freedom from government interference	5. Involvement in national economic plans; government influences business decisions
6. Individual corporation has little effect on environment	6. 'Gravitational' distortion by large companies
7. Chauvinism helps	7. Chauvinism hinders
8. Relatively stable business environment	8. Multiple environments, many of which are highly unstable (but may be highly profitable)
9. Uniform financial climate	9. Variety of financial climates ranging from overconservative to widely inflationary
10. Single currency	10. Currencies differ in stability and real value
11. Business 'role of the game' mature and understood	11. Rules diverse, changeable, and usually unclear
12. Management generally accustomed to sharing responsibilities and using financial controls	12. Management frequently autonomous and unfamiliar with budgets and controls

Source: Cain (1970), p. 58.

across competing projects, among different strategic business units; and determining the firm's attitude toward and actions in relation to entry into different markets (and withdrawal), acquisitions and strategic alliances. To accomplish these, the role of the tools of analysis become particularly crucial. Some of these tools are discussed in the following section.

GLOBAL STRATEGY PLANNING PROCESS

Although there are areas of commonalities in planning for domestic and international businesses, as indicated above, there are significant areas of difference which arise from the multiplicity and complexity of international business environment. Over the years, academics and practitioners have developed some very useful planning tools to guide the formulation of marketing strategies. The best known and perhaps the most widely used models include the Boston Consulting Group (BCG) Product Portfolio matrix and the General Electric (GE) Strategy Formulation Matrix, the Product Life Cycle, and the Generic Strategy Model. Although these models were proposed primarily for planning in domestic markets, they have been applied successfully within the context of international business, albeit with different analytical variables, and are now examined in the following sections.

The BCG matrix

The BCG matrix seems to have gained wide acceptance among managers and is known to have been applied in the analysis of the relative attractiveness of various markets, as shown in figure 9.1. Using two determinants – market attractiveness on the X-axis and the company strength on the Y-axis – a strategist is able to evaluate the sales potential in a market. Thus, the BCG matrix can serve as the backdrop for depicting a market size and sales potential measured by its attractiveness and the company strength. With the BCG as the analytical framework, market D will not be an attractive location for continued substantial capital investment because the firm is not strong enough to compete in a market that is very unattractive. On the other hand, the firm is strong in market A and developmental prospects are equally good. When applied in a domestic setting, market A in a BCG matrix would be described as the Star, and market D as the Dog. The benefits of the BCG as an international planning tool include the following:

- It provides a global overview of a firm's position in various markets in which it operates. It presents facts in such a graphic form that it makes for easy understanding by corporate executives.
- It is a useful framework for analysis and comparison of the performance of a firm's businesses in international markets.
- It is a good tool with which to formulate marketing and other operational objectives for specific markets.

Despite its simplicity, the BCG matrix as a planning tool in international management has been criticized by academics for being fundamentally flawed in a number of ways. These include the fact that:

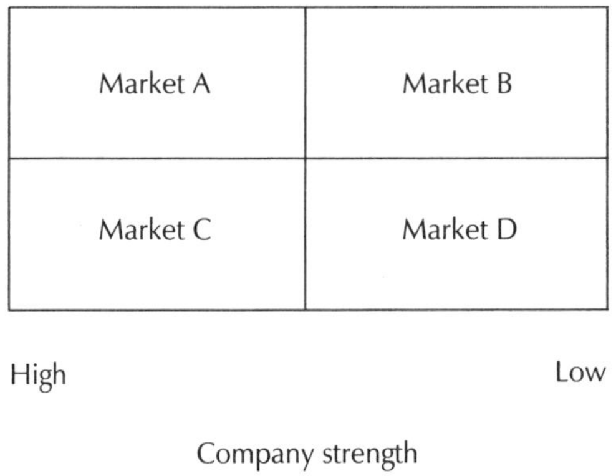

Market A	Market B
Market C	Market D

High   Low

Company strength

Figure 9.1 BCG market selection matrix

- It ignores the interdependence of international markets – for example, a production facility in a dog (market D) may be used to service market A or market B.
- It does not take into account the possible variation in input costs – materials, tariffs, exchange rates and transport. It seems to suggest that high market share and more production will result in decreased cost, and by implication, greater profitability in market C.
- The BCG matrix does not recognize a host of reasons other than profits that make firms remain in different markets. For example, access to technical information, the 'also present in a market' factor (the herd mentality of multinational firms) or preventing competition are very powerful considerations for a firm's presence in a foreign market.

Without disregarding the significance of these limitations, the full benefits of the BCG matrix could be captured by compiling and weighing all the variables which are important in order to reach a composite judgement. These will include the fit between the strategic direction of the firm and the political and socio-cultural imperatives in a market.

THE GENERIC STRATEGY MODEL

Michael Porter's generic strategy model is another analytical framework which has gained acceptance among managers and academics as a planning tool and has been applied extensively in industry analysis and strategic planning in domestic markets. However, Porter has continued to push the limits of its application to cover international strategy planning as well. Although similar to the generic strategy matrix, the international version is distinguished by the extent to which global activities require centralization/coordination, the need for a global strategy and the imperatives of country-centred strategy. This is depicted in figure 9.2. The resulting matrix exhibits five international strategy alternatives:

- global cost leadership – achieving international competitiveness through cost minimization;
- global differentiation – achieving international competitiveness through real or perceived differentiation advantage. This is usually enhanced by well-conceived positioning strategy;
- protected markets – using the benefits of host government protection to enhance ones market position;
- global segmentation – regional integrative strategy as the basis of international competitiveness;
- national responsiveness – this may be described as market (customer) rather than cost-driven approach as the key to achieving international success. With this strategy, the firm seeks to meet consumer requirements.

The main benefit of this model is that it provides a full range of strategies that international firms may adopt in pursuit of global success. It addresses some of the limitations inherent in the BCG model. It must be said, however, that these strategies are not written in tablets of stone and are subject to political, economic and cultural imperatives and the international orientation of the firm. The whole range of international strategic orientations are discussed in the subsequent section.

STRATEGIC ORIENTATION OF THE MNE

Multinational firms pursue international strategies that are best suited to their attitudes and predisposition to global business opportunities. These attitudes and predisposition are a function of a number of factors. According to Heenan and Perlmutter (1979) the strategic predisposition of a firm is shaped by the circumstances of its birth, the leadership style of its CEOs, its past administrative practices, and the myths and folklore that have endured in the organization. Heenan and Perlmutter developed the

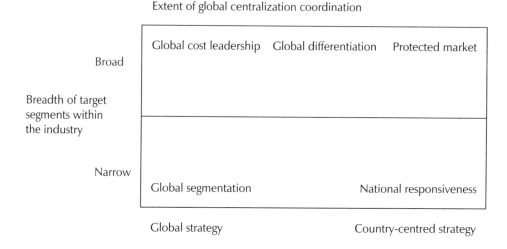

Figure 9.2 Strategic alternatives in an international industry
Source: Porter, M. C. Copyright © 1986, by the Regents of the University of California. Reprinted from the *California Management Review*, Vol. 28, No. 2. By permission of the Regent.

following strategic predispositions for understanding the operational characteristics of an MNE:

- Ethnocentrism: this is a strategic predisposition (value system) where all strategic decisions are guided by the values and interests of the parent. Such a firm is predominantly concerned with its viability worldwide and legitimacy only in its home country. This is based on the belief that home country management style and practices are superior to practices and styles found abroad.
- Polycentrism: this is a predisposition where strategic decisions are tailored to suit the cultures of the various countries in which the MNE competes. A polycentric multinational is primarily concerned with legitimacy in every country that it operates in, even if it means some loss of profits. This orientation may be described as national responsiveness and it is commonly found in mature industries.
- Regiocentrism: a predisposition that tries to blend the interests of the parent with that of the subsidiaries at least on a limited regional basis. A regiocentric multinational tries to balance viability and legitimacy at the regional level. With the emerging regional economic and political blocs, strategy is orientated to meeting the requirements of these blocs.

- Geocentrism: this is a predisposition that seeks to integrate diverse subsidiaries through a global systems approach to decision-making. A geocentric multinational tries to balance viability and legitimacy through a global network of its businesses. On occasion, these networks may even include the firm's stakeholders and competition. Geocentrism can be further classified as enclave or integrative geocentrism. The former deals with high priority problems to host countries in a marginal fashion; the latter recognizes that the MNE's key decisions must be separately assessed for their impact on each country.

Deriving from these characterizations is the EPRG profile (EPRG being an acronym for ethnocentric, polycentric, regiocentric and geocentric orientations). The EPRG profile describes the predominant predisposition of a multinational firm. Table 9.2 shows the orientation of the firm under different EPRG profiles. Furthermore, table 9.3 depicts a number of functional areas with the resultant strategy implications for the different EPRG profiles. Each profile dictates the behaviour of the firm in these functions. For example, in a polycentric multinational form, host country managers are given full autonomy to develop strategies and make decisions with little inputs from the headquarters. Although this scheme is useful in understanding the global strategy orientation of MNEs, it is only an approximate description of predispositions. In certain circumstances, a firm may choose a mixture of strategies in order to deal with unique situations. For example, the predisposition of a firm may be at variance with the strategy appropriate for the cultural, economic and political imperatives in a market.

GLOBAL STRATEGIC ALTERNATIVES

There is an ample literature on global strategy based on the works of academics such as Doz, 1980; Levitt, 1983; Porter, 1980, 1986, 1990; Ohmae, 1989; Wortzel, 1989; and others. The main thrust of these works is recognizing the bases for achieving and sustaining competitive success on a global scale. Porter (1980) identified these key success factors as cost leadership and differentiation which may be applied on broad or focused segments. But ultimately the design of international strategies has to be based upon the interplay between the comparative advantages of countries and the competitive advantages of the firm (Kogut, 1985). In the following section, we examine three broad global strategy alternatives

Table 9.2 International orientation of the firm under different EPRG profiles

Orientation of the firm	Ethnocentric	Polycentric	Regiocentric	Geocentric
1. Mission	Profitability (viability)	Public acceptance (legitimacy)	Both profitability and public acceptance (viability and legitimacy)	
2. Governance				
Direction of goal setting	Top down	Bottom up (each subsidiary decides upon local objectives)	Mutually negotiated between region and its subsidiaries	Mutually negotiated all levels of the corporation
Communication	Hierarchical, with headquarters giving high volume of orders, commands and advice	Little communication to and from headquarters and between subsidiaries	Both vertical and lateral communication with region	Both vertical and lateral communication within the company
Allocation of resources	Investment opportunities decided at headquarters	Self-supporting subsidiaries, no cross-subsidies	Regions allocate resources, under guidelines from headquarters	Worldwide projects allocation influenced by local and headquarters' managers
3. Strategy	Global integrative	National responsiveness	Regional integrative and national responsiveness	Global integrative and national responsiveness
4. Structure	Hierarchical product divisions	Hierarchical area divisions, with autonomous national units	Product and regional organizations tied through a matrix	A network of organizations (including some stakeholders and competitor organizations)
5. Culture	Home country	Host country	Regional	Global

Source: Heenan and Perlmutter (1979).

Table 9.3 EPRG profiles in different functional areas

Functional area	Ethnocentric	Polycentric	Regiocentric	Geocentric
Technology				
Production technology	Mass production	Batch production	Flexible manufacturing	Flexible manufacturing
Marketing				
Product planning	Product development determined primarily by the needs of home country customers	Local product development based on local needs	Standardize within region, but not across	Global product, with local variations
Marketing mix decisions	Made at headquarters	Made in each country	Made regionally	Made jointly with mutual consultation
Finance				
Objective	Repatriation of profits to home country	Retention of profits in host country	Redistribution within region	Redistribution globally
Finance relations	Home country institutions	Host country institutions	Regional institutions	Other global institutions
Personnel practices				
Perpetuation	People of home country developed for key positions everywhere in the world	People of local nationality developed for key positions in their own country	Regional people developed for key positions anywhere in the region	Best people everywhere in the world developed for key positions everywhere in the world
Evaluation and control	Home standards applied for persons and performance	Determined locally	Determined regionally	Standards which are universal, weighted to suit local conditions

Source: Heenan and Perlmutter (1979).

based on economic, technological, competitive and socio-cultural imperatives.

The open strategy approach

The traditional strategy which multinational firms have pursued for years may be described as the open strategy approach. This approach enables a firm to standardize or customize products and marketing programmes when and where it is necessary to do so, depending on the conditions and requirements of each market. The flexibility inherent in the open approach ensures: the recognition of socio-cultural and economic differences between markets – the principle of segmentation; and the application of the marketing concept – customer rather than cost driven. According to Porter (1986), competitive advantage is created and sustained through a highly localized process. Differences in national values, culture, economic structures, institutions and histories all contribute to competitive success. The firm modifies and adapts its intangible assets to employ them in each country and the outcome is determined by conditions in each country. Consequently, a firm should manage its international activities like a portfolio. Its subsidiaries or other operations around the world should each control the important activities necessary to do business in the industry and should enjoy a high degree of autonomy. The significant point here is that the firm's strategy in a country should be determined largely by the circumstances in that country.

The fundamental planning challenge for the multinational firm is one of balancing the economic imperative of global integration with the political imperative of prudent stakeholder management (Doz, 1980). Thus, setting a global strategy is a matter of adjusting as much as possible the business function – manufacturing, procurement, marketing, distribution and R&D – within the constraints of trade and investment barriers in a way that provides the best possible product/market fit (Wortzel, 1989). Despite the growing pressure for integrated global strategy, it would be an oversimplification to suggest that such a strategic approach to international management would be the panacea to the problems of increasing integration of international markets.

The globalization approach

The increasing pressure for globalization of business activities over the past ten years or so means that strategic planning and implementation have become progressively more complex. The focus of international planning is now firmly on global strategy. The concept of an integrated global strategy implies standardization of the planning and implementation of international activities with the attendant requirement for centralization of the decision-making process. The proponents of a global strategy argue that it offers the potential for synergy and greater competitive advantage which may be achieved through increased economies of scale in R&D and production techniques.

The unit of analysis under the global focus strategy is cost – economies of scale in R&D, production, packaging, branding, distribution and advertising. Perhaps the best known proponents of this strategic approach to international planning are the advertising agency Saatchi and Saatchi (they were quite successful in the 1980s designing advertising campaigns with global themes) and Theodore Levitt. The driving force in the argument for globalization of strategy is the commonality in the global markets and the convergence of standards and tastes which have arisen as a result of technological advance in most countries. These developments provide a source of linkages between countries. Therefore, the global firm must capture the benefits of these linkages in order to maintain competitiveness and success.

Porter (1986) suggest that the starting point for understanding international competition has to be based on industry-level analysis. Patterns of competition differ from industry to industry. Consequently, only a global strategy would be appropriate in dealing with global industries. A global industry being defined as an industry in which a firm's competitive position in one country is significantly influenced by its position in other countries. Strategic imperatives in a global industry imply that a firm must in some way integrate its activities on a worldwide basis to take advantage of the linkages among countries.

The 'glocalization' approach

The concept of glocalization which was first coined by Arvinda Phatak is fast gaining acceptance and popularity among academics as a half-way house between national responsiveness and a full shift towards globalization. This approach to strategic planning seeks to accommodate the need to recognize the merits of globalization while at the same time, being as responsive as possible at national levels. This is illustrated in figure 9.3. The strength of opinions for globalization is overwhelming. Kinichi Ohmae (1989) argues on the need for managers to adopt a proper international orientation in their strategic planning, suggesting that even though today's

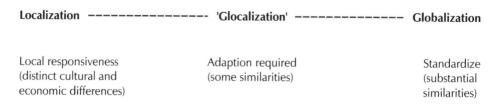

Figure 9.3 Spectrum of international competitive strategy

competitive landscape often stretches to a global horizon, managers see best what they know best: the customers geographically closest to home. He insists that effective global operations require a genuine equidistance of perspective. But even with the best of will in the world, managers find that kind of vision hard to develop – and harder to maintain.

On the other hand, competitive success in international markets may not depend entirely on cost rationalization but on firms recognizing the specific needs and requirements of consumers at national level. Even in his famous paper, Levitt (1983) recognized the need to think global but act local.

It has to be said that there is no denying of the economic benefits of globalization. The predominant question remains: at any cost? Ultimately, competitive success in international markets will depend on a firm's effectiveness in evaluating all the imperatives in its operating circumstances and its ability to respond accordingly.

SUMMARY

In this chapter, it has been shown that the concept of global strategic management is possibly the most important challenge facing corporate executives in the twenty-first century. An examination of the process of strategy planning revealed that, although the elements of strategy are the same in domestic and multinational business, the operational and environmental issues involved in global strategy planning are substantially different from those encountered in domestic strategy planning. The thrust of the debate in global strategy remains on localization versus globalization. The conclusion from this chapter is that, regardless of the 'label' that is attached to an international strategy, success will be determined by a firm's ability to recognize the unique host market characteristics and

EXHIBIT 9.1

No laughing matter as FedEx goes global

Federal Express, whose recent ads feature the shipping executive who boasts about slipping off to play golf while his boss listens behind a loo door, is finding that, when going global, humour does not travel well. The biggest US air express company, but so far a laggard overseas, FedEx has long been associated with funny advertising, from its fast talking pitchmen to the boss impersonating a secretary to check on a package. But now, the world's largest express transport company has changed its tune – and stilled its funny bone. 'Humour works better locally but doesn't always carry over. We have found that to tell our global story, we're better focusing on the brand imagery, and the fact that FedEx empowers customers in the global economy,' said Ira Bahr, senior vice-president and worldwide account director at Omnicom Group's BBDO, the ad agency for Federal Express since 1989. 'We've created a powerful and persuasive message that is very brand-differentiating and very strategic.'

The six commercials so far, with a dozen more to come within the next few months, focus on entrepreneurs doing business all over the world because of FedEx's delivery and warehousing inventory services. FedEx plans to spend around $45m on the campaign, close to what it spent last year.

The campaign, with minor modifications, is expected to run in twenty countries. It's their first global ad campaign and the first time FedEx hasn't customized its advertising to different parts of the world. 'The most important message that we have to deliver is that we've become a global company,' said David Schonfeld, vice-president of marketing. 'The global theme supersedes specific messages of the past. Our humorous ads have accomplished the objectives set, but no company can afford to leave its ad objectives untouched if the environment has changed.'

Discussion questions

1. In their pursuit of global aspiration, Federal Express is finding that, when going global, humour does not travel well. Explain why humour does not travel well.
2. To what extent can the new FedEx ads be described as truly global?

needs and doing whatever that is necessary to meet these needs. None the less, the maxim 'think global, act local', remains relevant in this age of globalization of business.

DISCUSSION QUESTIONS

1. Define the term strategy? Critically examine the difference between domestic and global business planning.
2. Identify and discuss the benefits of the BCG model in global strategy planning. What are the main limitations of this model as a planning tool?
3. Critically examine the relevance of the EPRG profile in global planning.

REFERENCES

Cain, W. W. 1970: 'International planning: mission impossible?', *Columbia Journal of World Business*, July-August, p. 58.

Doz, Y. 1980: 'Strategic management in multinational companies', *Sloan Management Review*, Vol. 21, No. 2, pp. 27–46.

Heenan, D. A. and Perlmutter, H. V. 1979: *Multinational Organisational Development: A Social Architecture Perspective*. Reading, MA: Addison Wesley.

Kogut, B. 1985: 'Designing global strategies: comparative and competitive value-added chains', *Sloan Management Review*, Summer, pp. 15–28.

Levitt, T. 1983: 'Globalization of markets', *Harvard Business Review*, May-June, pp. 92–102.

Ohmae, K. 1989: 'Managing in a borderless world', *Harvard Business Review*, May-June.

Porter, M. 1980: *Competitive Strategy: Techniques for Analysing Industries and Competitors*. New York: Free Press.

Porter, M. 1986: 'Changing patterns of international competition', *California Management Review*, Vol. 28, No. 2, Winter, pp. 9–40.

Porter, M. 1990: *Competitive Advantage of Nations*. New York: Free Press.

Taggart, J. and McDermott, M. 1993: *The Essence of International Business*. Hemel Hempstead: Prentice-Hall International.

Wortzel, L. 1989: *International Business Strategy Resource Book*. New York: Strategic Direction.

10

Corporate responsibility

INTRODUCTION

When the activities of Lonrho Mining Corporation in Africa were exposed in the press in 1972, the then UK Prime Minister, Edward Heath, in an answer to a question in the House of Commons remarked that: 'This is the unacceptable face of capitalism.' Since that statement was made, other events and developments such as the Bhopal disaster in India, *Exxon Valdez* disaster in Alaska, Chernobyl in Russia, *Piper Alpha* in the North Sea, Shell's activities in Ogoniland in Nigeria and the Robert Maxwell pension fund fiasco in Britain have contributed to highlighting the importance of corporate responsibility in the management of business operations.

The concept of corporate responsibility would not ordinarily be uppermost in the minds of management. The traditional view of management is that they are primarily responsible to their shareholders. The question of wider responsibility to society at large is still contentious. On the one hand, there are those (the classical school of thought) who believe that businesses should not assume any social responsibility beyond making as much money as possible for the owners of the firm. This school of thought boasts eminent scholars such as Milton Friedman. On the other hand, the opposing school of thought (the contemporary view) believes that businesses are important and influential members of the society and have an obligation to help maintain and improve society's overall welfare. Proponents of this view include Keith Davies.

The contemporary view stems from the knowledge that a firm cannot exist in isolation from the society in which it exists. The numerous stakeholders in a firm means that the responsibility of management extends beyond the idea of profit maximization for the owners. The stakeholders in a firm are the individuals or groups who have a stake in the consequences of management decisions and can influence those decisions. They include:

- subscribers of capital – shareholders and debenture holders;

- trades unions – workers have become better protected through the security of collective bargaining;
- consumers – who are entitled to safe products and healthy environment;
- government – which has a responsibility to protect the consumers and the public at large with legislation where necessary;
- suppliers to the firm.

Recent disasters such as those mentioned above have shown that no management can ignore the environment in which it operates, and the success of the firm may depend to a large extent on its public image. The attitude of the firm towards its employees form part of this image. When in December 1995, Marks and Spencer, the British clothes retailers, were accused in a television documentary of employing child labour in Morocco in order to reduce cost, the denial from the company was swift and unequivocal. Such is the importance that firms attach to their public image, particularly in this day of high consumer expectations. The concept of corporate responsibility is a huge area which covers a host of issues such as corporate governance, social responsibility and business ethics, and are discussed in the following sections.

CORPORATE GOVERNANCE

Corporate governance is a term that has generated a lot of excitement among politicians, business executives, shareholders and financiers (banks and other lenders) over the last ten years. Specific governance issues such as insider trading (the most celebrated cases being those of Ivan Boesky, the New York trader and Ernest Saunders and the other Guinness directors), hostile takeovers, and spectacular company failures have become common phrases in the language of business communities around the world. The pertinent question, however, is, what is corporate governance? What are its implications for senior management in public enterprises?

There seems to be considerable misunderstanding of what corporate governance is all about. Maw *et al.* (1994) note that almost every day when you read quality newspapers, you will find reference to the subject of corporate governance. Not all journalists know what that subject comprises, but they mention it all the same. Some commentators believe it is a fancy term for the way in which directors and auditors handle their responsibil-

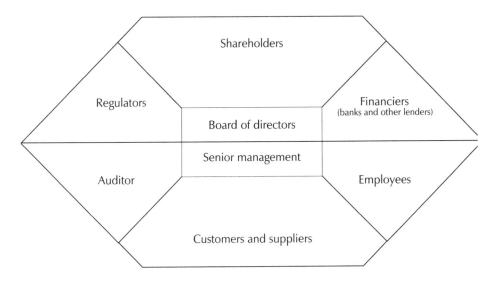

Figure 10.1 Interactions in corporate governance

ities towards shareholders. Others take it as being synonymous with corporate democracy. In this book, corporate governance is defined as a generic term that describes the nature of the relationships and interactions between all the stakeholders in an enterprise – shareholders, board of directors, senior management, employees, auditors, financiers, regulators and customers and suppliers. This relationship is illustrated in figure 10.1. Therefore, in principle, firms are run for the common good of all the stakeholders within the context of laws put in place to protect the rights of the third party – the employees, public and the environment.

In general, the issues in corporate governance are substantially similar in industrialized countries. However, approaches to the legal responsibilities and rights of stakeholders differ from country to country. Cannon (1994) suggests that the pattern and nature of corporate governance in specific nations or societies derives from the interaction of four broad forces: ownership pattern, board structure, regulatory situation and societal pressure. Emphasis on each of these forces is influenced by developments in the business community. For example, the destruction of the Brazilian rain forest and the environmental degradation in the Niger Delta region of Nigeria by Shell Petroleum have served to heighten societal pressure on the business community. Similarly, the death of Robert Maxwell in 1991 and the subsequent disclosure of the disappearance of the Mirror Group Newspapers pension fund led to calls for tighter statutory protection for stakeholders. It is argued that such protection should not be an obligation of corporate management, and that it must be left for the law. The broad framework for establishing the rights and responsibilities of shareholders and directors of a firm is provided in statutes. While shareholders provide capital, the directors are responsible for providing effective management to enable a firm to achieve its objectives and potentials.

There are important distinctions between governance and management. Deriving from these distinctions are the issues of separating ownership from control. In Tricker (1994), the following distinctions are offered:

> *Governance* is concerned with the intrinsic nature, purpose, integrity and identity of the institution, with a primary focus on the entity's relevance, continuity, and fiduciary aspects. Governance involves monitoring and overseeing strategic direction, socio-economic and cultural context, externalities, and constituencies ...
>
> *Management* on the other hand, is more of a hands on activity. In its traditional sense, management can be characterised as conducting or supervising actions with the judicious use of means to accomplish certain ends. Management primarily focuses on specific goal attainment over a definite time frame and in prescribed organisation.

More specifically, corporate governance focuses on the role of the board of directors *vis-à-vis* senior management as identified in figure 10.1. But what happens when there is a conflict between the strategic policy direction of the firm and social pressures? Is cross-membership of the board of directors and senior management necessarily harmful to the stakeholders? In some countries, the two-tier board of directors/senior management structure, as shown in figure 10.1, is kept separate to maintain checks and balances. In countries where a combined structure is permitted the societal pressure provides the counter-balancing influence. Despite these important safeguards, a number of important questions on issues of corporate governance still remain unanswered. For example, Tricker (1994) asks whether corporate decisions are being made in management and shareholders interests. Can boards of directors better serve the interests of shareholders and their governance responsibilities if they are somehow reformed or restructured? Who else has a stake in corporate governance? The specific roles of key stakeholders are outlined in the following sections.

Duties and responsibilities of directors

The duties and responsibilities of directors are clearly defined in statutes. Individually and collectively, members of the board owe a duty of care to the general body of shareholders. The board is responsible for ensuring that the affairs of the company are conducted diligently, legally and honestly; that the assets of the company are safeguarded and not misspent or misappropriated; that management is efficient and trustworthy; and that shareholders are kept informed. These duties place great responsibilities on the directors and are the justification for the 'fat cat' remuneration that they enjoy. With the spotlight of corporate governance, the job of a director will become ever more demanding in future.

Duties and responsibilities of regulators

The term regulator encompasses a wide range of regulatory bodies set up to control the conduct of public firms. In the United Kingdom such regulators include the Stock Exchange, OFTEL (regulatory body for the telecommunications industry), the Office of Fair Trading, and the Monopolies and Mergers Commission. It is the duty of the regulators to act as checks and balances against the powers of corporate executives and thus maintain confidence in public firms. This is achieved by receiving relevant and accurate information on a regular basis or when demanded.

Duties and responsibilities of auditors

As mentioned above, the board of directors has a duty to ensure that the assets of the company are not misspent or misappropriated. It is the responsibility of the auditors to ensure that the obligations of the directors are discharged as judiciously as possible. In the conduct of their duties, the auditors are entitled to unhindered access to company accounts and other relevant information that may required for proper scrutiny of a company's affairs. The role of the auditors is particularly important because shareholders, non-executive directors and regulators rely heavily on their reports as a better guide to a company's health.

THE ENVIRONMENT

The role of industry and commerce in the destruction of the environment has been widely identified as the most important challenge facing mankind. Chemical insecticides, fertilizers, concentrated single crop production, factory emissions, chemical additives such as phosphates in detergents, environmental degradation by oil companies, and the destruction of the rain forest are wreaking havoc with the environment. It is, therefore, not surprising that the environmental protection campaigners are directed at industry and commerce for being the main culprits. Table 10.1 illustrates a range of commercial activities and their impact on the environment. They have caused the problems and must play a pivotal role in tackling the issue. Environmental campaigners have, in recent times, succeeded in putting care of environment high up on the corporate governance agenda. In January 1996 the Royal Geographical Society voted at a conference in Glasgow, Scotland, to remove Shell Petroleum from its list of corporate patrons because of its environmental and political record in Nigeria. Arguments that Shell has helped the society with expeditions and cared for the environment failed to make any impact on the delegates. Shell's experience with the Royal Geographical Society serves to illustrate the kind of pressure that international firms are now facing on environmental matters.

There is no consensus on the view of business development and environmental protection on how to respond to the consequences of environmental degradation. Cannon (1994) suggests that it is possible to place the proposed responses to the environmental challenges along a spectrum which extends from corporations resisting proposals to change until forced by legislation and enforcement, to firms building their futures around internalizing environmental concerns. It is, however, becoming clear that the long-term solution to these concerns must be developed in collaboration with the industry. This realization is beginning to bear fruit in some countries which have encouraged the pursuit of the 'green' agenda. Terms such as 'ozone friendly', 'recycled paper' and 'biodegradable' are now used to connote environmental responsibility. This has been made possible by a combination of both voluntary and legislative controls. Cannon lists the following as some of the actions being taken by firms:

- internal reforms of business practices;
- long-term adjustment made to damaging social and economic activities;
- restrictions placed on certain activities or products;
- polluters pay for programmes by government;
- income from taxes employed to 'clean up';
- economic growth and industrialization limited to the amount that the area, community or planet can absorb;
- new technologies developed to correct harmful effects.

Table 10.1 Organizational implications of environmentalism

Organizational system	Environmentalists' concerns
Inputs	
Raw materials	Depletion of forests
	Harm caused by toxic materials like pesticides, solvents
Fuels	Depletion of oil, coal, natural gas
	Pollution created by fossil fuels, hazards of using nuclear energy
Throughputs	
Plant	Plant safety and accidents
	Risks to surrounding neighbourhoods
Workers	Occupational disease/hazards
	Work related injuries/ill-health
Wastes	Hazardous waste disposal
	Emissions of pollutants
	Emissions of environmentally destructive chemicals like CFCs
Transport	Risk of spills and losses in transporting hazard materials
Outputs	
Products	Product safety
	Health consequences of products such as tobacco, liquor, fats, beef, etc
Packaging	Garbage created by packaging
Servicing	Reliability, hazards of failure

Source: T. Cannon, *Corporate Responsibility*. Copyright © Pitman Publishing, 1994. Reprinted by permission.

The commitment of firms to these measures differs from country to country and depends on the regulatory regime in each country. The thrust of international responses to global problems is founded in laws and declarations as the basis for action by individual countries and the international community. It also provides the framework for legally binding international norms. International environmental laws are formulated to control human activities and preserve the integrity of the biosphere. The 1972 Stockholm Conference on the Human Environment has been described as an important watershed in the global environmental awakening. It not only led to the emergence of important legal principles and concepts but has resulted in the establishment of the United Nations Environmental Programme

(UNEP), an organization which plays a key role in shaping the international legal response to global environmental challenges. Multilateral treaties, agreements and guidelines emerged in such diverse areas as the protection of marine environment, the prevention of air and water pollution, and the regulation of trade in chemical and toxic substances.

Since 1982 UNEP has spearheaded the successful negotiation and conclusion of important international legal instruments, including those which address the challenges posed by the depletion of the stratospheric ozone layer, loss of biological diversity and transborder movements of hazardous wastes. In June 1992 the United Nations Conference on Environment and Development (UNCED) held in Rio de Janeiro provided fundamental guidance for, and created a new dimension to, future international action in the field of international law.

The international community's recognition that environmental problems transcend national boundaries has resulted in the development of an important new field of public international law known as international environmental law. Sands (1993) suggests that the growing realization that *ad hoc*, disparate and reactive policy responses by individual states or local communities will be wholly inadequate to address the growing environmental problems faced by the international community has been critical to the development of this new field. Environmental law now encompasses the development of new biotechnologies, places limits on international trade, development assistance, and intellectual property rights.

It is noteworthy that European countries are well ahead of the rest of the world in their awareness of environmental concerns. The green movement has been very active for many years and has representation at the European Parliament, where environmental issues are raised regularly. Furthermore, there are differences in the level of social responsibility with the European Union. The Scandinavian countries, Germany, Holland and France demonstrate the greatest commitment to environmental matters. Products and packages made of plastic are the normal target for attack by environmentalists.

Social responsibility comes at a cost. Developing environmentally friendly packaging materials, safer products, and supporting environmental education campaigns are expensive and affect profitability. None the less, a number of companies are facing up to their social responsibility with enthusiasm. While Body Shop is world famous for its environmental crusade, other companies such as the German automobile manufacturer, Volkswagen, are setting a new standard in environmental awareness. It aims to use 100 per cent reusable material in all its cars and vans. It is expected that in future, only those firms that are able to balance the desire for profitability with social responsibility will survive and prosper.

SUSTAINABLE DEVELOPMENT

The focus of the debate on environmental concerns since the Rio de Janeiro Conference of 1992 has been on the theme of sustainable development. Sustainable development has become a fashionable phrase in corporate vocabulary, with different interpretations. The term was in fact popularized by the World Charter for Nature, adopted by the United Nations General Assembly in October 1982. The Charter proposed 'to consolidate and extend relevant legal principles in a new charter to guide state behaviour in the transition to sustainable development' – sustainable development being defined as development that meets the needs of the present without compromising the ability of future generations to meet their own needs. But it was not until the Rio Declaration of 1992 that the term emerged as a common 'green' language which evokes sympathy from the leaders of the North and South alike, environmental movements, and international business executives.

One of the objectives of the Declaration was to promote 'sustainable and environmentally sound development in all countries'. The concept is particularly attractive to the South because of the realization among international leaders that sustained economic growth and development in developing countries requires the support of the international community. The role of the multinational corporations (as agents of economic transformation) in this process is very critical if this noble objective is to be achieved. Thus, the declaration puts further pressure on managers of multinational corporations. How they respond to this challenge remains to be seen. It is, none the less, expected that consumers will escalate the pressure on multinational corporations. As Faith Popcorn (1992) puts it, the consumers, in future, will want to know who you are before buying what you sell. Who you are will mean publicly stating your environmental policy.

HEALTH AND SAFETY ISSUES IN INTERNATIONAL BUSINESS

Allied to the debate on the environment are health and safety issues in international business. Accidents such as the *Exxon Valdez* in Alaska in 1988 and the Valujet air crash in May 1996 in the USA have left the public wondering whether firms are putting profit before safety. Firms have a responsibility to safeguard the safety of their employees, customers and the public in the course of their operations. Specific areas which have come under the close scrutiny of pressure groups include pollution from factory and automobile emissions, discharge of untreated sewage into the sea and the transport of hazardous products such as nuclear wastes.

Although there are wide ranging controls in place for these activities, enforcement is a matter of national prerogative. It is, however, worth stressing that the existing international conventions are still not legally enforceable. The government's determination and will to enforce environmental regulations are the most important instruments in countries where there is strict adherence to stipulated standards. The economic impact of regulatory regimes is normally an important consideration for governments. A number of approaches are being applied by western governments to encourage firms to adopt technologies and processes that are environmentally sound. Perhaps the most popular measure is what is generally known as the market-based approach. It includes fees, hybrid deposit–refund systems, and information disclosure requirements. A fee can be attached to each unit of emissions, effectively forcing the emitter to absorb the costs that the emissions impose on the society. Each emitter will be expected to reduce emissions to the point where its marginal cost of control becomes as expensive as paying the fee. Similarly, the deposit–refund system is like a fee with a rebate – those who generate a waste or purchase a product, must pay a deposit on the item, and when they deliver the item to a designated collection point for proper handling, they receive a refund. In the case of information disclosure, there is a requirement on the industry to report information about risks. Such data may include the quantity and content of discharges into the environment. It is expected that requiring a source to inform a local community of its toxic discharges will encourage the source to reduce those discharges. Requiring a firm to inform workers of risks they may face on the job – risks they may not have been aware of – can create a job market in which workers make informed choices.

There are indications to suggest that firms are now facing up to the challenge for environmental sanity with interest and commitment. The extent to which this new enthusiasm can be sustained depends largely on the economics of implementation.

ETHICS IN INTERNATIONAL BUSINESS

Ethics is concerned with principles of good conduct. In a complex field such as international business, the conduct of multinational firms is a

---

EXHIBIT 10.1

Shell searches its soul during troubled times

Royal Dutch Shell's management has succeeded in keeping a remarkably low profile in recent months considering the glare of publicity caused by the Brent Spar fiasco and the Ken Saro-Wiwa affair in Nigeria.

In a recent interview to the *Financial Times*, the President of Shell, Mr. Cor Herkstroter, admitted that the uproar over *Brent Spar* came as a surprise because Shell was convinced it was doing the right thing in trying to dump the installation in the North Atlantic. 'But we have learnt that there is a difference between feeling that you are right, and being perceived to be right. You have to take account of the views of the public and politicians. Those are not hard facts, they are things that move.'

Nigeria was different. Unlike the operational issues raised by *Brent Spar*, vital interests were at stake. Shell resisted public pressure to abandon a planned investment project after the execution of Ken Saro-Wiwa, the Ogoni activist. 'We want a constructive solution. Leaving Nigeria doesn't get you there. It is much more constructive to stay there and do the right things, such as reconciliation.' Shell has offered to clean up oil spills and reactivate community projects in Ogoniland if its staff were allowed back safely. But it is insisting all political factions support any agreement.

Had Nigeria and *Brent Spar* done lasting damage to Shell? Mr Herkstroter thinks not. 'But all this helped us to think about communication. We have to explain, to seek advice, to test opinions.'

Discussion questions

1. Why was public opinion an important factor in the decision not dump *Brent Spar* in North Atlantic?

Source: Adapted from *Financial Times*, 10 May 1996. p. 24.

---

subject of considerable interest to home and host countries, opinion leaders, consumers and environmentalists. Should international firms be allowed to adopt different standards in dealing with home and host markets? Should home governments ignore the conduct of their firms in international markets? Should profitability be placed before social responsibility? Is it ethically acceptable for multinational firms to promote materialism in traditional societies where materialism is alien? These are important questions regarding the conduct of multinational firms that need to be considered.

Bribery and extortion

One of the dilemmas which international business managers have to deal with relates the giving and receiving of business gifts. There is nothing unusual or new about business gifts; they have existed for as long as the concept of business itself. Gifts can be used to express mutual respect and appreciation in a business relationship and may take the form of entertainment and presents, particularly on special occasions such as birthdays and anniversaries. However, concerns have been expressed over the influence of 'gifts' on competition for business contracts. Thus, the following questions are pertinent in addressing the issue of business gifts. When is it ethically correct to give or accept business gifts? When does a business gift become bribe? When is it likely to be labelled as extortion? The answer to these questions lies in the motive of the person presenting the gift is.

Mahoney (1995) suggests that, in handling business entertainment and gifts, two fundamental questions need to be near the front of one's mind, quite apart from the obvious ones about not infringing the law or stated company policy. First, try to be quite clear about the motive behind the offering, which may not be good for one's self-esteem. The second is a sober realization of how one's power or influence may be solicited or expected in return for favours received. In some markets, giving and receiving gifts are an important part of the business culture and practice, particularly as a way expressing respect and friendship for business associates. In other markets, such expectations may be a well-entrenched part of the business culture. In that case, expectation of gifts becomes extortion rather than bribery. For example, in some countries, businesses are expected to contribute generously to the ruling parties as a guarantee of securing government contracts. Between 1990 and 1994, three successive governments in Japan collapsed as a result of corruption and bribery scandals. In October 1995, Willy Claes, the then Secretary-General of NATO, was forced to quit his post when he was indicted for accepting cash from Italian helicopter manufacturers on behalf of his party when he was Belgian finance minister, in return for a business favour. In 1995 South Korea was rocked by bribery scandal following the arrest, detention and subsequent confession of ex-President Roh Tae-Woo that he took bribes to the tune of US$400 million when he was president in return for business favours to big companies.

In extreme cases, 'protection money' is demanded. This practice was rife in Northern Ireland between 1970 and 1990, in post-communist Russia and in Italy. Although these practices are illegal, most host governments either pretend they are not happening or look the other way instead of taking decisive steps to stop them.

In markets where the practice is subtle, the difficulty is that in most cases, genuine business gifts and giving bribes to secure business favours are separated only by a very thin line. In recent years, most businesses with extensive global interests and operations have had to introduce policies on business gifts. These may include:

- outright refusal;
- declaring anything received in a designated register;
- insistence on giving or receiving only gifts of nominal value.

In the United States, the Congress requires that all firms and individuals lobbying on behalf of foreign governments and companies must register such interests and declare how much they are receiving for such services. In the United Kingdom, the lobby system is not so well developed. Members of Parliament are, none the less, required by parliamentary rules to register gifts and declare their business and consultancy interests outside their parliamentary work. In 1995 two Conservative Members of Parliament accepted cash to ask questions on behalf of a company during a parliamentary Question Time. The 'cash gift' was not declared or registered in the Members' Register of Interests, and the two MPs were duly suspended from parliamentary proceedings for a period of time. Similarly, in December 1995 Peter Davies, the Regulator of the National Lottery in the United Kingdom, came under considerable pressure to resign from his position after admitting accepting corporate hospitality and free flights from the US-based G-Tech – a major shareholder in Britain's lottery operator, Camelot.

These developments will no doubt heighten the calls for some form of regulatory business ethics by both home and host countries. Bribery scandals in the 1970s generated similar calls. It is noteworthy that the Lockheed bribery scandals in the USA in the 1970s provided the immediate impetus for the promulgation of the Foreign Corrupt Practices Act (1977) by the US Congress. This Act made it unlawful for American citizens to offer bribes to overseas officials. While the intentions of the legislation is wholly honourable, it has not succeeded in eliminating corruption in America's corporate culture. Indeed, most international business executives believe that bribery is universal as it is an entrenched part of international business culture.

SUMMARY

This chapter has examined the complex and changing nature of the issue of corporate responsibility in a dynamic business environment. Recent business disasters such as Bhopal and the *Piper Alpha* and environmental degradation in various parts of the world have generated many concerns about the activities of multinational corporations, raising accusations of double standards, lack of commitment to social responsibility and downright abuse of their considerable powers and influence in host countries. The chapter has also touched on the thorny issue of bribery and corruption in international business. A consistent theme to emerge from this chapter is the fact that, in future, the survival of firms will depend on their public image on social and environmental responsibilities.

DISCUSSION QUESTIONS

1. Examine the argument that there is no future for firms that fail to recognize their environmental responsibilities.
2. What is corporate governance? Examine the factors that have led to intense interest in the concept of corporate governance.
3. Describe the duties of the board of directors.
4. What is the relevance of the concept of sustainable development to social responsibility in global management?

REFERENCES

Cannon, T. 1994: *Corporate Responsibility*. London: Pitman Publishing.
Mahoney, J. 1995: 'Gifts, grease and graft', *Financial Times – Mastering Management Series*. Part 7, December 1995, p. 8.

Maw, N. G., Lord Lane of Horsell and Craig-Cooper, M 1994: *Maw on Corporate Governance*. Aldershot: Dartmouth Publishing.

Popcorn, Faith 1992: *The Popcorn Report*. New York: Harper Business.

Sands, P. 1993: *Greening International Law*. London: Earthscan Publications.

Tricker, R. I. 1994: *International Corporate Governance*. London: Prentice-Hall.

United Nations General Assembly Resolution 37/7 (1982), UN Doc. A/37/51.

World Commission on Environment and Development 1987: *Our Common Future*. Oxford: Oxford University Press.

11

Implementing and controlling multinational business strategy

INTRODUCTION

The implementation and control of business strategy are the most complex part of multinational business management. It is the efficiency and effectiveness with which these are handled that will determine whether the operation will be a success or failure. Implementing strategy entails the identification of key tasks to be performed, establishing critical success factors, and the setting of control procedures to monitor performance to ensure that any drift from the strategic plan is detected and corrected as soon as it occurs. In this chapter, we examine the range of issues that are critical to successful implementation and control of global business strategy.

IMPLEMENTING GLOBAL STRATEGY

Strategy implementation is the process by which strategies and policies are put into action, through the development of programmes, budgets and procedures. It is the sum total of the activities and choices required for the execution of a plan (Wheelen and Hunger, 1989). Strategy implementation cannot commence until the following issues have been determined. (1) The people who will implement the plan; their qualifications, previous experience, and training relevant to strategy implementation. It is important to recognize that implementing a multinational strategy is considerably more complex and difficult than in a domestic operation. (2) Tasks that must be undertaken in order achieve the desired results, contingency plans for unforeseen factors, and consideration for the uncontrollable external factors. (3) The method of operation such as the location of authority and control mechanisms necessary to minimize deviations from the planned action.

Strategy implementation has to conform to a set of systems which should have been addressed initially when the pros and cons of strategic alternatives were analysed. Jain (1990) suggests that three types of systems are needed – execution systems, monitoring systems, and control systems. He defines these systems as follows:

- Execution systems focus directly on the basic processes for conducting the firm's business. They include systems that enable products to be designed, supplies to be ordered, production scheduled, goods shipped, cash applied or employees paid.
- Monitoring systems are any procedures that measure and assess the basic processes. They can be designed to gather information in different ways to serve a number of internal or external reporting purposes: to meet regulatory requirements, to control budgets, to pay taxes, and to serve the strategic and organizational intent of the company.
- Control systems are the means through which processes are made to conform or are kept within tolerable limits. At the broadest level, they include separation of duties, authority limits, product inspection and plan submittals.

Unless these systems are designed properly, and their implementation supported by top management, the best planned strategy may not achieve its desired results. It is, therefore, not surprising that in a survey of company presidents and divisional managers by Alexander (1985), the following problems were revealed in order of frequency of occurrence:

1. more time needed for implementation than originally planned;
2. unanticipated major problems;
3. ineffective coordination of activities;
4. crises that distracted attention away from implementation;
5. insufficient capabilities of the employees involved;
6. inadequate training and instruction of lower-level employees;
7. uncontrollable external environmental factors;
8. inadequate leadership and direction by departmental managers;
9. poor definition of key implementation tasks and activities;
10. inadequate monitoring of activities by the information system.

ORGANIZATIONAL CONFIGURATION

The role of organizational configuration in the effective management of a multinational operation has been examined in chapter 8. The structure of an organization determines the relationships among the various parts, between the parts and the organization as a whole, and between the organization and its environment. In addition, it consists of a number of building blocks and coordinating mechanisms such as the location of authority for strategic and tactical (operational) decisions, method of communicating decisions, and means of enforcement of decisions (maintenance of control). Together, these elements make up the detailed configuration of an organization. The choice of a configuration to support an effective global operation depends among other things on the following:

- the international orientation of the firm (ethnocentric, polycentric, regiocentric and geocentric) and the relative importance of foreign and domestic market as perceived by management;
- the nature of the planning process in the firm;
- the volume of business generated overseas by the subsidiaries;
- the degree of diversity of the product;
- the operating structure of the firm, such as degree of divisional autonomy, division size, basis for divisional organization (region, function, product, customer, or process).

Thus, effective organizational design requires the skilful application of internal division of work, internal control and coordination, and the management of relations with the external environment. Effectiveness depends on the fit between the organization's part and processes that structural design determines. What needs to be done (the task) and how it gets done (the process) can be either facilitated or hindered, depending on the structure of this interaction (Ronen, 1986).

THE LOCATION OF AUTHORITY

The key debate on the location of decision-making authority in multinational enterprises centres on centralization versus decentralization. The degree of centralization of the decision-making process in an organization is determined by the extent to which directives are passed down from the headquarters. On the other hand, decentralization reflects the extent to which management is prepared to delegate some of the decision-making responsibilities to the subsidiaries. Ronen (1986) suggests that the degree of centralization and decentralization required in an organization is a function of the dynamic balance of controlling forces on one side and diversity and complexity on the other. Thus, the primary concern is how to maintain responsiveness, yet also provide coordination and control.

In highly centralized organizations, top management at headquarters tends to provide an autocratic style of leadership; it makes the decisions, communicates from headquarters to the subsidiaries, plans and sets goals at the highest levels, and exercises control (e.g. of budgets, performances, etc.). Centralization offers a number of important benefits to an enterprise. These would include:

- greater conformance to corporate goals and policies;
- better rationalization and utilization of resources;
- elimination of unnecessary duplication of functions, leading to greater cost-effectiveness; and
- easy to locate lines of authority and responsibilities.

As most multinational enterprises impose a direct and central control over their international affiliates, it is necessary to recognize that centralized control must be weighed against the lack of whole-hearted support for rationalizing systems experienced by a number of companies when local management feels its share of influence is limited or its achievement downgraded (Aylmer, 1973).

Discussions on decentralization are often focused on the premise that managers at the subsidiaries have a better understanding of the conditions in the countries in which they operate, than any one on the corporate or even regional level. Perhaps the best argument for decentralization is that decision-making occurs closest to the operation and environment, thus, enhancing flexibility, adaptability and timely decision-making. Other advantages include the following:

- It serves as a way of giving managers at subsidiary level, a sense of responsibility.
- It assists in training and developing managers for higher roles at the headquarters.
- Subsidiaries can operate with greater flexibility and speed, without unnecessary referrals to the corporate headquarters.

Other considerations include the degree to which operations are inter-related. Conglomerates tend to have fewer central controls, while firms

---

EXHIBIT 11.1

Rogue trader's boss fights to clear his name

Ron Baker, the former Barings executive charged with failing to exercise proper management controls over Nick Leeson, the rogue trader who broke the bank with debts of £830 million, is fighting to clear his name before a tribunal. The Securities and Futures Authority, the watchdog for brokers and futures dealers, has proposed to ban Mr Baker from senior City registers for three years. Mr Baker who was recruited to Barings from Bankers Trusts in April 1992 to head the corporate fixed income department, could also face having to pay thousands of pounds in costs.

Mr Baker has consistently maintained that he had no direct responsibility for any of Leeson's trading activities on the Far East money markets until 1 January, 1995, just weeks before the UK's oldest merchant bank collapsed and was rescued by ING, the Dutch banking and insurance group. Nick Leeson is currently serving a six-year jail term in Singapore.

Discussion questions

1. Why was Nick Leeson able to incur such trading losses without the knowledge of any of his superiors?
2. Explain why Mr Baker is being charged for failing to exercise effective management control over Leeson's activities in the Far East.

---

with a smaller number of foreign operations tend to have more centralized authority (Ronen, 1986). Rapidly changing or shifting markets also require greater decentralization of decision-making to ensure timely responses to opportunities and threats.

METHODS FOR COMMUNICATING DECISIONS

Multinational enterprises have a vast array of methods for communicating decisions to and receiving feedback from their global operations. Choices include the company journal, conferences and personal visits of top management to outposts. Increasingly a number of enterprises are relying on the electronic movement of data across national boundaries. This has been made possible by rapid adoption of advanced technological innovations in telecommunications and computers in industrialized countries. The choice of methods for communicating decisions has to be viewed within the context of their costs and effectiveness relative to other methods. Robinson (1978) offers a few guidelines on communicating decisions:

- All decisions made by a level higher than that implementing the decision, however the decision may be communicated initially, should be committed to writing (except those felt to be politically and/or legally vulnerable).
- Visits by decision-making authorities or their representatives should be on a regular periodic basis, not occasioned exclusively by crisis situations.
- Periodic conferences of key personnel of similar functions from both domestic and foreign operations are of great utility in developing universally valid strategies and in the delegation of tactical decisions to lower levels.
- Management training and development assumes greater importance for foreign operations because of the differences in cultural backgrounds, in the meaning of management, in the status of managers, and in the sources of management recruitment as one moves from one national society to another. Such training facilitates both the decentralization of decision-making authority and improvement in the quality and effectiveness of those decisions made at higher organizational levels.
- Periodic rotation of overseas managers to regional or corporate headquarters may be one of the most effective ways of communicating overall corporate goals and the rationale for corporate strategy, including the degree of control retained at each level.

MANAGING CULTURAL DIVERSITY

One of the most difficult problems in multinational operations relates to the question of how to manage cultural diversity in an enterprise, particularly at subsidiary level. The issue of cultural diversity in the workplace is highly sensitive and offers a variety of challenges to managers. Cultural diversity, at the simplest level, reflects the characteristics that may make one individual culturally different from another. Cultural diversity includes differences in race, ethnicity, national origin, language and religion (Ansari and Jackson, 1995).

Effective management of cultural diversity can mean changes to the working environment. In most cases, senior executives 'pretend' that appropriate steps are being taken simply by insisting that the enterprise offers the same treatment to all its staff, regardless of their ethnic or nationality background. Unfortunately, this 'culture-blind' attitude style represents a negative approach to the effective management of cultural diversity at the workplace; other approaches are required. Ansari and Jackson suggest that a diverse approach will recognize and respect differences in culture, and treat people in ways which bring out the best in them.

Although multinational companies are beginning to display some sensitivity to host country culture, headquarters executives still have to wrestle with one fundamental question. Should the management of the subsidiary be based on home or host country culture? There is evidence to suggest that multinational firms continue to encourage a monocultural workplace by ignoring cultural diversity. In her paper, Schneider (1988) argues that multinational companies are increasingly interested in promoting corporate culture to improve control, coordination and integration of their subsidiaries. Yet these subsidiaries are embedded in local national cultures wherein the underlying basic assumptions about people and the world may differ from that of national and corporate culture of the multinational.

The solution to the problem of cultural diversity does not lie in a simple either/or choice between home and host country cultures. Multinational enterprises will do better with a simple recognition of the benefits of cultural diversity at the workplace. But adoption of a consistent and monocultural approach to management by the multinational enterprises demonstrates, at best, a lack of understanding and appreciation of the benefits of effective management of cultural diversity at the workplace. At worst, it represents a determination to maintain a belief in the superiority of the home-country and corporate culture.

MANAGING CHANGE

With the ever-changing global economic and political environment, executives of multinational enterprises are now learning to cope with the specific problem of managing in a dynamic environment. Although a full discussion on the complex nature of management of change is beyond the scope of this book, it merits some examination. What is change management? Change management is not a distinct discipline with rigid and clearly defined boundaries. Rather, the theory and practice of change management draws on a number of social science disciplines and traditions (Burnes, 1992). Similarly, the theory borrows from a number of behavioural schools of thought. Burnes summarized the main theoretical underpinning of change management as follows:

- The individual perspective school: this focuses on the individual as the unit of analysis of organizational change. Its supporters believe that an individual's behaviour is the product of environment and reason. One of the basic principles of focusing on the behaviour of the individual is that it is believed that human actions are conditioned by their expected consequences. Behaviour that is rewarded tends to be repeated, and behaviour that is punished tends not to be. Therefore in order to change behaviour, it is necessary to change the conditions of which it is a function.
- The group dynamics school emphasizes bringing about organizational change through teams or work groups, rather than individuals. The rationale behind this is that because people in organizations work in groups, individual behaviour must be seen, modified or changed in the light of prevailing group practices and norm. Therefore, to bring about change, it is useless to concentrate on changing the behaviour of individuals. The individual in isolation is constrained by group pressures to conform. The focus of change must be at the group level and should concentrate on influencing and changing the group's norms, roles and values.
- The open systems school: this school sees organizations as composed of a number of interconnected subsystems. It follows that any change to any part of the system will have an impact on the other parts of the system, and in turn, on its overall performance. The objective of the open systems approach is to structure the functions of a business in such a manner that, through clearly defined lines of coordination and interdependence, the overall business objectives are collectively pursued. The emphasis is on achieving overall synergy, rather than on optimizing the performance of any one individual part *per se*.

The connecting thread through the various schools of thought is the behavioural change which is central to any organizational change.

Emphasizing the relevance of behavioural change, Burnes explains that to change anything requires the cooperation and consent of the groups and individuals who make up an organization, for it is only through their behaviour that the structures, technologies, systems and procedures of an organization move from being abstract concepts to concrete realities. However, effective management of change goes beyond the understanding of the agents of change. It requires an extensive analysis of the objective(s) of change, the process, the impact of any change on both the individuals and organization, and the impact of the external the environment on the change process.

For change management to be successful, the following guidelines are proposed by Burnes (1992):

- Change projects need to be considered in relation to the strategic requirements of an organization.
- Change should be planned and implemented in phases.
- Those most closely affected should be involved to make free and informed choices in order to gain their commitment.
- To be successful, change projects must allow those involved to make free and informed choices in order to gain their commitment.
- Individuals and groups will need to alter their behaviour if successful change is to be achieved.
- Cultural change is a necessary part of any change project.

These guidelines are particularly useful for multinational enterprises entering foreign markets by acquisition of existing businesses with set norms and practices. Changes in management philosophy and style, organizational culture and work practices are inevitable for companies that are absorbed into a larger global organization. Managing change in a multinational setting must recognize the issues raised under the section on managing cultural diversity at the workplace.

EVALUATION AND CONTROL

As multinational firms continue to spread the network and scope of their activities around the world, there is a need for an effective and continuous monitoring of these activities in order to ensure that the strategy is implemented as intended. Objectives may not be achieved unless adequate control mechanisms are in place. Control may be defined simply as the relationship and devices designed to assure that strategy (or policy) decisions are made by designated authority in conformance with corporate goals; that tactical (or operating) decisions conform to the selected strategies; and that actual operations are in harmony (Robinson, 1978). An effective control strategy must set out a system and pattern of information flow as well as the location of authority to ensure that there is an understanding of and harmony in the international operations of the firm. Such criteria should include not only revenue, profitability and other financial measures but also strategic control and the effect of its activities on the host country.

Financial control

Financial measures are the most effective and widely used techniques for evaluating the international performance of a firm. These include return on investment (ROI), budget analysis and historical comparisons. Daniels and Radebaugh (1987) suggest that the use of ROI as an evaluative measure for the performance of international subsidiaries may be inappropriate because of foreign currencies, different rates of inflation, different tax laws and the use of transfer pricing. Thus, both the net income figure and the investment base may be seriously distorted. Such a problem may be minimized by using other techniques that are more flexible and perhaps different from those used for domestic operation. Multi-domestic multinational corporations should use loose controls with their foreign units. The management of each geographic unit should be given considerable operational latitude, but be expected to meet some performance targets such as market share, productivity, public image, employee morale, and relationship with the host-country government (Wheelen and Hunger, 1989).

Strategic control

The design of the strategic control techniques in multinational enterprises should reflect the definition of business units and their expected contribution to the overall global objective. For the purposes of this discussion on strategic control, it is important to note the differences in approach between multinational and global corporations. On the one hand, multinational enterprises operate in each country with locally defined strategies and organizational structures. On the other hand, global enterprises operate with an integrated global strategy and are known to derive competitive advantage through coordination of an adopted strategy in all their international operations.

According to Dyment (1987), questions such as who earns profit, how much was earned, and whether this was the planned result, although important, reflect a standard approach to management control. He argues that in today's world of rapid communications, intensive competition and dynamic technological change, a different approach to management control is needed. A radically different approach is needed. Dyment contends that the global enterprise needs a system that measures and rewards performance on the basis of achieving strategic objectives that cross national borders, including the gains that come from intelligent selection of where in the world each value-added component should be located. He suggests that:

- For MNEs, the domestic information system (standard costs, monthly budgets, long-range plan and strategic plan) is modified to meet the legal and managerial situation of operating in a number of countries. These modifications usually reporting requirements for each country's fiscal and tax authorities and national budgets and five-year plans, against which actual results are compared. These plans and results may be forwarded to regional and international headquarters where they are analysed, additional information is often requested, and summary reports are prepared.
- Global enterprises have needs that are different from those of multinationals. The strategic information needed by global enterprises *must* cross international borders. The global enterprise executive must make economic decisions involving all aspects of the value-added chain from research and development, through manufacturing to distribution, with an integrated worldwide strategy.

Control of overseas operations has traditionally generated a lot of tension and disagreement between headquarters and the subsidiaries. There seems to be a perennial conflict in the understanding of what constitutes reasonable reporting requirements on the subsidiary managers. For example, Skinner (1968) observes that the headquarters executives feel frustrated by possessing a sense of responsibility which is thwarted by having 'only paper authority' over the field operations. He identifies headquarters executives' concerns as:

- the long time lag to get information from the field;
- decision-making at subsidiary level without adequate or proper consultation with headquarters;

- subsidiary executives tend to become 'too localized' to have global vision.

On the other hand, subsidiary executives often accuse headquarters staff of:

- undue interference and involvement in decisions that can be better made by those closer to the operation;
- inadequate delegation of authority;
- imposing onerous reporting requirements;
- excessive delay in obtaining getting headquarters to respond to simple requests from outposts;
- lack of understanding and sympathy from headquarters.
- excluding subsidiary executives in making decisions concerning the activities of the subsidiaries.

Although the conflicts between headquarters and subsidiaries may be a perennial one for multinational enterprises, it is highly unlikely that they will constitute a significant issue with a more integrated global strategy and coordination. MNEs must employ a better strategic control system, while at the same time recognizing the differences in the characteristics of the markets in which the subsidiaries operate. Similarly, subsidiary executives need to understand that they are a part of a bigger multinational organization. According to Skinner (1968), though the headquarters executives may hold the ultimate power to replace the overseas executive, 'this extreme action was not only distasteful but an impractical weapon because of their genuine problem in knowing enough of what went on abroad'. Skinner distinguished between headquarters' 'involvement' in overseas operations and the degree of 'command' exercised over those operations. By the former term, he refers to the functions performed by headquarters; by the latter term, to the 'how' of headquarters' involvement, from non-participant observation to a detailed reporting system and specific orders for conformance.

SUMMARY

The effectiveness with which multinational business strategy is implemented and controlled is the key factor in determining whether the strategy succeeds or not. In this chapter, it has been shown that the implementation of a multinational business strategy is a complex process which entails the identification of the key tasks to be performed, establishing critical success factors, and the setting of control procedures to monitor performance in order to ensure that any drift from the strategic plan is detected and corrected as soon as it occurs. In particular, the chapter has shown that:

- The best planned strategy may not achieve the desired results if it is not supported by adequate and relevant systems.
- The structure of an organization determines the relationships among the various parts, between the parts and the whole organization, and between the organization and its environment.
- The debate on the location of decision-making authority in multinational enterprises centres on centralization versus decentralization.
- The choice of methods for communicating decisions between headquarters and subsidiaries depends on their costs and effectiveness.
- Effective management of cultural diversity requires an approach which recognizes and respects differences as the key to bringing out the best in people.
- For multinational enterprises, there needs to be an understanding of the differences in the characteristics of global markets.
- Different control techniques are required for multinational and global enterprises.

DISCUSSION QUESTIONS

1. 'The effectiveness with which multinational business strategy is implemented and controlled is the key factor in determining whether the strategy succeeds or not.' Discuss.
2. Evaluate the arguments for the devolution of authority to subsidiary executives.
3. Critically examine the factors affecting the structural configuration of an enterprise.
4. Why might corporate goals be important in determining the degree of control retained by corporate headquarters over foreign subsidiaries?
5. Define cultural diversity. What approaches would you recommend for the effective management of cultural diversity at the workplace?

6. Examine the differences between strategic and financial control in international business.
7. What are the sources of conflict between headquarters and subsidiary executives?

REFERENCES

Alexander, L. D. 1985: 'Successfully implementing strategic decisions', *Long Range Planning*, June, pp. 90–102.

Ansari, K. H. and Jackson, J. 1995: *Managing Cultural Diversity at the Workplace*. London: Kogan Page.

Aylmer, R. J. 1973: 'Global marketing in the multinational corporations', in H. B. Thorelli and H. Becker (eds.), *International Marketing Strategy*. London: Penguin Books.

Burnes, B. 1992: *Managing Change: A Strategic Approach to Organisational Development and Renewal*. London: Pitman Publishing.

Daniels, J. D. and Radebaugh, L. H. 1987: *International Business: Environments and Operations*, 4th edn. Reading, MA: Addison-Wesley.

Dyment, J. J. 1987: 'Strategies and management controls for global corporations', *The Journal of Business Strategy*, Vol. 7, pp. 20–6.

Jain, S. C. 1990: *Marketing Planning and Strategy*, 3rd edn. Cincinnati, OH: South-Western Publishing.

Robinson, R. D. 1978: *International Business Management: A Guide to Decision Making*. 2nd edn. Hinsdale, IL: The Dryden Press.

Ronen, S. 1986: *Comparative and Multinational Management*. New York: John Wiley.

Schneider, S. C. 1988: 'National versus corporate culture: implications for human resource management', *Human Resource Management*, Vol. 27, No. 2, pp. 231–46.

Skinner, C. W. 1968: *American Industry in Developing Economies: The Management of International Manufacturing*. New York: Wiley and Sons.

Wheelen, T. L. and Hunger, J. D. 1989: *Strategic Management and Business Policy*, 3rd edn. Reading, MA: Addison-Wesley.

12

The future of multinational business

INTRODUCTION

The aim of this chapter is to examine the nature of the relationship between the MNEs and host countries. In doing so, it evaluates the impact of direct investment on the host country and the sources of conflict between the two parties. The main sources of conflict between the MNEs and host countries are identified as stemming from the technology transfer effect of direct investment, the influence of MNEs on sovereignty of the host country, accusations of cultural imperialism by the MNEs, and conflicts over equity ownership. Finally, the future of multinational business in the new world order is discussed. The impact of the so-called Third World multinationals and the contribution of the emerging economies in the new world economic order are analysed.

MNE AND HOST COUNTRY RELATIONSHIPS

As MNEs grow and spread across the world, most countries, especially the less developed ones, want to have the many benefits an MNE can bring: technology transfer, employment opportunities, tax revenues, and the opportunity for domestic business enterprises to build a partnership with powerful and well-connected foreign-based companies (Wheelen and Hunger, 1989). The downside of having multinationals in host countries is the financial drain of their presence through tax evasion and repatriation of profits. Wheelen and Hunger suggest that the host country has two choices to make: it can either allow the MNE to repatriate its profits to corporate headquarters – thereby draining the nation of potential investment capital; or it can allow the MNE to repatriate only a small portion of its profits – thereby making the country unattractive to other MNEs. It is, therefore, essential to examine the costs and benefits of regulations on the flow of inward direct investments.

It is the pros and cons of the presence of the MNEs in a host country that determine the kind of relationship that can be expected. Such relationships may be positive or negative. In a positive relationship, both the MNE and host country find accommodation for each other and strive to ensure that the presence of the MNE in the country brings about mutual benefits for all concerned. With a negative relationship, the objective on each side is to extract maximum benefit at the expense of the other. The sources of potential benefits and conflicts between MNEs and host nations are discussed in the subsequent sections.

Technology transfer effect

Although the technology transfer effect of direct investments by MNEs in a host country was discussed in chapter 7, it is sufficiently important to merit reiteration. The issue of technology transfer is a major source of conflict between MNEs and host countries, particularly the less developed ones. The abstract and proprietary nature of technology creates an atmosphere of mystery about it and can make its transfer a very complex issue (Monye, 1996b). The role of technology in economic development is well recognized and not contentious. It is the nature, motive and manner of its transfer that cause some degree of uneasiness in host countries.

Developing countries believe that MNEs have no regard for the concept of appropriate technology which host countries desire. These countries believe that in order to maximize the benefit of technology transfers, 'controls' are often applied on the conduct of MNEs and in particular, regulate the process and content of technology transfers. For the MNEs, the possession of firm-specific advantages in product or process technology is potentially the most important source of bargaining power.

Successful transfer of technology takes place when the need and motivation for such a transfer are felt by both transferee and transferor. For the transferor, the extent of the motivation will depend on its corporate desire to achieve, expand or defend an advantage, such as gaining or retaining access to materials, markets, manpower or other productive resources by instituting a presence in a host country. Host country motivation emanates from the desire to achieve economic development and enhanced material prosperity. In most cases, the development of an economy capable of satisfying a broad range of consumer demand is seen as a matter of national prestige, and the more advanced the product, the greater that prestige.

Thus, MNEs tend to exploit this desire for national prestige. The perceived importance of technology in a host country can be more important than its actual value and provides the MNEs with the opportunity to extract maximum benefits from any transfer negotiation (Monye, 1996b). But the relative bargaining power of the host country and the MNE has usually determined the outcome of transfer negotiations.

Sovereignty effect

A major source of tension between MNEs and host countries concerns the perceived impact of the presence of multinationals on the political and economic independence of the host nation. It is believed that because MNEs are financially independent with considerable size and influence, they cannot be controlled by the host countries. Moreover, concerns are often expressed that MNEs have the capacity to influence the direction of the host country's economic policy, thereby jeopardizing its sovereignty. Indeed, this point can be illustrated with the now too familiar case of ITT in Chile in the early 1970s. In this case, it was alleged that the CIA and ITT collaborated to topple Salvador Allende's government in 1973.

It is also feared that MNEs may lend themselves to being used by the home country government as agents in the conduct of its foreign policy. For example, the US government attempted to block the French from building their own nuclear capability by prohibiting IBM from selling the much needed equipment (Ronen, 1986).

Hood and Young (1979) suggest that it is difficult to establish criteria for judging the impact of the MNE on national sovereignty or autonomy. But it is recognized that greater foreign investment will increase the difficulties of host governments in pursuing independent policies. Hood and Young contend that the problems arise essentially because of the differences between the objectives of the multinational firm and the objectives of the host government. But for most host governments, the sovereignty of the nation cannot be compromised, and thus underscores the need to maintain their autonomy and exert influence over the activities of the MNEs.

Cultural imperialism

Multinationals are often accused of being agents of cultural change in host countries. These changes are most noticeable in lifestyles, consumer products and international advertising campaigns. In most traditional societies, multinationals are accused of exploiting advances in telecommunications systems to promote materialism, which is regarded as a symbol of the capitalist economic system.

The cultural damage to a nation resulting from rapid changes in lifestyle will continue to inspire strong negative feelings of outrage in a number of developing countries with rigid traditional values and, understandably, MNEs receive the blame. Often, such negative feelings tend to provide justification for taking strong actions against certain marketing activities of the multinationals such as bans on advertising campaigns promoting 'Western culture' at the expense of national values.

But with the increasing globalization of economic activities, cultural change in traditional societies is bound to continue. As Levitt (1983) argues, technology is a powerful force driving the world towards a converging commonality. He suggests that it has made isolated places and impoverished peoples eager for the allure of modernity, and almost everyone everywhere wants all the things they have heard about, seen, or experienced via the new technologies.

Conflict over equity ownership

Hymer (1960) emphasized that *control* is one of the factors that will motivate a firm to engage in direct rather than portfolio investment. Effective control of overseas subsidiaries can only be achieved with the ownership of the operation. Although control of a subsidiary can be effected without 100 per cent or even majority equity ownership, a substantial equity ownership offers the parent company a sense of security for its investment, and the freedom to influence the strategic direction and the day-to-day management of the operation. In effect, a strong equity base offers a certain guarantee that the parent company has the right to control the seats on the board and allocate human and other resources as it sees fit. In countries with stringent regulations governing the day-to-day conduct of foreign firms, effective control of the management of the subsidiary enables the parent company to circumvent certain rules such as repatriation of profits with transfer pricing.

From the host country's standpoint, 100 per cent or majority equity ownership by the parent company is unacceptable as it is not perceived to be in the interest of the country. The amount of equity controlled is often directly proportional to the control a developing country exerts over the company's action. Because the company's actions affect its economic development, equity control becomes an effective means of subordinating the MNE's actions to the national development plan (Ronen, 1986). The 1970s and early 1980s saw a raft of legislation in most developing countries designed to minimize the share of equity controlled by MNEs operating in those countries.

The loss of equity control and the influence for effective management of subsidiaries meant that MNEs began to consider alternative methods of servicing foreign markets. Consequently, the 1970s and 1980s witnessed a sharp increase in the popularity of international technology licensing and the franchising of trademarks and brand names (Monye, 1996a). However, as direct investments dried up, and with the structural adjustment programme embarked upon by most of these developing countries, limits on equity ownership are now being removed as incentives to attract FDI and regenerate ailing economies.

THE FUTURE OF MULTINATIONAL BUSINESS

International business as we know it today has come a long way. In chapter 1 it was shown that international production and the development of MNEs is rather a recent phenomenon. This is not to be confused with the history and development of international trade. It is remarkable that Hymer's 1960 work was the first attempt to explain why firms may engage in international production rather than invest abroad through the portfolio option. Earlier theories of international production concentrated on the behaviour of the US firms as units of analysis – understandable, given that American industrial capacity remained intact after the war, unlike that of most European and Asian countries. This post-war economic reality provided US firms with an advantage in terms of international development and expansion. As economic domination often leads to political domination, the rapid expansion of American MNEs raised fears in many nations that the United States might dominate the world economically (Ronen, 1986). In his book *The American Challenge*, Servan-Schreiber (1968) warned of the economic and political consequences of allowing America's international domination to continue unchallenged.

In 1946, European multinationals resumed economic activities and at the beginning of the 1970s, these firms were challenging the US multinationals internationally. By this time, the US multinationals no longer controlled the bulk of the global market. This is a remarkable achievement by the European and Japanese multinationals considering their post-war

EXHIBIT 12.1

The decline and fall of the G-7

The 1996 summit of the leaders of the Group of Seven industrial states which ended on Saturday, 29 June, in Lyons, France, was held amid sluggish growth, high unemployment and a sense that the baton of world economic leadership is slipping from their grasp. More than ever before, their economic weight risks being eclipsed by the brash new economies of the East and South.

The USA remains the world's dominant economic force, but its strength has been in relative decline for years. Half a century ago, the USA accounted for 50 per cent of global economic activity, as measured by gross domestic product. Now the International Monetary Fund expects China to draw even with the USA in the early decades of the twenty-first century.

The G-7 now account for only about 55 per cent of world output compared to 40 per cent for developing countries and 5 per cent for the transition economies. The G-7 share of world output will decline steadily during the next decade. The fact is developing countries have about 70 per cent of the world's land area, 85 per cent of its population, 45 per cent of its output and 15 per cent of stock market capitalization. 'One can no longer argue that the US leads the G-7 and the G-7 leads the world,' said Miron Mushkat, the Chief Economist at Lehman Brothers Asia Ltd in Hong Kong. 'It is a more equal relationship.'

As the industrial world slipped into recession in the early 1990s, for example, Western governments were powerless to halt the decline, economists said. Only the strengthening economies of the developing world, particularly Asia and Latin America, eased the force of recession. The developing world as a whole had a very big impact in moderating the recession. During the early 1990s when the global economy was relatively weak, it was kept stable by the emerging economies of the developing world, particularly Asia.

The World Bank's latest report on developing economies underscores the growing economic importance of what was once known as the Third World. Based on capital inflows and export growth, 'the fastest-growing regions over the past five years – East and South Asia, Latin America – also showed the largest advances in integration with the world economy,' the World Bank said. The Bank believes the stars of the developing world will put on a superior display of average growth in the coming decade that the G-7. It estimates the G-7 will grow an annual average of 2.8 per cent in the next decade whereas East Asia will expand 7.9 per cent annually, South Asia 5.4 per cent and Latin America 3.8 per cent.

Source: P. Torday, 'The passing glory of the west', *The Sunday Business*, 30 June 1996, p.19. Reprinted by permission.

technological and managerial handicaps. Although the seeming invisibility of the US firms and the feared global economic domination did not materialize, Franko (1978) observes that the menace of American economic imperialism, spearheaded by American multinationals, is an image still vivid throughout most of the world.

Over the last fifteen years, the so-called Third World multinationals have emerged and joined the fray. The excellent economic performance by developing countries during this period means that the right climate is being provided to Third World multinationals to strengthen their international competitiveness. World Bank statistics show that while the real GDP growth in G-7 states averaged 1.4 per cent from 1991 to 1993, East Asian growth averaged 9.4 per cent from 1991 to 1994, South Asia expanded by an average of 3.9 per cent and Latin America averaged 3.6 per cent. The magnitude of the threat from developing countries is illustrated in exhibit 12.1.

Three types of Third World multinationals can be identified: those from resource-rich countries such as OPEC members; those from skilled labour-rich countries such as the 'Asian tigers' (South Korea, Hong Kong, Singapore, Taiwan and Thailand); and those from market-rich rapidly industrializing countries such as Mexico and Brazil. With advances in technology and telecommunications, and the in-built natural advantages derived from factor endowment, these Third World multinationals will continue to pose a serious competitive challenge to the US and European multinationals.

Indeed, the trend towards globalization of business activities and the need to site production facilities in least-cost global locations will provide the Third World multinationals with natural leverage.

SUMMARY

In this chapter, it has been shown that while the benefits associated with FDI such as technology and capital transfers are desired, the impact of such investments on the sovereignty of the host nations can be fundamental. Specifically, the chapter has shown that:

- The relationship between the host country and the MNEs is determined by the expected mutual benefits to be derived from the presence of the MNE in the host country.
- The relative bargaining power of the host country and the MNE determines the outcome of technology transfer negotiations.

- Equity control in a subsidiary operation is a source of conflict between MNEs and host countries.
- International production is a recent phenomenon.
- The much feared domination of world economic activities by American multinationals did not materialize.
- The rise of the Third World multinationals is source of considerable concern for the US and European multinationals.

DISCUSSION QUESTIONS

1. Why should equity control in a subsidiary be a source of conflict an MNE and the host country? To what extent can the 'new open door' policy in most developing countries likely to enhance inward flow of FDI?
2. Examine the argument that the concept of appropriate technology is no longer relevant for developing countries as they believe that possession of advanced and sophisticated technology is a matter of national prestige.
3. 'Almost everyone everywhere wants all the things they have heard about, seen, or experienced via the new technologies.' Discuss.
4. Evaluate the likely impact of the third world multinationals of the global economic activities over the next thirty

REFERENCES

Franko, L. G. 1978: 'Multinationals: the end of US dominance', *Harvard Business Review*, Vol. 56, pp. 93–101.

Hood, N. and Young, S. (1979) *The Economics of Multinational Enterprise*. London: Longman Publishing Co.

Hymer, S. 1960: *The International Operations of National Firms: A Study of Direct Foreign Investment*. Cambridge, MA: MIT Press.

Levitt, T. 1983: 'The globalization of markets', *Harvard Business Review*, May–June, pp. 92–102.

Monye, S. O. 1996a: 'International market development', *les Nouvelles Journal of Licensing Executive Society*, Vol. 31, No. 1, pp. 1–7.

Monye, S. O. 1996b: 'Technology transfer negotiations: determinants of MNEs' bargaining power', *International Journal of Technology Transfer*, July/August.

Ronen, S. 1986: *Comparative and Multinational Management*. New York: John Wiley.

Servan-Schreiber, J. J. 1968: *The American Challenge*. New York: Athenaeum.

Torday, P. 1996: 'The passing glory of the west', *The Sunday Business*, 30 June, p. 19.

Wheelen, T. L. and Hunger, J. D. 1989: *Strategic Management and Business Policy*, 3rd edn. Reading, MA: Addison-Wesley.

Bibliography

Adler, N. J. 1984: 'Women in international management: where are they?' *California Management Review*, Vol. 26, No.4, pp. 78–89.

Akoorie, M. 1993: 'Patterns of foreign direct investment by large New Zealand firms', *International Business Review*, Vol. 2, No. 2, pp. 169–89.

Alexander, L. D. 1985: 'Successfully implementing strategic decisions', *Long Range Planning*, June, pp. 90–102.

Ansari, K. H. and Jackson, J. 1995: *Managing Cultural Diversity at Workplace*. London: Kogan Page.

Appleby, R. C. 1991: *Modern Business Administration*, 5th edn. London: Pitman.

Albaum, G., Strandskov, J., Duerr, E. and Dowd, L. 1989: *International Marketing and Export Management*. Wokingham: Addison-Wesley.

Ayling, D. 1988: 'Franchising in the UK', *The Quarterly Review of Marketing*, Summer, pp. 19–24.

Aylmer, R. J. 1973: 'Global marketing in the multinational corporations' in H. B. Thorelli and H. Becker (eds.), *International Marketing Strategy*. London: Penguin Books.

Bain, A. D. 1992: *The Economics of the Financial System*. Oxford: Blackwell Publishers.

Baranson, J. 1971: 'Automated manufacturing in developing economies', *Finance and Development*, Vol. 8, No. 4, pp. 10–28.

Becker, H. 1980 'Pricing: an international marketing challenge', in H. Thorelli and H. Becker (eds.), *International Marketing Strategy*, rev. edn. Oxford: Pergamon Press.

Bengtsson, A. M. 1992: *Managing Mergers and Acquisitions: A European Perspective*. Aldershot: Gower.

Bradley, F. 1991: *International Marketing Strategy*. New York: Prentice-Hall.

Brander, J. A. and Spencer, B. J. 1981: 'Tariffs and the extraction of foreign monopoly rents under potential entry', *Canadian Journal of Economics*, Vol. 14, No. 3, pp. 371–89.

Buckley, P. J. and Davies, H. 1979: *The Place of Licensing in Theory and Practice of Foreign Operations*, Discussion Paper, University of Reading, No. 47.

Buckley, P. J. and Ghauri, P. N. 1993: *The Internationalization of the Firm.* London: Academy Press.

Burnes, B. 1992 *Managing Change: A Strategic Approach to Organisational Development and Renewal.* London: Pitman Publishing.

Cain, W. W. 1970: 'International planning: mission impossible?', *Columbia Journal of World Business*, July–August, p. 58.

Cannon, T. 1994: *Corporate Responsibility.* London: Pitman Publishing.

Cantwell, J. 1991: 'A survey of theories of international production', in C. N. Patelis and R. Sudgen (eds.), *The Nature of the International Firm.* London: Longman.

Cateora, P. R. 1990: *International Marketing*, 7th edn. Homewood, IL: Irwin.

Cateora, P. R. 1993: *International Marketing*, 8th edn. Homewood, IL: Irwin.

Cateora, P. R. and Hess, J. M. 1988: *International Marketing.* Homewood, IL: Richard D. Irwin.

Caves, R. E., Crockell, H. and Killing, J. P. 1983: 'Imperfect market for technology licensing', *Oxford Bulletin of Economics and Statistics*, Vol. 45, No. 3, pp. 249–67.

Cavusgil, S. T. 1984: 'Differences among exporting firms based on their degree of internationalisation', *Journal of Business Research*, Vol.12, pp. 195–208.

Chandler, A. D. 1962: *Strategy and Structure.* Cambridge, MA: MIT Press.

Chatterji, D. and Thomas, M. A. 1993: 'Benefiting from external sources of technology', *Research-Technology Management.* Vol. 36, No. 6, pp. 21–6.

Contractor, F. J. and Sagafi-Nejad, T. 1981: 'International technology transfer', *Journal of International Business Studies*, Fall, pp.113–35.

Coyle, J. J., Bardi, E. J. and Cavinato, J. L. 1990: *Transportation.* New York: West Publishing.

Daniels, J. D. and Radebaugh, L. H. 1987: *International Business: Environments and Operations*, 4th edn. Reading, MA: Addison-Wesley.

Davies, H. 1977: 'Technology transfer through commercial transaction', *Journal of Industrial Economics*, Vol. 26, No. 2, pp. 161–75.

De Grauwe, P. 1989: *International Money: Post-War Trends and Theories.* Oxford: Clarendon Press.

De Mooij, M. K. and Keegan, W. 1991: *Advertising Worldwide.* London: Prentice-Hall.

Dicken, P. 1992: *Global Shift: The Internationalisation of Economic Activity.* London: Paul Chapman Publishing.

Dittrich, J. E. 1988: *The General Manager and Strategy Formulation.* New York: John Wiley.

Douglas, S. P. and Craig, C. S. 1983: *International Marketing Research.* Englewood Cliffs, NJ: Prentice-Hall.

Doz, Y. 1980: 'Strategic management in multinational companies', *Sloan Management Review*, Vol. 21, No. 2, pp. 27–46.

Dunning, J. H. 1977: 'Trade, location of economic activity and the MNE: a search for an eclectic approach', in B. Ohlin, P. O. Hesselborn and P. M. Wijkman (eds.), *The International Allocation of Economic Activity*. London: Macmillan.

Dunning, J. H. 1979: *International Production and the Multinational Enterprises*. London: Allen and Unwin.

Dunning, J. H. 1993: *Multinational Enterprises and the Global Economy*. Wokingham, UK: Addison-Wesley.

Dussuage, P., Hart, S. and Ramanantsao 1992: *Strategic Technology Management*. Chichester: John Wiley.

Dyment, J. J. 1987: 'Strategies and management controls for global corporations', *The Journal of Business Strategy*, Vol. 7, Spring, pp. 20–6.

Edwards, R. W., Jr. 1985: *International Monetary Collaboration*. New York: Transnational Publishers.

Eiteman, D. K. and Stonehill, A. I. 1989: *Multinational Business Finance*, 5th edn. Reading, MA: Addison-Wesley.

El Kahal, S. 1994: *Introduction to International Business*. London: McGraw-Hill.

Franko, L. G. 1973: 'Who manages multinational enterprises?', *Columbia Journal of World Business*, Summer, pp. 33–49.

Franko, L. G. 1978: 'Multinationals: the end of US dominance', *Harvard Business Review*, Vol. 56, pp. 93–101.

Giddy, I. H. 1994: *Global Financial Markets*. Lexington, MA: D. C. Heath.

Globerman, S. 1988: 'Addressing international product piracy', *Journal of International Business Studies*, Fall, pp. 497–504.

Griffin, T. 1993: *International Marketing Communications*. Oxford: Butterworth Heinemann.

Grimwade, N. 1989: *International Trade: New Patterns of Trade, Production and Investment*. London: Routledge.

Hallwood, P. and MacDonald, R. 1986: *International Money: Theory, Evidence and Institutions*. Oxford: Basil Blackwell.

Hallwood, P. and MacDonald, R. 1994: *International Money and Finance*, 2nd edn. Oxford: Blackwell.

Hallwood, P. and MacDonald, R. 1994: *International Money and Finance*, 2nd edn. Oxford: Blackwell.

Harrigan, K. R. 1985 *Strategies for Joint Venture Success*. Lexington, MA: Lexington Books.

Heenan, D. A. and Perlmutter, H. V. 1979: *Multinational Organisational Development: A Social Architecture Perspective*. Reading, MA: Addison-Wesley.

Heffernan, S. and Sinclair, P. 1990: *Modern International Economics*. Oxford: Basil Blackwell.

Hirsch, S. 1976: 'An international trade and investment theory of the firm', *Oxford Economic Papers*, Vol. 28, pp. 258–70.

Honeygold, D. 1989 *International Financial Markets*. New York: Woodhead-Faulkner.

Hood, N. and Young, S. 1979 *The Economics of Multinational Enterprise*. London: Longman Publishing.

Howells, J. and Wood, M. 1993: *The Globalisation of Production and Technology*. London: Belhaven Press.

Hufbuaer, G. C. 1966: *Synthetic Material and the Theory of International Trade*. London: Duckworth.

Hymer, S. 1976: *The International Operations of National Firms: A Study of Direct Foreign Investment*. Cambridge, MA: MIT Press.

Ietto-Gillies, G. 1992: *International Production: Trends, Theories, Effects*. Cambridge: Polity Press.

Jain, S. C. 1990a: *International Marketing Management*, 3rd edn. Boston: PWS-Kent Publishing.

Jain, S. C. 1990b: *Marketing Planning and Strategy*, 3rd edn. Cincinnati, OH: South-Western Publishing.

Jatusripitak, S., Fahey, L. and Kotler, P. 1985: 'Strategic global marketing: a lesson from the Japanese', *Columbia Journal of World Marketing*, Spring, pp. 47–51.

Jeannet, J. P. and Hennessey, H. D. 1988: *International Marketing Management: Strategies and Cases*. Boston: Houghton Mifflin.

Jenkins, R. 1989: 'The impact of foreign investment on less developed countries: a cross-section analysis vs. industry studies', Paper presented to the Academy of International Business, UK regional Annual Conference, at the University of Bath, 7–8 April.

Johanson, J. and Vahlne, J. E. 1977: 'The internationalisation process of the firm: a model of knowledge development and increasing foreign market commitments', *Journal of International Business Studies*, Vol. 8, No. 1, pp. 23–32.

Johanson, J. and Weidersheim-Paul, F. 1975: 'The internationalization of the firm: four Swedish case studies', *Journal of Management Studies*, October, pp. 305–22.

Kaikati, J. C. 1981: 'How multinational corporations cope with international trademark forgery', *Journal of International Marketing*, Vol. 1, No. 2, pp. 69–80.

Keegan W. J. 1989: *Global Marketing Management*, 4th edn. London: Prentice-Hall.

Keegan, W. J. 1970: 'Five strategies for multinational marketing', *European Business*, January, pp. 35–40.

Keegan, W., Moriarty, S. and Duncan, T. 1992: *Marketing*. London: Prentice-Hall.

Khambata, D. and Ajami, R. 1992: *International Business: Theory and Practice*. New York: Macmillan.

Kindleberger, C. P. 1969: *American Business Abroad*. New Haven, CT: Yale University Press.

Kinnear, T. C. and Taylor, J. R. 1991: *Marketing Research: An Applied Approach*, 4th edn. New York: McGraw-Hill.

Kogut, B. 1985: 'Designing global strategies: comparative and competitive value-added chains', *Sloan Management Review*, Summer, pp. 15–28.

Kojima, K. 1978: *Direct Foreign Investment: A Japanese Model of Multinational Business Operations*. London: Croom Helm.

Kotler, P. 1988: *Marketing Management: Analysis, Planning, Implementation, and Control*, 6th edn. Englewood Cliffs, NJ: Prentice-Hall.

Larreche, J. C. 1980: 'The international product/market portfolio', in H. Thorelli and H. Becker (eds.), *International Marketing Strategy*, rev. edn. Oxford: Pergamon Press.

Lau, R. 1994: 'Why everyone wants to know more about strategic alliances', *Broker World*, Vol. 14, No. 2, pp. 48–54.

Levi, M. D. 1990: *International Finance: The Markets and Financial Management of Multinational Business*, 2nd edn. New York: McGraw-Hill.

Levitt, T. 1983: 'The globalization of markets', *Harvard Business Review*, May–June, pp. 92–102.

Loudon, D. L. and Della Bitta, A. J. 1993: *Consumer Behaviour*, 4th edn. New York: McGraw-Hill.

Lovell, E. B. 1979: 'Appraising foreign licensing performance', *Studies in Business Policy*, New York Conference Board, No. 128.

Madura, J. 1992: *International Financial Management*, 3rd edn. New York: West Publishing.

Mahoney, J. 1995: 'Gifts, grease and graft', *Financial Times – Mastering Management Series*. Part 7, December 1995, p. 8.

Marsh, P. (1995) 'Management: tool of the team', *Financial Times*, 6 December, p. 14.

Maw, N. G., Lord Lane of Horsell and Craig-Cooper, M. 1994: *Maw on Corporate Governance*. Aldershot: Dartmouth Publishing.

McGee, J. S. 1966: 'Patent exploitation: some economic and legal problems', *Journal of Law and Economics*, Vol. 9, No. 1.

McKinnon, A. C. 1989: *Physical Distribution Systems*. London : Routledge.

Mead, R. 1994: *International Management: Cross Cultural Dimensions*. Oxford: Blackwell

Minchinton, W. E. 1969: *The Growth of English Overseas Trade in the Seventeenth and Eighteenth Centuries*. London.

Monye, S. O. 1996a: 'International market development', *les Nouvelles Journal of Licensing Executive Society*, Vol. 31, No. 1, pp. 1–7.

Monye, S. O. 1996b: 'Technology transfer negotiations: determinants of MNEs' bargaining power', *International Journal of Technology Transfer*, Vol. 21, Nos.1–2, pp. 54–60.

Norman, Peter and Nakamoto, Michiyo (1993) 'Tariff-cutting deal lifts hopes for Uruguay Round', *Financial Times*, 8 July, p. 2.

Ohmae, K. 1989: 'Managing in a borderless world', *Harvard Business Review*, May–June.

Oman, C. 1984: *New Forms of International Investment in Developing Countries*. Paris: OECD.

Onkvisit, S. and Shaw, J. J. 1983: 'An examination of the international product life cycle and its application within marketing', *Columbia Journal of World Business*, Fall, Vol. 18, pp. 74–87.

Onkvisit, S. and Shaw, J. J. 1989: *International Marketing: Analysis and Strategy*. London: Merrill Publishing.

Phatak, A. V. 1980: 'A note on currency problems in international marketing', in H. Thorelli and H. Becker (eds.), *International Marketing Strategy*, rev. edn. Oxford: Pergamon Press.

Phillips, C., Doole, I. and Lowe, R. 1994: *International Marketing Strategy: Analysis, Development and Implementation*. London: Routledge.

Pitelis, C. N. and Sugden, R. 1991: *The Nature of the Transnational Firm*. London: Routledge.

Pomfret, R. 1991: *International Trade: An Introduction to Theory and Policy*. Oxford: Basil Blackwell.

Popcorn, Faith 1992: *The Popcorn Report*. New York: Harper Business.

Porter, M. 1980: *Competitive Strategy: Techniques for Analysing Industries and Competitors*. New York: Free Press.

Porter, M. 1986: 'Changing patterns of international competition', *California Management Review*, Vol. 28, No. 2, pp. 9–40.

Porter, M. 1990: *Competitive Advantage of Nations*. New York: Free Press.

Posner, M. V. 1961: 'International trade and technical change', *Oxford Economic Papers*, Vol. 13, pp. 323–41.

Ricardo, D. 1971: *Principles of Political Economy and Taxation*. Harmondsworth: Penguin.

Robinson, R. D. 1978: *International Business Management: A Guide to Decision Making*, 2nd edn. Hinsdale: The Dryden Press.

Robock, S. and Simmonds, K. 1989: *International Business and Multinational Enterprises*, 4th edn. Homewood, IL: Richard D. Irwin.

Ronen, S. 1986: *Comparative and Multinational Management*. New York: John Wiley.

Root, F. R. 1987: *Entry Strategies for International Markets*. Lexington, MA: Lexington Books.

Root, F. R. 1990: *International Trade and Investments*, 6th edn. Cincinnati, OH: South-Western Publishing.

Rosenbaum, J. 1993: 'Strategic alliances in the global marketplace', *Managing Intellectual Property*, No. 35, December, pp. 17–25.

Rugman, A. M., Lecraw, D. J. and Booth, 1985: *International Business: Firm and Environment*. New York: McGraw-Hill.

Sakai, J. T. 1994: 'Japan as an attractive alliance partner', *Directors and Boards*, Vol. 18, No. 2, pp. 42–4.

Sands, P. 1993: *Greening International Law*. London: Earthscan.

Schneider, S. C. 1988: 'National versus corporate culture: implications for human resource management', *Human Resource Management*, Vol. 27, No. 2, pp. 231–46.

Servan-Schreiber, J. J. 1968: *The American Challenge*. New York: Atheneum.

Skinner, C. W. 1968: *American Industry in Developing Economies: The Management of International Manufacturing*. New York: Wiley.

Sodersten, B. and Reed, G. (1994) *International Economics*, 3rd edn. Basingstoke: Macmillan.

Sparrow, P. and Hiltrop, J. M. 1994: *European Human Resource Management in Transition*. London: Prentice-Hall.

Stern, P and Stanworth, J. 1988: 'The development of franchising in Britain', *National Westminster Quarterly Review*, May, pp. 38–48.

Taggart, J. and McDermott, M. 1993: *The Essence of International Business*. Hemel Hempstead: Prentice-Hall International.

Teece, D. J. 1976: *The Multinational Corporation and The Resource Cost of International Technology Transfer*. Cambridge, MA.

Terpstra, V. 1983: *International Marketing*, 3rd edn. Chicago: The Dryden Press.

Tew, B. 1988: *The Evolution of the International Monetary System 1945–88*. London: Hutchinson.

Thayer, J. D. 1994: 'The tender trap', *Journal of European Business*, Vol. 5, No. 3, pp. 34–8.

Thunman C. G. 1982: *Swedish Licensing in World Markets*, Research Reports, Marketing Techniques Centre, Stockholm, No. 11.

Tookey, D. 1969: 'International business and political geography', *British Journal of Marketing*, Vol. 3, No. 3, pp.18–29.

Torday, P. 1996: 'The passing glory of the West', in *The Business Sunday*, 30 June, p. 19.

Torrington, D. 1994: *International Human Resource Management*. London: Prentice-Hall.

Toyne, B. and Walters, P. G. P. 1993: *Global Marketing Management: A Strategic Perspective*, 2nd edn. Needham: Allyn and Bacon.

Tricker, R. I. 1994: *International Corporate Governance*. London: Prentice-Hall.

Turnbull, P. 1987: 'A challenge to the stages theory of the internationalization process', in P. J. Rosson and S. D. Reed (eds.), *Managing Export Entry and Expansion*. Westport, CT: Greenwood Publishing.

UNCTC 1992: *World Investment Report: Transnational Corporations as Engines of Growth*. New York: United Nations.

UNCTC 1993: *World Investment Report: Transnational Corporations and Integrated International Production*. New York: United Nations.

United Nations General Assembly Resolution 37/7 (1982), UN Doc. A/37/51.

Vernon, R. 1966: 'International investment and international trade in the product cycle', *Quarterly Journal of Economics*, Vol. 80, pp. 190–207.

Vernon, R. 1977: *Storm Over the Multinationals: The Real Issues*. Cambridge, MA: Harvard University Press.

Vernon, R. 1979: 'The product cycle hypothesis in a new international environment', *Oxford Bulletin of Economics and Statistics*, Vol. 41, pp. 255–67.

Vernon, R. and Wells Jr, L. T. 1991: *The Economic Environment of International Business*, 5th edn. Englewood Cliffs, NJ: Prentice-Hall.

Vernon-Wortzel, H. and Wortzel, L. H. 1991: *Global Strategic Management: The Essentials*, 2nd edn. New York: John Wiley.

Welch, L. S. and Luostarinen, R. 1988: 'Internationalization: evolution of a concept', *Journal of General Management*, Vol. 14, No. 2.

Wells, L. T. 1972: *The Product Life Cycle and International Trade*. Cambridge, MA: Harvard University Press.

Wheelen, T. L. and Hunger, J. D. 1989: *Strategic Management and Business Policy*, 3rd edn. Reading, MA: Addison-Wesley.

Wilson, A. 1982: *Aubrey Wilson's Marketing Audit Check Lists: A Guide to Effective Marketing Resource Realisation*. London: McGraw-Hill.

Wind, Y., Douglas, S. and Perlmutter, H. 1973: 'Guidelines for developing international marketing strategies', *Journal of Marketing*, Vol. 37, pp. 14–23.

World Commission on Environment and Development 1987: *Our Common Future*. Oxford: Oxford University Press.

Wortzel, L. 1989: *International Business Strategy Resource Book*. New York: Strategic Direction Publishers.

Young, S. 1987: 'Business strategy and the internationalisation of business: recent approaches', *Managerial and Decision Economics*, Vol. 8, No. 1.

Young, S., Hamill, J., Wheeler, C. and Davies, J. R. 1989: *International Market Entry and Development*. Hemel Hempstead: Harvester Wheatsheaf.

Index